Degrees of Risk

Degrees of Risk

Navigating Insecurity and Inequality in Public Higher Education

BLAKE R. SILVER

The University of Chicago Press
Chicago and London

The University of Chicago Press, Chicago 60637
The University of Chicago Press, Ltd., London
© 2024 by The University of Chicago
All rights reserved. No part of this book may be used or reproduced in any manner
whatsoever without written permission, except in the case of brief quotations in
critical articles and reviews. For more information, contact the University of Chicago Press,
1427 E. 60th St., Chicago, IL 60637.
Published 2024
Printed in the United States of America

33 32 31 30 29 28 27 26 25 24   1 2 3 4 5

ISBN-13: 978-0-226-83474-0 (cloth)
ISBN-13: 978-0-226-83476-4 (paper)
ISBN-13: 978-0-226-83475-7 (e-book)
DOI: https://doi.org/10.7208/chicago/9780226834757.001.0001

Library of Congress Cataloging-in-Publication Data
Names: Silver, Blake R., author.
Title: Degrees of risk : navigating insecurity and inequality in public
     higher education / Blake R. Silver.
Description: Chicago ; London : The University of Chicago Press, 2024. |
     Includes bibliographical references and index.
Identifiers: LCCN 2023050475 | ISBN 9780226834740 (cloth) |
     ISBN 9780226834764 (paperback) | ISBN 9780226834757 (ebook)
Subjects: LCSH: College students—United States—Social conditions—21st century. |
     Uncertainty. | Security (Psychology) | Equality. | Education, Higher—United States.
Classification: LCC LB3605 .S568 2024 | DDC 378.1/980973—dc23/eng/20231106
LC record available at https://lccn.loc.gov/2023050475

♾ This paper meets the requirements of ANSI/NISO Z39.48-1992 (Permanence of Paper).

For Nader

Contents

Prologue ix

1 Welcome to the Ivory Casino 1

2 Precarious Pioneers: Deploying Resilience
for an Uncertain Journey 21

3 Risk Minimizers: Using Resistance
to Alleviate Insecurity 47

4 Opportunity Maximizers:
Building an Enterprising Self 77

5 Insulated Explorers: Flexibility and the
Pursuit of Self-Discovery 103

6 Amplifying or Alleviating Insecurity:
The Role of Universities 125

7 The Lessons of Precarity 152

Acknowledgments 177
Appendix: Methods 181
Notes 187
References 205
Index 225

Prologue

"From the get-go, it was uncertain," Daniel stated, while reflecting on his college experience with a laugh. His humor was a thin veil for deeper concerns. As our conversation progressed, the precarity of his situation became apparent. Sitting in his room in front of a giant photograph of the New York City skyline, Daniel told me the story of how his parents immigrated to Manhattan in the latter part of the twentieth century.[1] "My father is a humble cab driver, and my mom's a preschool teacher. . . . We're not middle class; we're a working-class family." Though his father attended a university in Afghanistan, his degree went unrecognized by employers in the United States, and his mother concluded her education after high school. Daniel described what it was like growing up with limited financial resources: "Spending your entire life working class, sometimes you have concerns like 'how am I going to get food on the table?' My parents have those concerns." His expression was earnest, almost desperate, as he described college as "my ticket out . . . it's my ticket to the middle class."

In his fourth year of study but still unsure about when he'd graduate, Daniel described a perilous trek through higher education. He arrived at college undecided about his field of study and chose information technology (IT) on a whim when his orientation group "swung past the IT room. . . . I stumbled into it basically. . . . And the next thing I know, I was an IT major." Since this happenstance encounter, Daniel had stuck with the major. "It's the hill I chose to die on," he declared, "as soon as I signed myself away to it, I haven't really thought about any other major. All I've thought about is how I can get this degree and get into the workforce." His goal was to "burn through my courses and hopefully get to graduation sooner or later."

Despite this steadfast commitment to his major and his education, Daniel struggled through college. He recalled,

> It was actually a lot rougher than I'd thought. . . . I didn't realize there would be a set path they wanted us to go through the courses, so at first, I was just burning through my gen ed requirements and not worrying about how many IT classes I took. But also, the first semester, I remember some counselor told us that, "hey you guys are new, you're not used to the college curriculum, so maybe just do 12 credits instead of the 15," which is the standard. . . . So, it's not been the smoothest.

Believing that it was prudent to begin with a limited number of credits and postpone courses in his major in order to focus on general education requirements, Daniel missed important prerequisites and fell behind schedule for a four-year graduation.

Trying to recover and make progress toward his degree, he subsequently failed a required course. Unfamiliar with the process to remain in the major and retake the class, Daniel again found himself in a fog of confusion when he was suddenly "removed from all my IT courses [for the coming semester] because they assumed I had been terminated." Scrambling to get back into the major and enroll in classes, he sent a flurry of "emails back and forth" in what became "a good one- or two-month process." The result was disheartening: "By the time I had gotten myself cleared [for registration], I was only able to take one class that semester, so that was kind of a big wrench in my wheel."

Daniel chalked these challenges up to the structure of a big university. He explained, "It's just bureaucracy, so you know, I had to email someone, and they had to email someone, and they had to email someone, and it had to go all the way from the top back to me." Though he recalled this process with a chuckle, his sense of powerlessness was palpable as he told me, "You're just trying to get ahold of someone and they're like 'okay, I've got to talk to my guy,' and their guy has to talk to someone else." Finishing his thought, Daniel's eyes settled on his desk as silence filled the room. He looked defeated, exhausted.

Summing up his time in college thus far, Daniel described semesters riddled with uncertainty: "There have been a lot of new experiences and a lot of things I didn't expect. . . . There was a lot of things I basically had to find along the way." He couldn't help feeling like he was "going at it solo," a sense he attributed in part to his family's lack of firsthand experience with US higher education. More importantly, however, the university had offered little

PROLOGUE

guidance on how to navigate college. He noted, "It's a lot more confusing than one actually thinks. . . . If they could make a '[College] for Dummies' book, that would be really useful."

Without the guidance he desired, Daniel often felt assailed by insecurity. In addition to his academic performance and progress to graduation, this insecurity affected his home life, finances, and plans for the future. He'd recently lost a job working at a pharmacy when the local branch closed. While management offered to relocate him to a store in a nearby city, Daniel explained why he couldn't take them up on that offer: "I don't have a car; I can't walk to [that city]." Without a steady source of income, his $15,000 in college debt would grow even faster in the coming semesters. His prospects of repaying this money hinged on securing a well-paying job after graduation, something that felt far from certain:

> The biggest [obstacle] is my lack of connection to the industry, because I'm going from a first-generation family into a society where arguably the easiest way to get into the workforce is if you know someone. I don't know someone; I'm just me. So, my biggest concern is how am I going to escape that pile of résumés when ten or twenty of those résumés are going to have the name of someone within the company or even their own relative works for the company? Like how do I get out of that stack when there are people who are related to the section manager?

Having heard about peers' struggles to secure desirable jobs in the tech industry, Daniel anticipated that similar challenges might stymie his attempts. As he reflected on his college experience and looked toward the future, there seemed to be no end to the insecurity that had marked his journey thus far.

I asked about some of the lessons he'd learned in college. Without hesitation, he replied, "The most important things are to be diligent and resilient." Illustrating determination to pick himself back up when he was knocked down, Daniel reflected on challenges encountered and errors made: "could've, should've, would've—it's the past, right? . . . It's important to have that resilience and that diligence, definitely." He saw contemporary higher education as a place where these traits were essential for survival:

> In the university, the teacher's not running after you, you're running after the teacher. . . . It was structured in high school. When we were going for our electives, we had a sheet of paper that would tell us what courses we were taking, "this is what you're doing." . . . But when we got to university, it's like, "look, we're not going to tell you how to do anything. Everything you do is up to you." . . . At the end of the day, every decision you make is on you.

Though hard work and independence are often framed as positive qualities, Daniel's story illuminated the oppressive nature of these lessons. While staff and administrators at his university extolled the virtues of developing "grit" and "resilience," they failed to acknowledge that the need for such traits was often driven by gaps in available support.[2] Navigating the precarious world of higher education, he increasingly felt alone and internalized the pressure to be self-reliant.

As we concluded our discussion, Daniel offered a glimmer of hope, a vision for a different kind of educational experience. Although his own journey through college was chaotic, he'd heard about institutions that sheltered students from these types of insecurities. He explained:

> I know that some of my friends from the United Kingdom, when they go to university, they still have that high school structure where they tell you what courses you're going to take and what you're going to do. . . . You're on a path. . . . I would argue that if some institutions adopted the European or the UK model, it might be helpful for a lot of students, because they could jump into something a lot more familiar and a lot less flexible. And that's the thing. We have this idea that flexibility is a great thing, but in some ways, it can be a choke point. It's information overload.

Daniel's suggestion seemed simple enough. Couldn't universities like his create structure to assist students through their undergraduate studies?[3] Couldn't they replace the abundance of choice and the paralyzing flexibility with clear guidance to combat uncertainty and shepherd students to graduation? Couldn't they offer more support? These possibilities sounded reasonable, almost obvious. Yet higher education in the United States continues to move in a very different direction.

This book explores college students' experiences with insecurity in higher education. Most research on insecurity takes a focused look at one or two of its manifestations, perhaps job instability, family churn, or the dissolution of social safety nets.[4] Such research has revealed crucial insights about the causes and consequences of the uncertainties that shape daily life. To understand the insecurity college students confront today, however, we must cast a wider net. These students face pervasive uncertainty driven by challenges many of them encounter financing college, navigating its flexibility, finding needed resources, anticipating an unpredictable labor market, and recovering from the disruptions generated by the COVID-19 pandemic, to name a few. Exploring any one of these factors by itself could engender valuable insights, and yet it would also produce an incomplete understanding of students' day-to-day lives. Students encounter various forms of insecurity that are experienced together, not in isolation from one another. Such is the nature of contemporary precarity. In short, this project does not aim to trace the source or outcome of a particular manifestation of uncertainty or instability. Rather, it attempts to understand broader patterns in how students interpret and navigate the insecurity that abounds in college today.

1

Welcome to the Ivory Casino

Higher education is often described as an "ivory tower," a place of privilege, insulated from the trials of the outside world. Scholars and journalists alike refer to a "campus bubble" that supposedly offers students a safe place to learn, explore, and find themselves as they transition from adolescence to adulthood.[1] In theory, the resources available within colleges provide abundant opportunities for guided growth and development. And there is some evidence to support this notion. Research on higher education documents the proliferation of resources and services capable of reducing uncertainty and facilitating the transition to adulthood.[2] Academic advisors are available to provide guidance as students select fields of study and navigate course offerings. Career development professionals can assist with finding internships or planning for postcollege opportunities. Clinicians are employed to meet students' health-care needs. Numerous student affairs personnel have the capacity to connect students with financial aid, tutoring, coaching, and other types of assistance. Though college budgets are often limited, spending on administrative support is extensive and growing by the year.[3]

But are college students truly sheltered from the precarities of the outside world? Research suggests they are not.[4] Approximately 25 percent of students who enroll in college today don't return for a second year.[5] Though the bachelor's degree is often described as a four-year program of study, most colleges and universities publicly advertise their six-year graduation rates. Even these numbers are often unimpressive. The national average completion rate for students who begin their studies at public four-year universities is a meager 67 percent, meaning that one in every three students who start college at these institutions will not possess a bachelor's degree six years later.[6]

The risks of a leaky pipeline to graduation are compounded by the need to borrow money to pay for college. The average undergraduate today receives over $4,000 in federal loans each year.[7] Media coverage often focuses on the ways student debt constricts the opportunities of college graduates. But what these accounts miss are the consequences that begin well before completing a degree. For many students, taking out loans for large sums of money foments a great deal of stress.[8] Furthermore, debt can be especially challenging to repay for those who do not graduate.[9] In short, when it comes to affording and completing higher education, insecurity abounds. A minority of students make it to graduation in a timely manner with limited debt. Others flounder in college, struggling to complete their degrees or becoming encumbered by exorbitant student loans with steep interest rates.

Some would argue that it's not just the acquisition of a diploma that insulates college-going youth from insecurity but also the skills and experiences they gain along the way. After all, colleges emphasize that the preparation they offer for adulthood goes beyond the provision of a credential, that it's about what students learn and how they grow in the process.[10] Yet research calls these claims into doubt as well. For instance, studies of labor market outcomes show that individuals who attend college but do not obtain a degree receive few benefits.[11] In fact their incomes on average are only marginally higher than those of high school graduates.

Moreover, research on student experiences and outcomes suggests that promises to support the types of learning and development needed for labor market success are often unfulfilled. Despite the widespread belief that college imparts skills young adults need to succeed in white-collar jobs, the reality is more complicated. Reporting on the results of an assessment of learning administered at twenty-four colleges and universities, Richard Arum and Josipa Roksa found that at the end of their second year of undergraduate study, nearly half of the students displayed no measurable progress in tests of critical thinking, complex reasoning, and written communication.[12]

Similarly, in contrast to promises of personal growth, college students' developmental opportunities are constrained by racist and sexist assumptions about self-presentation.[13] To fit in with peers, students frequently adopt and maintain simplistic roles throughout their time in college. As they take on cookie-cutter identities to shield themselves from marginalization—becoming "the funny guy," "the quiet one," "the mom of the group," and so on—most gain little experience with other kinds of roles.[14] In the end, large numbers of students do not benefit from the types of learning or development often attributed to higher education.

I argue that far from being sheltered from insecurity, college students today traverse incredibly precarious terrain. While the metaphor of the ivory tower calls to mind a site of refuge, many students find that their experiences challenge this vision. Daniel, for instance, noted that his path to adulthood might in fact have been smoother had he begun full-time work after high school, "become a tradesman," or joined the military. He'd even considered leaving the university to pursue one of these options. But still enrolled, Daniel feared leaving college would amplify uncertainty, a fear that was justified given the well-documented struggles of those who leave college without a degree.[15]

Hoping that higher education will alleviate insecurity, youth increasingly enroll in college following high school graduation.[16] When I asked Rick about why people go to college today, he responded succinctly: "to reduce your risk." And yet he and his peers discovered that rather than being sheltered from insecurity, they'd entered a high-stakes environment filled with uncertainty. They found public higher education to be more like a casino than an ivory tower. Placing bets of time, energy, and money, students waited for the results. Hands were dealt, dice were rolled, and roulette wheels were spun. Some held their breath apprehensively, while others enjoyed the thrill. A few placed small bets to minimize risk, and others played at every table, hoping to increase their odds of a win.

Recently, the COVID-19 pandemic brought many of the precarities of higher education front and center. As campuses closed and classes moved to virtual instruction, the uncertainties confronted by students—related to finances, technology, academic performance, and a range of other factors— became more visible.[17] This led commentators to speculate about a new era of insecurity for underresourced colleges and universities.

"It feels unpredictable every single semester," Dee announced emphatically. Her university tended to attribute insecurity and uncertainty to the pandemic. Administrators blamed public health guidance, technology vendors, state policies, and the virus itself for the precarity that complicated students' lives.[18] But as Dee was well aware, uncertainty in higher education was about more than the pandemic. She described struggling to afford college, unexpected changes in her financial aid package, challenges finding academic advising, and other obstacles to accessing university resources. In other words, the pandemic was just the most recent event exposing the ways uncertainty is woven throughout the fabric of public higher education.[19] Rather than being the sole cause or manifestation of insecurity, COVID-19 illuminated a broader truth: that uncertainty is built into these settings, shaping student experiences in profound ways. But if insecurity in college isn't new, if it's not the temporary result of a global pandemic, then where did it come from?

The Sources of Insecurity

Sociological perspectives on higher education illuminate the ways student experiences are influenced by broad social forces and structural conditions.[20] One of the most consistent trends of the last fifty years has been the amplification of insecurity in a variety of social contexts. While societies have always confronted degrees of danger and risk, changes during the twentieth century—including social, political, and economic transformations—brought about new kinds of precarity.[21] In practical terms, this meant that things like job security and tight-knit communities were replaced by unstable employment, fragile connections, and other kinds of contingencies.[22]

Sociologists refer to these trends in various ways. Some highlight the adoption of individualistic, neoliberal policies that amplify instability, while others depict society in a state of churn, where daily life is in flux.[23] Sociologist Allison Pugh used the phrase "insecurity culture" to capture the demands for individual responsibility and flexibility created by trends toward deregulation and privatization.[24] Regardless of the terms used to describe this new form of social organization—neoliberal, churning, or insecure—there is widespread consensus that a shift from general stability to pervasive uncertainty has occurred. This uncertainty shows up in a variety of arenas relevant to social life. For instance, scholars document its influence in the labor market, families, communities, and civic life.[25]

These changes have had profound implications for education broadly and higher education in particular. Implementation of neoliberal policies resulted in the erosion of government support for various social provisions, including state funding for colleges and universities.[26] In turn, many postsecondary institutions cut budgets, came to rely on contingent faculty workforces, and raised tuition to exorbitant levels.[27] The increasing costs of college far exceeded inflation, with tuition becoming the main source of funding for higher education. As recently as the latter half of the twentieth century, students in many states could pay the cost of college attendance by working approximately twenty hours a week at a job paying minimum wage. Today, by contrast, students would need the equivalent of one to two full-time minimum-wage jobs to cover the same expenses.[28] Government policy has simultaneously replaced grant funding with loans, placing the risk of college attendance in the laps of students and their families.[29]

Related shifts in the relationship between students and institutions of higher education amplified uncertainty. In response to declining government support and declining support for higher education by the American public at large, most colleges—especially those with limited resources—were compelled to employ market-based strategies comparable to those of commercial organizations.[30] This involved two major shifts. First, institutions felt pressure to market higher education as an individual investment in a private good. We can see the results of this marketing in the ways institutions aim to "sell" their amenities in college viewbooks, online advertisements, and at admissions fairs.[31] Second, students and their parents were repositioned as consumers, a trend that shapes the ways they encounter and interact with institutional representatives.[32]

This marketization of higher education coincided with a decline in the doctrine of in loco parentis (Latin for "in the place of a parent"), which long reflected a shared understanding that colleges and universities had a responsibility to monitor students' welfare in the absence of parents.[33] Rather than serve as surrogate parents, institutions began treating students as consumers, paying greater attention to (affluent) students' preferences and desires. In this context, colleges came to emphasize choice and individual responsibility over structured resources and intentional support.[34]

In our 2019 article, Josipa Roksa and I described the "do-it-yourself" environment within universities that resulted from this conception of students as consumers.[35] Taking the senior year of college as our focus, we explored how soon-to-be graduates navigated the transition to postcollege life. The university we studied offered abundant services for this transition, including a career center, job fairs, financial literacy workshops, a career library, and graduate school information sessions to name a few. And yet these services were disconnected from students' curricular experiences and day-to-day lives such that many were unaware they existed, and less than a quarter of the students we interviewed reported utilizing any of them.[36] We quote a student named Nate, who summed up these patterns: "I feel like at [the university], because of the atmosphere of the school, you sort of have to do it yourself. . . . Like the university is there and they're not going to just come help you out. You have to go through the university to figure out all of the options that they have."

The do-it-yourself environment caters to a specific version of young adulthood that presumes that students desire flexibility and choice over structure and intentionality and that they will therefore select optional resources from a menu of possibilities.[37] Such an approach contrasts with the construction of guided pathways where structured resources are integrated into programs of study to ensure that all students have the support they need to succeed in college. Although guided pathways have a range of benefits, they remain rare.[38] Instead, a lack of structure wins out in the ivory casino, where positive experiences and outcomes are the assumed results of ample opportunities for exploration.

There are several reasons why these trends might create challenges for students. To begin with, the contemporary journey from adolescence to adulthood is a period of great uncertainty.[39] Through the middle of the twentieth century, this transition typically occurred in relatively short order in the United States as youth acquired traditional markers of adult status—completing education, finding employment, leaving the parental home, and forming families—in their late teens and early twenties.[40] Today, these markers are spread out and lack the linearity they once had. Individuals start and stop schooling; they find and lose employment more frequently; they move out of their parents' home and return again multiple times over the course of their twenties.[41]

The shifting nature of the transition to adulthood is tied to the onset of broader forms of precarity. This is especially true of the obligation many young people feel to extend formal education well beyond high school graduation.[42] As employment became more insecure, individuals encountered pressure to continue their education for longer periods of time to remain up-to-date and "marketable" in their fields.[43] In other words, students go to college to get jobs. And yet institutionalized connections between school and work are limited in the United States, requiring individuals to navigate these transitions with little help from their colleges.[44]

While insecurity is increasingly prevalent, public colleges and universities today are rarely equipped to offer structured support for the transition to adulthood.[45] Further, many within higher education seem to misunderstand the challenges confronted by contemporary students. Drawing from interviews with faculty, staff, and administrators, sociologist Pamela Aronson showed how these institutional representatives tended to individualize the uncertainties confronted by students, focusing on individual capabilities and dispositions.[46] For instance, rather than recognizing influential structural conditions, Aronson found that most faculty and staff pointed to issues like a lack of motivation to explain students' struggles. The result is that early adulthood is more precarious than it once was, but colleges and universities lack the resources and understanding needed to buffer students from insecurity.[47]

Studying Precarity in College

Given the extent to which elements of insecurity culture—such as uncertainty, instability, and individualism—have taken root in public higher education, it is surprising how little is known about the ways college students interpret and navigate this context. Although knowledge about the experiential core of college life has expanded since 2010, research on how students encounter insecurity lags.[48] *Degrees of Risk* illuminates this understudied but crucial element of higher education, addressing a number of interconnected questions. How do college students today confront insecurity? Where does it figure into their perceptions of what higher education represents and why they traverse this path? What types of strategies are employed to navigate insecurity in college? What might colleges do to mitigate insecurity?

To answer these questions, I looked primarily to students and their stories. This book grows out of more than one hundred ethnographic interviews conducted over the course of the 2020–2021 academic year at a public institution I refer to as Commonwealth University, or CU for short.[49] Commonwealth University offered a rich site to explore the ways college students experience and deal with insecurity. The institution is representative of what Laura Hamilton and Kelly Nielsen call "the new university."[50] Resulting from the fiscal constraints imposed by neoliberal policymaking, new universities are public institutions with limited resources that enroll student bodies with greater representation of racially and socioeconomically marginalized students.[51] These relatively young institutions did not benefit from the largesse that characterized earlier eras of higher education when colleges serving primarily affluent White student bodies formed and grew. Instead, they expanded at a moment of fiscal austerity and were positioned to serve groups of students historically disenfranchised by public education, including students of color, low-income students, and first-generation college students.

Places like CU are rarely examined in sociological research on higher education.[52] Sociologist W. Carson Byrd critiques the tendency for research to "overwhelmingly focus" on "highly selective institutions that are also the most well-resourced institutions in the nation."[53] This emphasis on elite settings is partly responsible for the ways student experiences with insecurity have been overlooked and obscured. As scholars fixate on the lives of youth at Ivy League schools and elite liberal arts colleges, it's easy to miss the uncertainties confronting students whose institutional homes don't have multibillion-dollar endowments capable of smoothing the road ahead. Yet four-year public institutions make up the largest sector of postsecondary education. Nearly half of all college students in the US study at these schools (7.6 million to be precise), surpassing enrollments in four-year private institutions (3.3 million) as well as combined enrollment in public and private two-year institutions (4.8 million).[54] Neglecting these sites means missing the realities of higher education for students today.

The student body of CU reflects the diversity of the surrounding region and state. This diversity made it possible to interview students from a range of sociodemographic groups. Nearly 60 percent of undergraduates identify as students of color. Approximately one-third are from low-income families,

TABLE 1.1. University and sample demographics

Student characteristic	Commonwealth University (%)	Study sample (%)
Socioeconomic status		
First-generation college students	40	43
Pell Grant eligible	30	34[a]
Race/ethnicity		
Asian or Asian American	24	20
Black or African American	12	13
Hispanic or Latinx	18	17
White	41	36
Multiracial, other race/ethnicity	5	13
Gender		
Women	49	52
Men	50	45
Nonbinary or agender	Unknown[b]	3

[a] This number is an imperfect approximation of Pell eligibility. While students' access to financial aid was discussed, not all participants were aware of the specific grants they received. It is possible that some Pell recipients did not report this source of financial aid, and others who referred to grants for low-income students may not have received Pell Grants specifically. Other studies have similarly documented challenges of gathering self-reported information from students on income or financial aid status (Bowman and Hill 2011; Smith and McCann 1998). For this reason, I primarily rely on parental education and occupation to describe students' socioeconomic status.
[b] At the time of this study, CU did not publish data on students' identification beyond the gender binary.

and 40 percent are first-generation college students whose parents have not completed a bachelor's degree. Surveys of CU students indicate that approximately four in ten grew up in households where a language other than English was spoken.[55] In total, 104 students took part in this study. Table 1.1 shows how my sample compared to the demographics of the broader university.

With the pandemic constricting campus life, interviews were conducted over a videoconferencing platform. Though interviewing from a distance can be challenging and contingent on the whims of spotty internet connections, this approach offered an invaluable window into students' lives. My research assistants and I were able to virtually join participants in the spaces they occupied each day, understanding them in situ. From the settings where they lived, worked, and studied, many were able to point to evidence to support their claims. Grant gestured around a mostly empty corner of the student union to illustrate how quiet his study space was during the pandemic. Isabelle, Finley, and Olivia each gave me tours of the posters adorning the walls of their living spaces, explaining their significance. And when Jonah described the distractions that came with trying to learn in close proximity to his parents and siblings, there were frequent interruptions to illustrate his point. These virtual meetings offered entry into the social worlds of students in a way that interviews at the campus coffee shop could not match.

To bring additional context to the interviews, I gathered an archive of materials about life at CU. This archive included content from university websites, social media posts, press releases, campus newsletters, and other announcements referenced by students. I wrote field notes to process these materials and analytic memos connecting them to the experiences described in interviews. In doing so, it was possible to gain a more detailed understanding of the specific institutional arrangements encountered by CU students over the course of their college journeys.[56] A close analysis of interview transcripts, archive materials, and field notes illuminated the patterns described in this book. The methods appendix offers additional details about the choices and procedures that guided the research.

Ethnographic interviews like the ones conducted for this study are not meant to quantify experiences or tell us how prevalent they are. Rather, interviews are valuable because of the way they help us understand processes that shape broad social patterns, the emotions that result from lived experiences, the lenses through which participants see the world, and the stories people tell to make sense of their lives.[57] In this study, I set out to talk with students about their college journeys and how they interpreted and dealt with the insecurity that has become so pervasive in contemporary higher education. I heard about the anxieties of choosing and changing majors, of selecting and failing courses, of finding and losing funding. I listened as students described the risks of transferring institutions, taking online classes, or failing to find an internship. I learned about the uncertainties woven throughout attempts to look for guidance on these matters. And I discovered that students encountered and managed insecurity in very different ways.

Insecurity and Inequality in College

Connecting with a diverse group of students afforded the opportunity to be attentive to inequality. While insecurity may be a fact of life for most college students today, not all of them are equally equipped to deal with it. As social scientists have observed, individualistic and uncertain climates create "winners" and "losers" in ways that correspond with durable inequalities.[58] Describing his research on the transition to adulthood for college-going youth, Richard Settersten argued that "the trend toward individualization means that personal characteristics and resources have become increasingly important in determining how young people fare, thereby exacerbating the risks faced by those from disadvantaged backgrounds."[59] In other words, in a context where colleges and universities take little responsibility for student welfare, preexisting inequalities are amplified.

Illustrations of this dynamic can be seen in the divergent experiences students from different socioeconomic backgrounds have navigating higher education. In their longitudinal study of students at a flagship university, Elizabeth Armstrong and Laura Hamilton found that working-class and lower-middle-class youth confronted notable obstacles on their path to a college degree.[60] Without consistent advising, tasks like choosing majors, navigating remedial coursework, and becoming socially involved on campus posed serious risks for these students. Mistakes in any arena could derail one's progress.

Rather than being able to count on structured guidance from institutions, students today often turn to individual resources for support in their college journeys.[61] Socioeconomically advantaged youth benefit from the insights and social connections of their families, occasionally filling in the gaps with strategically chosen university resources. Their affluent parents act as "college concierges," smoothing the path through higher education.[62] But the families of low-income, first-generation, and working-class (LIFGWC) college students usually cannot offer the same resources. Ambiguities in programs of study, financial aid, and faculty expectations create uncertainties that these students frequently struggle to navigate.[63]

The financial risks of college are also elevated for less socioeconomically advantaged students. Though many assume grants and scholarships make college accessible for those who otherwise could not afford to attend, student borrowing is prevalent even among low-income youth who are eligible for Pell Grants.[64] Low-income students are actually more likely to take out loans than their peers from other income levels, and they experience high levels of stress about borrowing, worrying about their prospects of successful repayment.

Further, emerging evidence suggests that experiences with insecurity in higher education are not race neutral.[65] Having encountered prejudice and discrimination in a range of settings, students of color and their families may find uncertainty to be especially perilous. Efforts to mitigate risk often follow. For instance, students of color tend to select majors and engage in career planning in pursuit of more stable postbaccalaureate opportunities.[66] Research suggests this pattern applies across socioeconomic backgrounds. While socioeconomically advantaged White parents often encourage exploration and flexibility, socioeconomically advantaged parents of color may advise students to make firm commitments in order to avoid uncertainty.[67] Despite efforts to plan and minimize insecurity, Black and Latino students frequently confront barriers to success in higher education driven by discrimination, prejudice, and histories of exclusion.[68]

In sum, a lack of structure and intentionality on the part of universities can magnify disparities between college students such that individuals' social locations and the corresponding resources they bring with them to college become incredibly consequential. And as the examples above show, these resources are not just economic ones. Social theorist Pierre Bourdieu described multiple forms of capital that can be leveraged for success in specific settings.[69] Two of the most relevant to research on education are social and cultural capital. Social capital refers to an individual's network of parents, peers, neighbors, faculty, staff, and other mentors who can facilitate success as well as the obligations and loyalties built into those connections.[70] Cultural capital is similarly wide ranging and includes information, comfort, familiarity, and dispositions that can help one navigate an institution.[71] For instance, knowing how to locate academic support services or being comfortable attending faculty office hours are examples of cultural capital that might benefit students in college.

In 2005 Tara Yosso expanded thinking about the impact of sociocultural resources in education with the introduction of her theory of *community cultural wealth*.[72] In addition to recognizing the influence of traditional forms of social capital and cultural capital, this framework accounts for a range of previously neglected resources. Specifically, in addition to social and cultural capital, Yosso describes (1) "aspirational capital," or the capacity to sustain hopes for the future despite obstacles; (2) "linguistic capital," which includes abilities derived from experiences communicating in multiple languages or styles; (3) "familial capital," a sense of communal support, encouragement, and shared history; (4) "navigational capital," an ability to navigate through multiple types of institutions, including those characterized by inequality and marginalization; and (5) "resistant capital," observed in behaviors and strategies for opposing oppression.[73]

Going beyond the narrower focus on social class that characterized earlier scholarship on capital, Yosso's work explains how race and ethnicity intersect with socioeconomic background to inform these sociocultural resources. For instance, she explains how students of color and students from immigrant families may draw from experiences of racial and ethnic marginalization to build navigational capital or resistant capital.[74] As the concept of community cultural wealth makes clear, though inequality often takes predictable forms, capital is not the sole domain of middle- and upper-middle-class White students.[75] Students of color, including those from LIFGWC families, bring unique resources for succeeding in higher education. These resources are informed by histories of resisting marginalization as well as experiences moving between and communicating across cultures.[76]

Race-conscious theories of sociocultural resources like Yosso's help illuminate the ways socioeconomic status, race, ethnicity, and additional dimensions of lived experience come together to inform how resources are acquired, leveraged, and received by various audiences.[77] This work shows how students' access to resources is an artifact of histories of racism, nativism, ethnic prejudice, and other forms of oppression. Similarly, the way faculty, staff, administrators, and other gatekeepers interpret a student's use of these resources is driven by that student's social location.[78] The same displays of middle-class cultural capital may be valued differently depending on whether the student in question is Black or White, for example.

Collectively, the contributions of Bourdieu, Yosso, and others who have followed in these traditions provide crucial tools for understanding how inequality might show up in students' capacities to manage insecurity. Though early research on capital and higher education focused somewhat narrowly on college access and outcomes, work since 2010 has delved into students' experiences within college. These studies have shown that theories of capital are applicable to understanding topics such as how students become involved on campus, respond to academic difficulties, interact with faculty members, and find professional opportunities.[79] I argue that these theories can also tell us a great deal about the tools students bring to bear on insecure contexts where individualism, uncertainty, and instability abound.

Some might bristle at seeing the theories of Bourdieu and Yosso employed side by side. In the minds of many, their work is opposed—part of separate scholarly camps. Bourdieu's theories foreground the role of social structure in reproducing inequality. Those operating in the cultural capital tradition are sometimes accused of employing a "deficit perspective" that fixates on what students lack and blames students for their own failures.[80] This critique in some ways misses the point of sociological analysis. Bourdieu theorized how institutions are designed to unequally reward the cultural resources of students from various socioeconomic backgrounds. He noted that this system is arbitrary and serves to reproduce inequality in a way that benefits those in power as they seek to pass advantages on to their children. Put simply, sociological work in this tradition is clear: institutions are to blame.[81] What the critics get right is that interpretations of Bourdieu's work are sometimes translated into inequitable efforts to change students rather than institutions.[82] Programs to equip students from first-generation and working-class families with middle-class cultural capital abound, while systematic efforts to change institutional norms and practices are comparatively rare.

By contrast, Yosso's work emphasizes capacities for resistance and resilience, foregrounding agency. Such perspectives can be empowering for students. But because of this tendency, those who rely on the explanatory power of community cultural wealth are sometimes charged with missing the broader mechanisms that perpetuate inequality.[83] In too many cases, a narrow focus on assets and resilience leaves unexamined the specific ways colleges and universities foster environments where LIFGWC students need to expend tremendous amounts of time and energy to succeed while their socioeconomically advantaged peers can navigate their educational journeys in more leisurely ways.

We need both perspectives. To appreciate the complex dynamics involved in dealing with insecurity, concepts are needed that can illuminate agency as well as constraint.[84] Exploring how resources relate to inequality in insecure educational contexts requires acknowledging the questions that students confront on a regular basis. Can I afford college? Did I select the right school? Should I transfer? Will I choose the right major, opportunities, and classes? Can I succeed on my path, meeting my goals? Will I be rewarded with stable employment? In short, will college pay off? Based on what we know about inequality, it is reasonable to expect that not all students will answer these questions in the same way.

A Road Map for Uncertain Journeys

Insecurity is at the heart of contemporary public higher education. *Degrees of Risk* shows how it shapes college students' experiences, how they respond to its presence, and how specific features of the university often exacerbate it. Though they encountered it in a range of ways, few students could escape this insecurity. It influenced every corner of college life, and a great deal of inequality arose from disparate capacities to manage it.

As I conducted interviews, I met students who were situated in very different ways in relation to the uncertainty that pervaded CU. There were LIFGWC students like Daniel, introduced in the prologue, who were assailed by insecurity. I refer to them as *precarious pioneers*. These students, whose stories are explored in greater detail in chapter 2, arrived in college with few transferable resources at their disposal. Without much in the way of money, social networks, family support, or familiarity with dominant culture, pioneers often felt on their own and were struggling to navigate an insecure climate. As pioneers thought about their journeys through college, they described uncertainty as a fact of life that was impossible to avoid. Instead, they worked to be resilient, recovering each time they were thrown off course.

A Black student named Ellie was like Daniel in many respects. She grew up in a working-class family and was a first-generation college student. However, her encounters with insecurity were different. She spoke of uncertainty as a type of risk that needed to be carefully managed and mitigated when possible. Ellie drew from elements of community cultural wealth in the form of durable aspirations, experience resisting marginalization, and familial support to avoid a variety of hazards. She described herself as a focused and cautious student who was dedicated to doing well in her courses but unlikely to become involved outside of the classroom. I refer to LIFGWC students like Ellie as *risk minimizers*, and their experiences form the basis for chapter 3. Though they worked diligently to chart a safe path through college, their aversion to uncertainty came with costs. Seeking the safe route didn't always position students well for success within or beyond college.

Others were situated in relation to insecurity in very different ways. Wanda, a Latina student, was a continuing-generation college student (meaning she had a college-educated parent) and grew up in an upper-middle-class family. She saw the abundance of choices available at CU as beneficial, offering the chance to distinguish herself from her peers. Taking advantage of opportunities to intern, study abroad, conduct research, and add minors and concentrations to her program of study, she treated insecurity as a game she could win. Socioeconomically advantaged *opportunity maximizers* like Wanda leveraged economic, social, and cultural resources to build résumés that would demonstrate merit. As chapter 4 shows, these students described how their efforts were targeted to alleviate concerns about discrimination on the basis of race, gender, religion, sexual orientation, ability, and immigration histories. Wanda, for instance, talked about the vulnerability she felt encountering racial prejudice on campus that she anticipated would affect her opportunities within and beyond college. Yet maximizers' extensive involvement was sometimes stressful, and their experiences with marginalization often left them feeling anxious about the future.

Finally, there were individuals like Calvin, a continuing-generation White student from an upper-middle-class family. He viewed uncertainty as desirable—a spark for self-discovery. Comfortable with insecurity and sheltered from its most damaging consequences as a socioeconomically advantaged White man, he was positioned as an *insulated explorer*. Basking in the flexibility afforded by CU, students like Calvin could engage in leisurely exploration without pressure to build impressive résumés. They claimed to appreciate the excitement of being surprised and saw bumps in the road as opportunities to learn more about themselves. While the university encouraged such exploration, few students could afford to engage in it. Chapter 5 takes an in-depth look at these patterns.

These young people encountered the insecurity of the ivory casino in different forms, and they managed it in different ways. Daniel struggled to stay afloat, while Calvin savored opportunities for discovery. Ellie sought shelter from uncertainty, while Wanda leveraged flexibility to reproduce her parents' socioeconomic advantages. These responses were not random; they were informed by students' intersectional social locations, their corresponding resource configurations, and the contours of their university, as depicted in tables 1.2 and 1.3.

If we take seriously Bourdieu's contention that schools are responsible for the inequality that emerges within educational settings, it becomes necessary to ask questions about the university's role in producing these patterns.[85] Like many colleges, CU operated with structures, policies, and practices that administrative leaders and most students seemed to take for granted. Sociologists often refer to these organizational features as *normative institutional arrangements*.[86] Such arrangements stem from tendencies of institutions to model themselves after their high-status peers and are often assumed to represent best practices even when little evidence exists to support their efficacy.[87] They can be observed in characteristics of the university that influence how students experience higher education and include things like average class sizes, advisor caseloads, communication strategies, and the organization of student services. Sociologists Rashawn Ray and Jason Rosow note that these arrangements function as "boundaries that shape social interactions and establish control over social environments."[88] I argue that we can better understand how students are encountering insecurity in college if we simultaneously consider the form and impact of normative institutional arrangements.

It would be easy to blame this insecurity on cuts to state funding, rising inequality, or a global pandemic. Factors such as these are clearly influential. But precarity doesn't just seep into colleges and universities from the outside, a product of external forces beyond their control. Postsecondary institutions also play a direct role in producing and perpetuating it. The practices and policies they use to organize education amplify uncertainty, instability, individualism, and anxieties about the future.

Responding to the marketization of higher education, colleges cater to a specific subset of affluent students and families. The way a university like CU is situated in relation to these individuals has everything to do with the context of fiscal austerity surrounding public education today, which positions students as customers rather than learners.[89] Though public universities

TABLE 1.2. Characteristics of students' relationships to insecurity

Student type	Student demographics	Resource configuration	Interpretation of insecurity	Navigational strategies
Precarious pioneers (26%; $n = 27$)	Low-income, first-generation, and working-class students	Few economic resources, little familiarity with higher education, and limited family support; they rely on capacities for resilience	Seen as dangerous but unavoidable; feel assailed by insecurity	Being resilient when insecurity creates setbacks, "picking yourself back up"
Risk minimizers (25%; $n = 26$)	Low-income, first-generation, and working-class students	Few economic resources and little familiarity with higher education, but familial support equips them with community cultural wealth	Seen as risk that has to be carefully monitored and avoided when possible	Using available resources to minimize insecurity, seeking a safe route through college
Opportunity maximizers (36%; $n = 37$)	Socioeconomically advantaged students who have been marginalized on the basis of race, gender, sexual orientation, ability, or immigration	Economic and social capital come together with elements of dominant cultural capital in the form of college knowledge	Seen as complex (stressful but also advantageous), offering various opportunities to be leveraged for protection against marginalization	Using resources and opportunities to win at a game of merit, producing demonstrable achievement through strategic engagement
Insulated explorers (13%; $n = 14$)	Socioeconomically advantaged students who feel insulated as members of advantaged groups (often White men)	Economic, social, and dominant cultural capital, including both college knowledge and ease	Seen as desirable, providing the context for broad personal growth and development	Basking in insecure environments, emphasizing exploration in pursuit of personal development

TABLE 1.3. Sociodemographic characteristics of student types

Student characteristic	Precarious pioneers % (n)	Risk minimizers % (n)	Opportunity maximizers % (n)	Insulated explorers % (n)
Parental education				
First-generation college students	85 (23)	81 (21)	3 (1)	0 (0)
Continuing-generation students	15 (4)	19 (5)	97 (36)	100 (14)
Family income				
Low income	78 (21)	73 (19)	3 (1)	0 (0)
Middle or high income	22 (6)	27 (7)	97 (36)	100 (14)
Social class background				
Working class	67 (18)	62 (16)	3 (1)	0 (0)
Lower-middle class	22 (6)	27 (7)	3 (1)	0 (0)
Middle class	11 (3)	8 (2)	32 (12)	29 (4)
Upper-middle class	0 (0)	4 (1)	62 (23)	71 (10)
Race/ethnicity				
Asian or Asian American	26 (7)	19 (5)	24 (9)	0 (0)
Black or African American	15 (4)	12 (3)	16 (6)	7 (1)
Hispanic or Latinx	22 (6)	31 (8)	11 (4)	0 (0)
White	30 (8)	27 (7)	27 (10)	86 (12)
Multiracial, other race/ethnicity	7 (2)	12 (3)	22 (8)	7 (1)
Gender				
Women	48 (13)	62 (16)	60 (22)	21 (3)
Men	52 (14)	35 (9)	38 (14)	71 (10)
Nonbinary or agender	0 (0)	4 (1)	3 (1)	7 (1)

Note: Please see the Methods appendix for additional details on the definition of various sociodemographic categories.

ostensibly exist primarily to educate state residents, these institutions are increasingly beholden to affluent out-of-state families capable of affording full tuition.[90] Where an in-state student might pay $12,000 annually to attend CU, out-of-state tuition exceeds $35,000 a year. Out-of-state students are also more likely to live on campus and pay for the auxiliary services such as housing, dining, and parking that make up important revenue streams for many colleges today.[91]

An emphasis on the desires of affluent out-of-state students may be surprising at a school like CU, where the typical student wasn't from a wealthy family and didn't grow up hundreds of miles away. Most undergraduates were middle or working class and arrived at the university from nearby cities and counties. Moreover, CU sometimes described itself as a "diverse" and "accessible" university with a focus on supporting upward mobility. The university website featured stories about the successes of LIFGWC students. In a single week in May, three profiles were posted to its homepage. They featured a "first-generation student" from a college access program, a student from an upwardly mobile immigrant family, and a low-income student who "overcame challenges" including "financial hardships."

Nonetheless, the focus on affluent students and families shapes institutions like CU in fundamental ways. With these individuals in mind, colleges make assumptions about what their priorities and desires might be, and university personnel come to rely on normative institutional arrangements that cater to them. These arrangements, in turn, coalesce to determine which types of broad pathways through a university are most visible and accessible. Armstrong and Hamilton note that when an institution "structures the interests of a constituency into its organizational edifice, we say that it has created a 'pathway.'"[92] They give examples of pathways focused on social engagement, professional preparation, and upward mobility, and they illustrate the concept with a helpful comparison: "Just as roads are built for types of vehicles," they observe, "pathways are built for types of students."[93] Chapter 6 delves into the normative institutional arrangements that shaped the types of pathways available to students at CU.

At many institutions today, it is believed that socioeconomically advantaged students and their families see college as a venue for unencumbered exploration and self-discovery. In her book *Degrees of Inequality*, Ann Mullen shows that while many students think of postsecondary education as a means of career preparation, the most socioeconomically advantaged youth view going to college as an opportunity to grow through self-actualization and self-exploration.[94] These dispositions align with an emphasis on flexibility, which can be seen in the proliferation of curricular, cocurricular, and extracurricular options on many college campuses.[95] With a title that acknowledges its connection with Mullen's work, *Degrees of Risk* shows how catering to affluent students leads higher education administrators to weave flexibility and choices into organizational arrangements at the expense of structured guidance, creating complex and risky pathways through college.

The result is that CU and schools like it tend to share several features characteristic of insecurity culture: they are flexible and unstructured, providing resources in a laissez-faire way on an extensive menu of options, rather than integrated throughout curricular requirements. These institutions therefore work best for students who have sufficient stores of economic resources—to pay for tuition, fees, books, technology, extracurricular activities, and other expenses—as well as dominant social and cultural capital to help them navigate the abundance of choices and opportunities available at the university.

Many young people do not have access to all of these resources. This created problems for students like Daniel and Ellie, as they tried to succeed in a university that wasn't built for people like them. These youth confronted normative institutional arrangements that functioned to amplify insecurity. In contrast to flexibility and choice, Daniel and Ellie would have appreciated structured guidance. Even the socioeconomically advantaged maximizers like Wanda were sometimes frustrated by the absence of particular types of resources (like robust support for students with marginalized identities). But in addition to shaping the types of policies and practices that exist within an organization, a focus on a narrow subset of affluent students also informs which resources are absent, underfunded, or understaffed.[96] Over the course of the study, it became apparent that many CU students struggled because potentially beneficial resources had limited visibility (i.e., they weren't widely known or publicized), didn't employ proactive practices, or were decentralized and disconnected from the curriculum.

There were also noteworthy exceptions to the patterns described above. At universities as large as CU, there are usually some programs that take a different approach to student support, scaffolding journeys through higher education. While they may be comparatively rare, it is important to examine and learn from these exceptions. The latter portion of chapter 6 does just that in order to consider how certain programs can function to bolster security, helping to mitigate uncertainty and provide stability for a broader range of students.

Collectively, the findings presented in this book expose a series of lessons for students, scholars, and higher education leaders. Chapter 7 brings these insights together. It begins with an overview of the problematic lessons students described learning at CU. As they confronted rampant insecurity, they acquired individualistic perspectives or *selectively sociological imaginations* that contributed to the reproduction of inequality. The LIFGWC students who adopted individualistic perspectives described learning to see struggles as the result of individual deficits rather than learning to connect their experiences to broader social, historical, or political contexts. Meanwhile, I use the term *selectively sociological imagination*, building from the work of C. Wright Mills, to characterize a pattern whereby more socioeconomically advantaged students used contextualized explanations of their own experiences but failed to extend those explanations to understanding the experiences of others.[97] They thoughtfully described how their social locations were shaped by an intermingling of privilege and oppression but quickly turned to individualistic explanations of the struggles confronted by others.

The second portion of chapter 7 explores lessons for scholars, showing how the concepts presented in this book offer new ways to conceive of insecurity, inequality, and the relationships between the two within public higher education. Finally, understanding how college students encounter insecurity and the challenges presented by normative institutional arrangements devised for affluent students helps to unearth strategies for redesigning universities. This last chapter concludes with lessons faculty, administrators, and policymakers can use to build institutions capable of supporting success for more diverse groups of students.

2

Precarious Pioneers:
Deploying Resilience for an Uncertain Journey

When I met April, she had been in college for more than a decade, attending four different postsecondary institutions over the course of that time. A White, first-generation college student from a working-class family, she experienced college as a whirlwind of precarity. Describing her experiences at CU so far, she noted,

> There was a lot of uncertainty around finances, around housing, even food security sometimes. . . . I lived in my car for two months. . . . I was basically living in my car on campus and showering at the gym. . . . Sometimes it's been one of those things where I've had to make decisions between taking care of getting my textbooks and getting clothes that I need or shoes or whatever. I remember I wore one pair of sneakers for almost five years. They had holes in both soles because I was buying textbooks, because textbooks are just so expensive.

In the times when April did have housing or finances, she shared them with family. Currently juggling two jobs, she noted, "I work because I need to. . . . I still [financially] support my father to an extent and my siblings for a little while lived with me—off and on, different siblings—so there was never really an option to just be a student."

April's uncertain financial situation wasn't the only source of insecurity she encountered in college. She also struggled to understand and navigate the university bureaucracy:

> It was tough trying to find the resources I needed at CU. . . . And when I did, it was a little bit overwhelming. Like the person I talked to . . . gave me about twenty different things that I needed to get in touch with, or find more resources for, or call and see and maybe get directed somewhere else. . . . It's a lot to navigate. It's overwhelming.

April went on to explain how her struggle to find resources and support amplified the uncertainties she experienced in college. It often felt like she was making this journey on her own with little sense of what would happen next. Though she described navigating the university as "overwhelming," she was quick to absolve CU of blame: "I have to also acknowledge that something that may be overwhelming for me might not be overwhelming for somebody else. . . . Perhaps they have [resources] set up perfectly for the average student, and I just don't fall into that."

I refer to individuals like April as *precarious pioneers*. These students were assailed by insecurity in higher education. As first-generation college students who came from low-income and working-class families, pioneers experienced college as new and frequently hostile terrain.[1] Bombarded by uncertainty and instability, they struggled to chart a course at CU, and their trajectories through higher education were frequently derailed by the precarity that shaped their lives on and off campus. Nonetheless, pioneers drew on personal resources to be resilient and persist in their studies even in the face of long odds.

As April's words illustrate, pioneers often characterized themselves as atypical students. They believed their experiences were unusual, and as such, they sometimes thought the university couldn't be expected to organize student services in ways that worked for individuals like them.[2] Yet experiences like April's are far more common than is often acknowledged. In fact, about a quarter of the students I interviewed at CU fell into this group. Pioneers' sense that their challenges with insecurity were unusual came not from any statistical reality but rather from their isolation and alienation at a university that expected students to thrive in an insecure environment where flexibility and choices were prioritized over structured guidance. This chapter illuminates the experiences of a group of students who are frequently invisible in higher education.

Encountering and Interpreting Insecurity in College

Beliefs about the "typical" student are skewed toward more affluent youth who have historically been the focus of research on college students, popular culture portrayals of university life, and efforts to market higher education.[3] Nonetheless, the past decade has witnessed expanding understandings of the experiences of LIFGWC college students. Today, for instance, we know more about these students' pathways to higher education as well as the factors that shape their transition from high school to college and their persistence to graduation.[4] This literature has begun to illustrate how postsecondary institutions themselves generate, and frequently limit, these pathways. In their book *Paying for the Party*, Elizabeth Armstrong and Laura Hamilton explain how many of the barriers confronted by LIFGWC students can be attributed to a "blocked mobility pathway."[5] They note that such barriers are commonplace at institutions that fail to provide sufficient resources for student support. Though students who receive extensive support from their parents and hence do not need to work—as much or at all—tend to fare well in these settings, their less socioeconomically advantaged peers have very different experiences.

Scholars have also uncovered valuable insights about how LIFGWC students become involved on campus and the challenges they encounter finding a sense of belonging in college settings that cater to more affluent youth.[6] We have even learned a great deal about the diverse ways these students navigate relationships with family and their home communities.[7] Despite this progress, little is known about how LIFGWC students are encountering and interpreting the insecurity that characterizes higher education today. The stories of precarious pioneers help to fill this gap.

Pioneers entered CU with a vision of college as a place that could offer a guided path toward upward mobility and stable adulthood. As other scholars have found, the promise of middle-class employment was a crucial part of this understanding.[8] This was clear when pioneers replied to my inquiry about why they chose to attend college. Kim, a Black LIFGWC student, responded succinctly, "for better opportunity, better jobs," and Kwang, a low-income, first-generation Asian student, noted that, "education, for me, was a ladder to a better life." College seemed to offer the promise of an escape from the insecurity that characterized their childhood and adolescence.

Yet pioneers were frequently disappointed when they discovered that their journeys through college could feel even more precarious than their high school years. A White first-generation student named Grant summed up this realization, describing higher education as "a roller coaster, because college is so much new stuff. There's more happening, more highs and more lows." He acknowledged that while life was filled with uncertainty, in college there was "more unexpected stuff," making uncertainty "more common, more frequent." Similarly, Alvin, a Black student from a low-income family, noted that, "I'm used to unpredictability in life. . . . But college brings it to a whole new level."

Instead of a structured route to a bachelor's degree and middle-class adulthood, these youth found that college was an unpredictable setting. Choices and opportunities abounded, but there was little guidance to be found on how to handle these possibilities. Was it safe to change one's major, adopt a new concentration, get involved in a student organization, work an unpaid internship, or study abroad? Should students take twelve credits a semester or fifteen?

Would it be wise to postpone graduation in order to complete a minor? Could they find help preparing for exams, paying tuition, choosing a career, accessing technology, or receiving testing accommodations? In a university where options were wide ranging with little structure, navigating higher education was complex to say the least.

The distance between students' initial conceptions of what college would be like and the reality they discovered at CU was difficult to process. Bernadette, an Asian LIFGWC student, said, "It's so unpredictable what was going to happen each day of college. . . . I didn't understand how different it was going to be [from high school]." She explained how the uncertainty that seemed inescapable at college was, "negative because I personally don't like things that happen unpredictably. I would like to know exactly what's going to happen." This realization gave students pause as they began to wonder whether graduation would ever arrive, and if it did, whether their degree would open doors to a job. Sam, a Middle Eastern LIFGWC student, explained,

> If you don't have a college degree, you're screwed, but just because you have a college degree doesn't mean you're going to get a six-figure salary. . . . Like, you have a degree, cool, but so does that guy who chugs beer every night with his frat. Getting a degree doesn't do as much as it used to. . . . That's why I have a lot of stress and frustration with paying all this money, because it's not giving me the life that I was promised college would get me. It's just getting me to a door that everyone is trying to squeeze through.

Sam's frustration stemmed from the discrepancies between his initial conception of college as a structured route to middle-class employment and the reality that his journey at CU had unearthed: going to college offered a chance for upward mobility but no guarantees.

This insecurity could have powerful effects on the ways precarious pioneers experienced higher education. After noting that life at CU often felt uncertain, Andre, a White first-generation and low-income student, told me about his feelings toward this type of environment: "The uncertainty part affects me a lot. . . . It's always going to make you question how good you are, how worthy you are, if you're going to make it. . . . You don't know if you are going to do well in those classes. . . . Those uncertainties really prevent me from even studying sometimes." As his quote illustrates, an insecure climate fomented feelings of doubt and uncertainty, feelings that could sometimes be paralyzing. Though the extent of this insecurity came as a surprise for most pioneers, they had few resources to dispel uncertainty, and many quickly came to take it for granted as an unavoidable part of college life. As Bernadette summarized, "It is what it is."

Economic Insecurity in College

"I don't think it should cost so much just to get an education. I was told all my life, 'you need to go to college to get a good job,' not 'you need to get a good job to go to college.'" With these words, Kevin, a Black LIFGWC student, summed up the frustration expressed by many of his peers. Though it was common knowledge that college could be expensive, he'd heard that ample financial aid was available for low-income students. He also attended a community college before transferring to CU. Having thought that choosing public colleges would be a smart financial decision, Kevin was shocked by how quickly his tuition and fees added up. Before long he had maxed out on federal loans and was borrowing money from his cousins to try to remove a registration hold CU had placed on his student account.

The pronounced insecurity pioneers encountered related to a range of factors. Perhaps the most foundational of these was economic insecurity. Pioneers typically came from low-income, working-class families with little in the way of financial resources. Like April, they sometimes experienced housing and food insecurity that amplified the instability of their college journeys. Alyssa slept on friends' couches before moving in with her boyfriend's family, and Jyoti lived in her professor's basement for a semester. Daniel, introduced in the prologue, felt the impact of material deprivation in a variety of ways, with concerns that ranged from whether he and his family would have enough food to where he could do his academic work when the COVID-19 pandemic caused campus to close temporarily. Daniel noted, "I went from being in the classroom [and the library] to being at home learning, and I didn't have a desk in my room. I'd be sitting on my bed . . . streaming courses. So, I got an office chair and I'd use my bed as a desk. . . . I'd be hunched over writing notes. . . . But I got through it."

This economic precarity created barriers that limited students' ability to fully engage in their courses. Unable to afford textbook purchases, pioneers tried to succeed in classes using borrowed copies, old editions, and even YouTube videos to substitute for course texts. Funding technology needs proved similarly challenging. Kim, for instance, confronted a series of tech-related obstacles to doing her homework and participating in online classes:

> As far as having access to technology . . . for me, internet could be spotty. And because of our parents' situation . . . bills wouldn't be paid sometimes. So, I didn't have WIFI for about a week, and I had to use our neighbor's— I had to go over to his house and be in his basement to use his WIFI to do my classes. . . . I also have no webcam. My computer is very old . . . and some teachers really want a webcam [for class participation].

Even smaller expenses could add up. Kim expanded on her remarks, emphasizing that the costs of engaging in college went beyond laptops and in-home Wi-Fi to basic materials that many faculty and students took for granted. "Even paper—I know that's a weird thing to bring up. . . . But paper is a cost." She told me about one of her strategies for "penny pinching" in a math class that required frequent use of scratch paper: "I would use a picture frame . . . with a piece of paper in the back and write on the glass [with a dry-erase marker]. I would just write on the glass and then wipe it off."

Struggles with economic insecurity meant that pioneers also experienced financial uncertainties that affected their ability to remain enrolled at CU. Dee, a Latina LIFGWC student, noted, "The most unpredictable part of my college experience has to be the financial situation." This unpredictability took two main forms. First, there was the surprise that "some of these classes are just more expensive than I thought." Then there was additional confusion about why her financial aid package changed after she transferred to CU from a community college: "I know that FAFSA was helping me for quite a while, but now I feel like they're not. Although I'm going to a more expensive school, I feel like they're paying less and less of my classes." The result was a precarious financial situation that necessitated tough decisions about how to proceed. Dee recalled,

> I would have to choose like, okay do you want to skip the semester and work more? Or do you just really want to try and get that loan or maybe push it working full-time and going to school and paying these off, even though you might be paycheck to paycheck? Or lastly, but I really wouldn't want to, is ask my parents for money. . . . I had thought this year I wasn't going to go to school. I didn't go last semester, and I thought I wasn't going to be able to go this semester.

Having already taken a semester off when she couldn't pay fall tuition, Dee was glad to be enrolled in classes again for the spring term. Yet the prospect of having to pause her studies again in the near future was very real. Averse to private loans and reluctant to ask her parents for money at a time when her mother was unemployed and her father's landscaping work was their only source of income, she was hoping that her new job would get her through the coming semester.

Even when they were able to remain enrolled in classes, pioneers found themselves in recurring situations where financial constraints threatened to throw them off course. A clear example appeared in Miguel's account of his college journey. A Latino LIFGWC student, Miguel joined me for an interview on a Wednesday morning in early November. Recalling how, "I came in a little blindly; I did not know everything [about how to fund college]," he described a series of crises that ensued in the form of recurrent

> moments where I was like, "maybe I shouldn't continue for next semester." . . . I passed all of [my classes], maybe with a C or B in there, but I managed to get through all my classes. But there was a point in the first-semester freshman year where I was not really sure if I was going to be able to come back the next semester. . . . It was really bad actually. It was my first semester of first year, and I just didn't think I was ever going to come back after. . . . It was a very stressful time. . . . I paid most of [my bill] off the first semester and then I realized I was a little short on it and I wasn't going to be able to manage to pay off all of it.

This realization brought shock and panic. Miguel recalled, "I didn't come in with the full knowledge of how much exactly I was going to pay. So, I just figured it out like halfway through [the first semester] and I was like, 'I've got to hurry up and earn that money.'"

Miguel took extra shifts at "random jobs," making a series of small payments to his account. Realizing that he was going to fall short on funds, he visited the financial aid office. "They basically said my last option was just to get more and more loans," but having already maxed out on federal loans, he realized, "I didn't have the option of getting private loans. . . . I was never going to get approved for them." Miguel was probably correct in this assessment. While federal loans don't require a credit score, private lenders typically require a cosigner who meets a certain score threshold. In this way, many LIFGWC students find their options for financing college are limited even if they are willing to consider additional loans.

Things were thrown further into limbo when the university sent Miguel's remaining bill to collections along with a late payment penalty. He began to wonder what would happen next. "I didn't know what was going to happen. . . . [My family members] weren't supporting me either, so I was on my own and had very few people around. . . . I thought I was going to be homeless actually. . . . In a homeless shelter or something. It was a very extreme situation."

Three days from the deadline to reconcile his bill before being dropped from spring classes and housing, Miguel had a fortunate encounter. Breaking into a smile, he recalled:

> At the last minute, I met someone—a friend of a friend—it was a total stranger. I told him my situation, and three days before [the deadline] he loaned me $800, and that's how I made it past the finish line. . . . So yeah, a stranger basically saved me. . . . It was a very last-minute thing.

Unfortunately, this was far from his last brush with precarity. The pattern continued for Miguel, who summed up a recurring problem: "I work summers trying to make money, and I spend it all in the fall." These accounts were common among pioneers. As noted in chapter 1, while just a few decades ago many students in the US could pay the full cost of college attendance with a part-time job paying minimum wage, that would be far from feasible today.[9] This insecurity followed Miguel right up to the moment of our interview, when he acknowledged, "Actually, for next semester I'm thinking I might have to take it off too. . . . It's like a repeat of the freshman first semester." His sense that the struggles of prior semesters were repeating themselves was disheartening. Yet for pioneers, this feeling was a familiar one; precarity was not a momentary challenge, it was omnipresent.

The causes of financial insecurity went beyond not having money. Struggles to understand a complex system for obtaining grants, loans, and other funding opportunities also played an important role. Sam painted a picture of CU's new student move-in day when he learned about a balance for "tens of thousands of dollars" that had appeared on his student account. "It was a big price tag, and I had just moved in, and I had a huge freak out. I was like 'oh my god, I can't go to college,' you know, it was a lot of anxiety." He traced this confusion to inequality in the availability of information about financial aid:

> I didn't know how loans worked. I didn't know how financial aid worked. I didn't know any of that stuff. I didn't know you had to fill out more documents and turn it in or all this stuff. And they don't really teach you about that in high school—at least for me—I didn't know about that. And of course, my friends' parents, they went to college so they kind of knew that stuff. I was a first-generation, and so I had no idea how to do any of that.

Struggles to comprehend college financing followed pioneers throughout their studies. Just as students began to feel they understood the system, new information would catch them off guard. A White LIFGWC student named Amal recalled how he learned to carefully calculate the cost of each semester. Yet the quirks of financing tuition seemed to stymie his efforts to budget. He described college costs as unpredictable, explaining,

> I expected my summer semester to cost less than half a regular semester. . . . I'm in-state, so the tuition is usually 7K [per semester, including student fees], but for summer I'm taking seven credits, not sixteen—not that many, just seven credits—and it's four thousand dollars, so it's more than half my full semester. My first reaction was "bullshit," but what are you going to do?

Compounding this challenge, Amal and other pioneers frequently discovered that their financial aid packages did not extend into the summer term, meaning that bills had to be paid without the help of grants and federal loans. The absence of predictability as it pertained to the costs of college intensified uncertainty for pioneers.[10]

Lost in the Do-It-Yourself University

While economic insecurity was central to shaping the college journeys of pioneers, these students also encountered uncertainty that had little to do with financing college. This insecurity was generated by the contours of a university that expected and rewarded middle-class social and cultural resources. Chapter 6 delves into the normative institutional arrangements of the university in greater detail, but here I offer an in-depth account of pioneers' specific experiences in this context.

Commonwealth University provided a clear example of the "do-it-yourself" environment that Josipa Roksa and I theorized in our study of college seniors.[11] Expecting students to arrive possessing familiarity with higher education and comfort navigating its expansive bureaucracy, this do-it-yourself environment offered resources through a buffet of choices. Orientation videos, university web pages, and newsletters alluded to resources that were "endless" and could be "leverage[d] . . . in reaching your goals." A brochure for prospective students promised that at CU, "you'll have the help you need to shine." Throughout their interviews, however, students described the distance between these resources and their daily experiences, characterizing them as inaccessible in a variety of ways. The university provided little structured support connected to classes or other requirements, contributing to pioneers' sense that this institution wasn't built for people like them. After all, most pioneers were first-generation college students whose parents had little to no firsthand experience with higher education, and most of them came from working-class families whose cultural resources were rarely recognized by the university.[12]

Uncertainty was pervasive from the moment pioneers set foot on campus as they selected classes, chose majors, and navigated faculty expectations. Jonah, a Black LIFGWC student, noted that many individuals at CU attributed uncertainty to the pandemic. Yet he recognized that its roots ran deeper:

I can't blame it on COVID. During the start of my freshman year, it felt very unpredictable because I was like, "okay, I don't know if I can do this major because it's so rough. I don't know if I can really pull through with that degree in [computer science] at the end of the day. I'm not good enough" . . . And that's when I became uncertain a little bit of like "can I really do this major? Am I really fit to be here in college? Do I have the brain power, the intellectual capacity, to really be a college student?" So, in that regard, I was really uncertain.

In this moment, Jonah wasn't just unsure about whether he'd chosen the right major but even about whether he could "really be a college student." As time went on, he continued to have doubts about his academic progress: "I don't know if that four-year plan is really feasible anymore based on where I'm at right now. I think I have my doubts every semester. . . . I'm like, 'can I really do this?'"

Straining to navigate these academic obstacles, Jonah might have benefitted from tutoring, advising, and mentoring. And CU certainly had relevant services available. But when I asked whether he'd received support from any university resources, Jonah frowned, pressing his hand against his forehead. After a long pause, he replied, "I mean, I haven't interacted with the university as much. . . . I feel like right now, I don't know who to go to for advising. I know we have an email [account]. . . . But how helpful is emailing about your academic things? How helpful can that really be?" The prospect of having to disclose his academic struggles through a message to a generic email account was too much for Jonah, who couldn't help "feeling like I'm lost." He speculated about more direct and personalized alternatives, "I'd rather [have a meeting with] a set person I have, and they're going to help me through finding those classes and things like that." While this wish seemed reasonable, Jonah—currently in his third year of study—confessed, "I still don't know my advisor."

The impersonal nature of the do-it-yourself environment showed up even in the ways students learned about the consequences of academic struggles. Lance, a first-generation Asian student, provided an illustrative example. Like Jonah, he recalled how academic challenges sparked uncertainty in his first semester on campus: "My first semester at CU . . . coming from [a] small town; I don't have any of the skills that the students [at CU] would have, and I don't think my high school prepared me enough. . . . I got put on academic probation after my first semester." Having a GPA "below 1.0" brought about all sorts of anxieties. But the worst part was the way he learned about his academic probation status: "I opened my junk mail in my dorm, and I saw a letter from academic affairs . . . saying, listen, you're on academic probation. You really screwed up last semester, so we're limiting you to 13 credits this spring semester." The pain of this moment was still felt fresh as Lance remembered the feelings of uncertainty that washed over him.

> When I first opened that letter, I was [wondering], first of all, am I still on track to graduate? That's number one. Number two is like, I know CU graduates, especially STEM graduates, have a high job placement probability; however, it's not ever going to be 100%, and there's always a chance someone falls through the cracks. . . . So, my other thought was [how will this affect employment opportunities]? The third thing was my [work-study job]. Am I going to get dropped from [that job]? And the fourth thing was like, what's my mother going to think of this?

As these thoughts raced through his mind, Lance reflected on the impersonal nature of this email that ended up in his spam folder. In many ways, it seemed like a metaphor for the way he felt at CU: lost, on his own, and at a distance from the faculty, staff, and administrators who made decisions about his fate. Near the end of his sophomore year, Lance had yet to connect with any faculty or staff who could help him navigate higher education.

Academic challenges are a common element of the transition into college for many youths, especially those coming from underresourced high schools.[13] These challenges can include obstacles related to academic preparation, interpreting faculty expectations, navigating group work with peers, and feeling a sense of belonging in the classroom.[14] Jonah, for instance, contrasted his experience in computer science courses with classmates who "have been coding since they were ten years old." As his example shows, some of the obstacles encountered by pioneers began long before students arrived in college. But academic struggles were also amplified by the insecure climate of CU, where pioneers often perceived they were navigating these struggles on their own.

Even transfer students with prior experience at other types of postsecondary institutions had similar challenges with the do-it-yourself environment. For example, Dee recalled the uncertainties that came with navigating her first year at CU after transferring from a local community college. She described how this uncertainty connected to her identity as a first-generation college student: "My transfer experience was kind of difficult, just because I didn't have anybody to reference to. My parents obviously didn't go to college, neither did my siblings. . . . It was kind of confusing."

The confusion Dee experienced ran the gamut from determining which courses to take to figuring out how to get a parking pass for a lot near her classes. Many of these challenges caught her by surprise in part because, as Dee recalled, staff at her transfer orientation

> mentioned some [support] programs that I would really like to consider, but each time I'm trying to look for these people or bring up the topic, nobody really knows what I'm talking about. . . . Whenever I call the student offices, or anybody in general who I feel like should know, they don't really know much—they know as much as I do on the topic. They're like, "I don't know. Here, I'll transfer you to somebody else," and by the time thirty minutes have passed, I've already been transferred through fifteen people.

Though she'd successfully navigated community college, CU felt expansive and unwieldy. Without resources and human connections built into their programs of study, students like Jonah, Lance, and Dee traversed precarious terrain.

CONTINGENT FACULTY, CONTINGENT CONNECTIONS

One of the most frequently cited examples of growing insecurity in higher education is the proliferation of contingent faculty employment.[15] Though full-time, tenured and tenure-track faculty members were once well represented as instructors in postsecondary institutions, things have changed over recent decades. In 1975, full-time faculty accounted for 55 percent of instructional staff at postsecondary institutions, with more than four in five of those faculty in a tenured or tenure-track position. By the early twenty-first century, there was a new majority, with part-time faculty and graduate students making up approximately 60 percent of college and university instructors while full-time, tenure-line faculty accounted for less than a quarter of the total.[16] Publicly available data indicate that CU's employment of instructional faculty has followed similar trends. In addition to creating challenges for faculty themselves, who cannot count on consistent pay, benefits, and job security, CU's reliance on part-time faculty brought liabilities that affected students. Pioneers felt the impact most acutely.

Part-time faculty often lacked important institutional knowledge. Amal discussed his experience with an adjunct instructor who was "hired two weeks before the semester." By the middle of the term, he felt "completely unprepared" for his course exams. These exams were created by the department rather than the instructor, who seemed similarly surprised by their content. "Excuse my language, but as soon as I saw the questions, I was like, 'what the shit? what does this mean?' It was that uncertain point of no one knew what was going to happen with that class or where it was going to go." This left him in a state of confusion, wondering, "What's next? . . . What do I do? What do I do afterwards?" Amal eventually learned from classmates that there were online resources summarizing the material their instructor hadn't covered, but it was not easy to recover from failing these initial exams.[17]

Moreover, because many part-time and adjunct faculty worked multiple jobs across multiple institutions, they sometimes seemed less accessible to pioneers who primarily relied on email correspondence—rather than office hours—to communicate with faculty.[18] Renee, a White first-generation college student from a low-income family, recalled moments of struggle in a class where she would

> email the teacher, and he didn't respond too often, because he had two or three different emails and he worked at [another organization too]. So, he was always busy as well. We'd have to be like, "Hey, I sent you an email. Did you get it?" And he's like, "No, I'm sorry. I've been busy." And sometimes he still wouldn't see it after that. So, it's been hard.

Coming from families without much firsthand college experience, pioneers could have benefitted from the consistency and institutional familiarity of full-time faculty mentors. Yet these mentors were hard to come by at a university where so many instructors were employed on a part-time basis.[19] As they tried to learn from contingent instructors who were only loosely affiliated with the university, pioneers felt unmoored.

PRECARITY BEYOND THE CLASSROOM

Pioneers also encountered uncertainty as they tried to navigate challenges beyond the classroom. Commonwealth University employed a range of student affairs and counseling personnel to support their college journeys and their broader transition to adulthood. These resources included the university's centers and offices for counseling, career services, diversity and inclusion, new student services, learning services, LGBTQ+ students, veteran support, and alcohol and drug education, to name a few. Each of these units possessed resources capable of reducing the insecurity students encountered. Yet pioneers were often unaware of these resources or had limited access to them.

As Kwang approached the end of his second year at CU, he shared that one of his primary sources of uncertainty had to do with coming out to his parents. Having recently begun a romantic relationship with another student, Kwang worried about how they would react. "It's kind of a worry always in the back of my head. Because if I bring my partner, who is a guy, to meet my family, it could lead to a very bad falling out." Given that he lived at home and relied on his family for food and housing, the consequences of this type of falling out were significant.[20] "It's very anxiety inducing. . . . That's been incredibly stressful, all the time. That's one of the things I have difficulty separating from my education. It's on my mind constantly." While these stressors were affecting Kwang's academic performance, he had not sought support at the university. "The university can't have much of a part in it, so I don't seek out resources," he explained with a sigh. Although CU had relevant services, including a range of workshops, LGBTQ+ center staff, and electronic resources devoted to the coming out process, Kwang was unaware of their existence.

Even when pioneers were informed about resources, they frequently struggled to access them. Sometimes this had to do with the complexity of university bureaucracy. Numerous pioneers described instances of hearing about a resource from a friend only to be sent from one office to the next on a quest to locate its gatekeepers. These resource scavenger hunts were frustrating and exhausting. In other moments, pioneers found that access to resources was moderated in a way that limited their benefit. For example, Rosalyn, a multiracial first-generation college student, detailed the impact of her mother's cancer diagnosis. "It has not been easy. That's for sure. Seeing her scared and afraid of what's going to happen made me worried. . . . During the whole process of her recovering, I fell off my academics for a while because of that. . . . I couldn't get myself to focus on anything." But when Rosalyn reached out to CU's counseling center, "they tried to send me somewhere else." Having previously used her six allotted sessions, the center informed her she would have to seek counseling outside the university. These types of limits on student access to counseling services are common in higher education, especially at large universities.[21]

Some pioneers also found it uncomfortable to approach a university resource for help. For instance, Alyssa, a White LIFGWC student, was aware that she could reach out to the university's financial aid office to ask questions about funding her education, yet she seemed uncomfortable doing so. This was apparent as she described confusion over what happened to one of her grants:

> I used to have a [fund name] grant that [the university] would give me, but I don't have that this semester, I guess because of COVID, but I don't really know. I didn't ask. I figured everyone's probably spamming the financial department, so I just let it go, although I should probably check into it.

Though Alyssa desperately needed this grant, she was reluctant to reach out to financial aid when she sensed they might be busy. Instead, her father took

PRECARIOUS PIONEERS

out a parent PLUS loan to cover her remaining tuition and fees.[22] Chapter 6 expands on the ways CU's policies and practices exacerbated these barriers to accessing resources.

ON THEIR OWN

As they struggled with uncertainty in this do-it-yourself environment, pioneers felt alone, adrift in an uncaring bureaucracy. They perceived a gulf between students like themselves and faculty, staff, and other administrators. Kevin summed up these sentiments:

> I do wish there was more of a direct line between [faculty and administration] and the students. . . . At community college, you kind of knew most of the teachers, and the dean actually would talk to the students and stuff. But here, I have no idea who presides over the college, and I don't really get that feeling whether they care or not honestly.

Having transferred from a small, tight-knit community college, Kevin longed for the sense of connection he'd experienced in a setting where "you kind of knew most of the teachers" and the dean. Without these connections, it was hard to tell whether anyone at the university cared about him.

In line with April's words, quoted in the opening of this chapter, pioneers frequently attributed their sense of being on their own in college to the notion that they were "atypical" students. For some, this implied that CU was "doing the best it can" and couldn't be expected to make changes that would meet their needs, but for others, it led to a sense of frustration with a university they felt had let them down. The sting of alienation was sometimes made worse by students' impression that CU administrators liked to talk about what they were doing for LIFGWC students without following through to provide meaningful support. Miguel explained:

> I have a feeling that they preach a lot about "oh yeah, we do a lot for first-generation students, we do this and this," but when you actually go ask in person for the help, they usually turn you down. . . . I would say divert some of that spending on programs for preaching, "we're going to do this this and this; we support you." Those support things, they're good if they work, but they're basically just words that come out of their mouth. They're not actually following through.

From Miguel's perspective, CU administrators knew the right things to say, but had little intention of making good on their promises to support first-generation college students.

As they struggled to succeed at a university that seemed uncaring and inauthentic, pioneers sometimes felt betrayed. Times when the university left them adrift could have lingering impacts as students carried the pain and isolation of these moments through their college journeys. Sam illustrated this point when he discussed the way CU's climate of uncertainty undermined his affiliation with the university.

> I completely get people who are like, "yay [school mascot], yay CU!" like they love their school, right. But for me, that first year, I never bought one hoodie from the bookstore. I never had one CU poster or anything like that, no CU gear at all . . . because I was like, "you guys are robbing me." . . . It made me not appreciate school as much or have school spirit. . . . I always thought that I was weird for that. . . . A lot of people don't talk about that. They're like, "you're crazy, school spirit, yay, go CU!" . . . Every time I have to pay part of the payment plan, I feel like I'm cutting an arm off, literally. . . . Especially considering the uncertainty revolving around after college for me, which is like, "is this degree worth it, am I going to get a job with this degree?" I might not.

Though uncertainty seemed to accost pioneers at every turn, from their perspective, CU was uninterested in helping to minimize that uncertainty. Sam's impression that his feelings were unusual—"I always thought that I was weird for that"—made his sense of isolation all the more pronounced. When other students expressed their school spirit, he felt alone.

The Impact of Personal Resources

Pioneers' encounters with precarity in college were shaped not just by the structure of university resources but also by the personal resources at their disposal. Research has examined the forms of capital students bring with them to college. Yet the picture painted by these studies has been limited in some ways. Perhaps most notably, this research portrays LIFGWC students as either lacking capital or as benefiting from extensive familial support. The first perspective, couched in theories of social reproduction, argues that students from less socioeconomically advantaged backgrounds arrive at college without the dominant social or cultural resources expected by universities and hence are set up for failure.[23] Research in this vein tells a story of how these students are disadvantaged by middle-class institutions, which work against social mobility. A second perspective, drawing from theories of community cultural wealth, posits that the families of LIFGWC students are tight-knit and provide extensive support that counteracts the exclusionary expectations of universities.[24] The story here is one of the marginalized triumphing over oppressive institutions. Although both perspectives illuminate crucial elements of inequality, they also miss important complexity.

Research in the social reproduction tradition often assumes LIFGWC students enter college without applicable resources due to a lack of the middle-class cultural capital rewarded by many institutions.[25] And it was certainly true that pioneers encountered unique challenges navigating the college setting. As the previous section illustrates, CU was organized in a way that created hurdles for students whose parents weren't familiar with the contours of higher education and the array of institutional resources and opportunities available. Coming from LIFGWC families, pioneers struggled in this environment and faced very real resource constraints.[26] Daniel, for instance, summed up this situation, noting that "Being from a working-class family means that—especially with parents that have never gone to university in the US—I didn't have that net to navigate when I was going through university." Others described how being an LIFGWC student could restrict social networks. April recalled, "There was a time there where I had very few social resources around me, mostly because I didn't want people knowing that I was living in my car." Her experiences align with the findings of studies suggesting that LIFGWC students face an uphill battle finding support networks on campus.[27] Notably though, even in the face of these obstacles, pioneers managed to persist in their studies, challenging the notion that they were without resources.

Another strand of research on the experiences of LIFGWC students emphasizes the ways community cultural wealth can help them succeed in college.[28] Tara Yosso defined community cultural wealth as "an array of knowledge, skills, abilities and contacts" that marginalized students, including students of color, low-income students, working-class students, and students from immigrant families, use to persist in oppressive institutions.[29] Most of these forms of cultural wealth rely on close connections with supportive families. For instance, *familial capital* includes a "sense of community history" fostered by strong communal bonds, while *resistant capital* refers to the capacity, typically taught by parents and other family members, to oppose inequality and subordination. The interviews conducted for this study affirmed that many LIFGWC students did in fact benefit from supportive families and assets that derive from communal experiences resisting marginalization.[30] Chapter 3 will delve into the experiences of a group of students with access to such resources. Yet pioneers didn't fit this model.

Pioneers usually portrayed their parents as less engaged in their college journeys, like the bystanders described by Laura Hamilton in her book *Parenting to a Degree*.[31] Miguel's family migrated to the US when he was in elementary school, and neither his parents nor his older brothers extended their education beyond high school. When he prepared for college applications, Miguel didn't even mention his plans to his mother or father. "It's always a little rocky with family," he acknowledged, "we don't really talk about [college] stuff, it's just something I do on my own. I basically just ventured into college on my own. I did applications without telling them." Similarly, Kwang's impression that his parents were "not LGBT-friendly" often dissuaded him from looking to them as a source of support, and April described her family as skeptical of the value of higher education. "None of my family, with the exception of one grandfather ever went through any kind of higher education. . . . He went to seminary, and that was about the highest education level in my family. . . . So higher education was not seen as necessary or sometimes even helpful to being able to live the life you wanted to live."

The experiences of students like Miguel, Kwang, and April complicate essentialist assumptions that all LIFGWC students arrive in college with extensive community cultural wealth to support their success. The reality is that the LIFGWC students I interviewed were a diverse group.[32] While some benefitted from familial support and related community resources, for pioneers, this type of support was not something they could take for granted.[33] Instead, they relied on personal capacities for resilience.

DRAWING FROM PERSONAL RESOURCES TO BE RESILIENT

Renee's college journey began with disappointment after learning that she was rejected from the only university she applied to—one she'd assumed was a safe bet—because her high school transcript was not received on time. After initially forgetting to submit the transcript, she made an unsuccessful last-minute attempt to fax the document the evening it was due. As a result, her application was marked incomplete. News of the rejection was not easy to digest, but she quickly applied to community college and began an associate degree instead. When challenges funding her education arose, Renee recalled, "I applied for weeks and months for scholarships and never ever received one. I went though, like, fifteen different websites; took surveys, wrote essays, did all that and I never heard back from anybody." In the end, she found an off-campus job to help pay tuition.

While Renee worked diligently to push through a range of challenges at community college and eventually transferred to CU, precarity quickly took hold there as well. "My GPA's kind of tanked since I've transferred, and I'm working on getting that back." Focused on bringing up her grades, Renee was often overwhelmed. As each semester began, she felt the crushing weight of uncertainty: "it's like that . . . every semester. It's kind of unsure how I'm going to figure out how to study; unsure how the tests are going to be held; unsure if I'm going to get a good grade."

Struggling to communicate with her professors (who "don't respond [to emails] too often") and her family ("without context, it's hard for them to understand"), Renee relied on her own resilience to push through college. She described her sense that she was "juggling everything" alone:

> I'm trying to take it day by day with the current classes and my current stresses. . . . I am a very hard-working person. Doing my best to . . . bring my GPA up . . . and then a part-time job on the side, and then my home stresses as well. And my family, my friends are going through some things, so I'm dealing with that as well.

After being laid off from her job, she took out loans to fund her final year of college, "I'm forcing myself to graduate. . . . It's been really stressful because I'm in six classes." With a course credit overload, Renee tried to press ahead to graduation.

Pioneers' activation of personal resources to support resilience was especially evident when they discussed recovering from encounters with uncertainty and instability. For them, being resilient meant accepting precarity as an unavoidable part of college life and pushing through difficult times with positivity and determination. Catherine, a first-generation Latina student from a working-class family, summed up her philosophy for navigating CU:

> We are literally full of uncertainty, and we've just got to learn to live with what we have right now and make the best of it. . . . Anything can happen at any moment. I'm just going to do what I can to keep myself going, because thinking negative won't get me anywhere. . . . [When things go wrong] you adapt and move forward.

Eric, a Latino first-generation student from a working-class family, described a similar approach to handling challenges at CU: "For me, I just push through it." And Alvin claimed that "if there's an uncertainty that I'm facing currently, I have to think about how I need to really persevere through it. In day-to-day life, things can happen that I won't be ready for. . . . I tell myself to slow down, think positive; it's going to get better." As their words made clear, pioneers saw determination and persistence as a necessity in a university that was "full of uncertainty."

An emphasis on resilience went hand in hand with an orientation toward self-reliance. Tara illustrated the ways students' struggles with the do-it-yourself environment at CU encouraged them to depend on personal resources rather than institutional ones. Having heard about the university's Career Services Center and its mission of supporting students with professional development, Tara decided to seek them out. Yet her experience with this office took a painful turn when her self-presentation was critiqued by a staff member.

> Last year, I was trying to apply for this [opportunity], so I went to career services to check my résumé and make a cover letter. . . . I walked in and they directed me to this guy . . . and he was just critiquing everything I was doing, my behavior and how I was acting and . . . I don't know how to describe it. I started crying and then I left. And I just never went back to any CU resources. It was a very bad experience.

Tara summed up her takeaway from this encounter: "So, I'm just going to use my own resources." Similarly, Miguel recalled, "I tried all the resources I could at CU [financial aid office], and they let me down. They didn't pay attention to my case. . . . But I managed it, and I'm still here." Though some students may have turned to family resources for support, this was not a viable option for pioneers whose communication with parents was limited. As Kwang put it, "It's all down to me."

Feeling like they were on their own, unable to depend on family or the university for support, pioneers were compelled to adopt a neoliberal self, one that emphasized individual responsibility.[34] In doing so, these students adhered to what Allison Pugh refers to as a *one-way honor system* "that dictates strict rules for themselves" without attempting to hold the institution—in this case, the university—accountable for its shortcomings.[35] Though students were often frustrated with CU, they made clear that the ultimate responsibility for success rested on their own shoulders. In the end, rather than pushing back against the do-it-yourself environment, pioneers engaged in self-blame. Renee illustrated this tendency when she proclaimed that her "biggest obstacle" to success was herself. Even after expressing his disappointment with the university, Sam's voice became soft as he professed, "I also never really reached out for help all that much, so that kind of is on me."

When they found themselves in a bind, pioneers turned inward, refashioning themselves to meet the moment. Eric claimed that resilience was about learning how to adapt to uncertainty. "I think I could have tried harder [to push through struggles]. . . . If it does happen again, I know it's going to be my fault for not learning from it." And Dee said, "I feel like I can do better. I need to work on myself." While this tendency to individualize blame for difficulties was painful for pioneers, it also provided a sense that they possessed the capacity to overcome challenges, to pick themselves back up when knocked down. In short, adhering to the one-way honor system and its individualistic tendencies made the exercise of resilience seem more feasible. Rather than focusing on their frustrations with the university, pioneers repositioned themselves as the responsible parties.

As part of their efforts to be resilient, pioneers explained the importance of holding fast to their ambitions. They leveraged what Tara Yosso calls "aspirational capital," or "the ability to maintain hopes and dreams for the future, even in the face of real and perceived barriers."[36] Jyoti provided a clear example of how aspirational capital helped students persist in their studies. She encountered a range of challenges during her first three semesters at CU and struggled to find resources. Compounding these struggles, her father had a medical emergency that required open-heart surgery. As her family contended with financial hardship, Jyoti began a new job that further compromised her academic performance. Feeling an acute sense of "burnout," she took a leave of absence. Recalling moments during that semester off when she contemplated transferring and "almost wanted to drop out," Jyoti described how her eventual return to CU was driven by "really holding on to my dream of being an art therapist and doing art therapy." Despite the odds, she held fast to her hopes for the future.

THE LIMITS OF RESILIENCE

The resilience and determination shown by pioneers was impressive to say the least. Their stories made clear that these students did in fact bring important resources to the journey through higher education. They did not usually possess the types of social or cultural capital valued by the university or the consistent familial support received by some of their peers, but pioneers had assets in the form of determination to work through challenges, endure uncertainty, and hold fast to their aspirations for the future. Even though their progress was frequently interrupted, they used capacities for resilience to persist in their studies. Yet there were also limits to the help these personal assets could provide at a place like CU.

The shortcomings of self-reliance in the contemporary university are rarely discussed. Fortunately, research on K–12 schools has begun to expose the limits of resilience. In his study of all-male schools, sociologist Freeden Blume Oeur observes that while an emphasis on resilience in high school settings is commendable for highlighting student agency, "this framing accepts as unassailable virtue precisely that which needs to be historically situated."[37]

Focusing on students' capacity for persisting in the face of great odds leaves unexamined the broader social patterns that create obstacles for these youth in the first place, leaving the structural drivers of inequality unchanged.

Drawing from increasingly popular literature on "resilience," "grit," and "growth mindsets," college personnel preach the virtues of individual responsibility.[38] By this logic, students who have the "right attitude" will succeed in their journeys through higher education. And yet these proclamations are disingenuous. Institutions like CU might laud students for self-reliance and independence, but their actual practices reward those who seek help and make demands of university services.[39] Because CU's do-it-yourself environment allocated resources in a self-serve manner, advantages accrued to students who knew where to look for support and how to piece resources together. Chapter 4 delves into the experiences of opportunity maximizers who took this type of approach. Pioneers, by contrast, found that being resilient only carried them so far.

Although capacities for resilience aided students in recovering from setbacks, these personal resources provided less assistance with planning for the future. Kim acknowledged these limitations when she described herself as a student who frequently needed to push through crises. "The best thing I can do is use my endurance," she professed, and Dee acknowledged her tendency to focus on cleaning in unpredictable moments: "It's not like I can hide from [uncertainty]. It's not like I can really hide from [those situations]. I just face them head on. If I'm super stressed, I start cleaning my room more. . . . I just clean, clean, clean, and I'm like 'well at least I'm productive.'" Kim and Dee struggled to anticipate future challenges or generate strategies for addressing those challenges proactively. Instead, they used the resources they had, focusing on recovering from current crises rather than worrying about the future.

Pioneers were conscious of differences between themselves and their peers who had the capacity to develop detailed plans for navigating the insecurity of college. Rupa, an Asian LIFGWC student, contrasted herself with classmates:

> I know people who are like "I have to have a plan, and I have to have everything ready." . . . I don't feel that way. I take it day-by-day. I'm not saying I'm so great; I'm just so behind on everything that I take everything day-by-day. I look at my calendar and I say, "what can I do this week?" . . . My whole life is uncertain, so I don't think [challenges come] as any shock.

Sarina, an LIFGWC Latina student, finished recounting a series of upheavals in a similar way, announcing that she was "going day-by-day." This phrase, "day-by-day," was a refrain for many pioneers, a mantra that provided a modicum of comfort. It offered a prescription for where to focus one's energy (in the here and now), while acknowledging the seeming impossibility of heading off insecurity. Though they recognized the advantages that could accrue for students who were able to plan ahead, circumventing some of the worst manifestations of precarity, Rupa and Sarina needed to "take everything day-by-day."

Moreover, pioneers' emphases on resilience and individual responsibility offered few tools for seeking help from others. As sociologist Lisa Nunn has argued, being self-reliant can be both an asset and a liability in the contemporary university.[40] Participants in her study were reluctant to seek guidance from professors, who, they perceived, valued independence and personal accountability. Yet Nunn shows that, in reality, faculty are often willing to make exceptions to policies or provide additional guidance for students who ask for help, advantaging those who are comfortable making such requests. Pioneers worried that asking for an exception or a change to standard practice would disappoint their professors or be met with indifference. In either case, they were reluctant to make requests for support. Though Kim had come to the realization that she needed "to get better at reaching out or just kind of emailing professors" for help, the do-it-yourself environment offered little guidance on how to do so.

On the Road without a Map

What comes next for pioneers? Interviews with these students offered a partial account of their college journeys, an opportunity to learn about their present circumstances and past experiences. But these conversations also raised questions about their futures. In some ways, pioneers could be viewed as success stories who persisted in the face of significant odds. This was in part due to the nature of my sample. I only interviewed students who were currently enrolled at CU. There were also individuals whom I didn't have an opportunity to talk to, those who started working toward an undergraduate degree but didn't persist beyond their first year.[41] Making it to the second year of college increases one's odds of graduation, but as pioneers made clear, precarity does not end.

Mindful of the fact that insecurity had been woven throughout their journeys thus far, the pioneers in this study recognized that there were few guarantees about the future. Miguel wondered whether he'd be able to return to CU next semester, while others questioned whether they'd ever complete a bachelor's degree. Eric was in his sixth year of undergraduate study but was still unclear about his progress toward graduation. "I also feel uncertain on how I'm on track with the degree—if I'm doing everything well or if I'm going to be able to graduate with what I'm doing or the classes I'm taking and stuff like that." This type of uncertainty lingered even in students' final semester of college. Renee, who was just weeks from graduation, explained: "Trying to graduate . . . has been really stressful. If I don't pass either one of the two attempts for this exam, then I will not be able to graduate, and that's been really high pressure on me."

Additional insecurity manifested in pioneers' discussions of their postbaccalaureate lives. Looking beyond graduation, they experienced a mixture of hope and dread as inspiring ambitions mingled alongside paralyzing uncertainties. They held fast to dreams for a better life, but they also saw few opportunities to escape the precarity that had followed them through college thus far. Catherine illustrated the resulting combination of emotions:

> I think [the future is] exciting. I think it's very exciting. I'm kind of scared, because I don't know what I'm going to do after graduation, but I'm really excited. I can't believe that college went by so fast. I never imagined it would go by this fast. It feels like I was just a freshman yesterday.

Reflecting on how her undergraduate years had flown by, Catherine claimed to be enthusiastic about what the future might hold. Nonetheless, her apprehension about not knowing "what I'm going to do after graduation" felt more urgent each day.

> I can't find anything that relates to my major. That's what kind of worries me as well, because I don't know what I want to do after graduation. . . . You know, honestly, I have no idea. . . . I feel bad about feeling like this, because I'm majoring in criminal justice, and like, I don't know if I'm going to be doing anything that's criminal justice related. . . . We'll see what comes along the way.

Her sense that the future was insecure amplified the stress of this otherwise exciting moment.

Catherine's conclusion that "we'll see what comes along the way" was illustrative of a broader pattern in pioneers' discussions of postbaccalaureate life: these students' visions of the future were often vague. Kim was less than a year from graduation, but when I asked about what she would do after finishing her degree, her response was ambivalent: "I'm still trying to figure that out before I get [to graduation]. I'm not even sure. . . . I'm just doing the best I can, just looking. I'm worried I won't find anything. . . . That's kind of my main worry is finding employment, finding housing, you know." She claimed to be considering a range of pathways including working in art galleries, museums, and health-care settings. Yet with a major in communications and no experience working in these fields, her prospects were limited.

Even students like Jyoti, who professed to have a specific career aspiration, often had few concrete plans for working toward that goal. After describing how she was holding on to her dream to become an art therapist, Jyoti acknowledged that she did not plan to enroll in graduate school for art therapy following graduation.

Challenges anticipating and planning for the future were fueled by several factors. First, with few mentors and resources at the university, pioneers sometimes lacked a sense of what they might do with their degree. Jonah, for instance, was about to enter his fourth year at CU, but when discussing his future, he noted,

> There's so many ways I can take my major. It's not one set route of when I graduate, this is what I'm going to be doing for sure. I could just as easily get the degree and become a software developer, or I can make my own apps and I can do my own thing if the company route is just, let's say I'm finding it tough to find a job. . . . There's not a set, fixed route I can go . . . because my major is just so flexible.

Jonah wanted to appreciate this flexibility, and he described how it contributed to some students' sense of excitement about the future. Yet having such a broad set of options left him "stressed . . . worried about finding a job." He had also considered going to graduate school, but this option felt full of uncertainty as well:

> I'm worried that graduate school is going to be very rough and tough, and I'm not going to be able to do it. Because I'm barely surviving undergrad. Grad is a step up from undergrad; it's up there. So, if I can't do it now, then am I going to be able to do grad school?

In other words, options like attending graduate school, which may have helped pioneers to fine-tune their aspirations, felt ominous after struggling through undergraduate study. This may have been exacerbated by the challenges pioneers encountered finding mentorship from faculty.[42]

Furthermore, pioneers' vague sense of the future was compounded by the same precarities that made planning difficult during their undergraduate years. As they took life "day-by-day" in order to survive the onslaught of insecurity, they struggled to make concrete plans for their next steps. Alyssa, for instance, acknowledged, "So, I haven't quite sat down and researched actual jobs that exist, even though I probably should. But I'm kind of just going along as I can and figuring out what I like to do and what I might be interested in." Though she felt that planning for the future was something she "probably should" be doing, Alyssa described the paralyzing fear that stopped her whenever she thought about life after graduation: "of course I want to think like I'll have an opportunity, but there's always a fear, what if I don't? I know a lot of people don't get good ones that they actually want in their major right away."

Though their peers featured in the coming chapters relied on a range of social resources to guide their transition out of college, pioneers were different. They described how the lessons they learned in college encouraged them to project their self-reliance into the future as they envisioned an independent adulthood. Summarizing what CU had taught him about life, Miguel described college as an "independentizing experience," adding that "relying on yourself, without relying on others, is a very good thing I've learned here." And Jyoti affirmed that college "taught me the importance of independence." The next chapter shifts to examine the experiences of a group of LIFGWC students whose durable networks of community support helped foster very different capacities for dealing with insecurity in higher education.

3

Risk Minimizers:
Using Resistance to Alleviate Insecurity

Noah was soft spoken. When we sat down for an interview one afternoon in April, he was friendly but succinct as he offered a frank assessment of his journey through the first two years of college. It appeared that he had much in common with the pioneers described in the previous chapter. Coming from a working-class and low-income family, Noah entered college with few of the dominant social, cultural, or economic resources expected by CU, and he encountered many of the same insecurities described by pioneers.[1] After initially declaring a major in electrical engineering, he struggled in his first-semester courses, sensing that he was behind his peers and wasn't learning enough. Other challenges followed. Navigating financial aid, interpreting faculty expectations, and transitioning to online classes at the start of the COVID-19 pandemic proved to be especially difficult. Yet he described managing this insecurity in a very different way from the precarious pioneers.

When he "saw that the job growth for [electrical engineering] is not that high in the future," Noah became concerned about the employment prospects of his major, deciding that "I didn't really want to risk it and be an electrical engineer and not have job security." Seeking to avoid economic insecurity and lessen the chance that he might fail courses and "then repeat [them] again and again," he decided to change his major to information technology. He conferred with his new advisor to develop a plan for navigating coursework:

> I had to meet with my advisor and ask what classes I need to take for next semester, having consulting on what would be the best options. . . . Because I don't want to like overdo it and take six classes or so. I just need to consult with them if I should do [each class] . . . or if this is the correct classes I need to take for next semester.

Enlisting the information technology advisor for "consulting," Noah engaged in careful planning as he worked to assess the feasibility of his course selections each semester. In this way, he tried to map out a safe path through his new major.

He approached financing college with the same level of caution and detailed planning, taking part-time jobs in fast food and at an online retail warehouse. "I try to minimize the amount of debt after school. So that's basically why I [work so much], just to pay the college off." His extensive work schedule left little time for extracurricular activities, unpaid internships, study abroad, or other cocurricular experiences. In fact, Noah was generally skeptical of these kinds of opportunities, which he saw as risky and as having the potential to throw him off course. He pushed back against the insecurity at CU—exemplified in abundant choices and a lack of structure—by focusing on a narrow set of essential tasks to exercise control over his journey through college. Noah thought about the insecurity he saw in higher education as a series of risks, which he believed could be anticipated and avoided—or at least mitigated. He summed up his feelings on this matter, noting, "I don't like to take risks much. . . . Just knowing that I could probably fail, I wouldn't take the risk."

Encounters with insecurity play an important role in youth culture. In her book *Fast Cars, Cool Rides*, sociologist Amy Best illuminates the social worlds of young people who cruise and race cars, interpreting their encounters with risk in a range of ways.[2] She shows how navigating "cultures of risk" shapes youths' identities. On the surface, telling stories about confronting insecurity offers an occasion to perform femininity or masculinity in ways that increase one's social status.[3] Yet Best argues that something deeper and more complex is also happening here. For many socioeconomically marginalized youths, risk narratives become "a way to manage, if not control, the uncertainty of their future."[4] As one builds a repertoire of encounters with insecurity where harm was successfully averted, it becomes possible to conceive of oneself as having greater agency. By narrating their capacity to deal with a risky environment, youth may assert control over their own futures.

In a comparable way, LIFGWC students in this study drew from their experiences in a university laden with risk to project a capacity to deal with uncertainty. The pioneers featured in the previous chapter emphasized their ability to endure insecurity and recover from crises, but there was another group of LIFGWC participants, like Noah, who managed risk in a very different manner. This chapter explores the experiences of these *risk minimizers*, who drew from a unique set of resources to navigate the insecurity of CU, anticipating and working to avoid its potential harms. They did this by resisting the complexity and flexibility that characterized their university, focusing instead on identifying safer, simpler routes through college. Minimizers used their skill navigating an insecure environment to plan for uncertain futures and reduce instability.

Becoming "Planners"

Like pioneers, minimizers saw uncertainty and instability as problematic elements of higher education. Victoria, a first-generation White student, said the environment she faced at CU was "negative for sure. . . . It's disruptive because I want to focus my energy into my studies, and things that make you feel uncertain detracts you from that. That's why I don't like uncertainty." Minimizers described how this type of insecurity was prevalent at CU, especially when compared with their previous educational settings. Marc, a Latino LIFGWC student, recalled,

> I remember during that transition from high school to like the first month of college, or so. It was really, really strange, for me, because it kind of felt like the whole world really didn't care about what was going on with you. Every college student is really independent, and they're the ones seeking their own success and education in different ways. It's not like in high school where they're telling you [what] you have to do.

Similarly, Patrice, an LIFGWC Latina student, noted that while she occasionally felt unsure about her progress when she was at community college, "now at CU, I'm of course uncertain of everything." As she struggled to find information and navigate the university, she concurred with pioneers' assessment that—in contrast to high school and some community colleges—CU was a place where insecurity abounded.

Like other LIFGWC students, minimizers found this insecurity especially disappointing because they had hoped higher education would be a reliable way to pursue upward mobility. "Just getting a good, decent-paying job is the value of college for me," Noah claimed, and others described their hope that obtaining a degree would be a way to secure "a better life" in the future. Minimizers had expected that college attendance would offer a safer route to a stable, middle-class adulthood. Many of these sentiments were summed up by Rick, the White first-generation student from a working-class family who was quoted in the first chapter, when he stated that "the main purpose of college, I'd say, [is] to reduce your risk." Ignacio, a Latino LIFGWC student, offered a similar perspective; he described higher education as "the safest of all the options."

Though minimizers' perceptions of insecurity were similar to pioneers' in many ways, they differed in how they tried to manage it. Where pioneers viewed instability as unavoidable, depicting college as an environment where they had to work hard just to stay afloat, minimizers thought of themselves as having the capacity to head off insecurity, mitigating its most harmful consequences with effective organization. They often claimed to be "planners." When describing herself to one of my research assistants, Sarah, an Asian LIFGWC student, said "I like to plan everything ahead of time." Quinn, a White first-generation student, similarly acknowledged that "I am a planner—I have to be." Summing up her approach, she noted,

> Life is uncertain anyways. You don't know what's going to happen, and with this type of environment [at college], you have to have your ducks in a row to be prepared. . . . It's really just all preparation. That helps with the uncertainty. . . . I never expected anything like this—to be so busy, to have an experience like this—there's no slacking off. . . . I formulate plans in my head all the time and adjust as needed. I start preparing for today, so I have things ready for today, just to take enough of the load off. So, whenever a surprise or a drive-by comes through, I'm ready to go and I don't have to worry about some of the other tasks I have to deal with on a daily basis.

Quinn's belief that "life is uncertain" was echoed by most minimizers. Lucas, a Latino LIFGWC student, observed, "there's always going to be some uncertainty. . . . Anything can happen at any time. . . . I always like to say, 'the plan is blah blah blah,' because anything can happen in life, but I will always strive to be going in the right direction." Victoria returned to a similar refrain, repeating the phrase "anything can happen" throughout her interview. This sense that life was unpredictable—even more so in college—led them to plan for contingencies.

BRACING FOR AN UNCERTAIN JOURNEY

This proclivity to plan showed up in minimizers' journeys to and through college. For some, efforts to minimize risk in higher education began years before they even enrolled. An Asian and White LIFGWC student, Minh described herself as "very self-motivated. I'm definitely not like a procrastinator. I'm very organized, so I like to plan out when I'm going to do all my work. . . . I'm hard working and organized." She traced these dispositions to her high school years:

> Since probably my sophomore year in high school, I've always mapped out exactly what I'm going to do, and like how long it's going to take me in col-

lege. . . . I had like my whole four-year plan for college already written out back in my sophomore or junior year of high school. So even if there is—I know there is—a possibility that things are going to change, I still like to have a plan just so I know exactly how it can go.

Having clear plans allowed Minh to think ahead to college, outlining specific pathways that accounted for various contingencies that might arise.

For other students, efforts to minimize risk ramped up as they transitioned into higher education and persisted throughout college. A Latina, first-generation college student from a low-income family, Emily described herself as "organized" with "good attention to detail." Her wariness toward uncertainty was evident from the beginning of her interview when she described her decision to select CU for its proximity to home: "I was going to live at home for the most part, because I just couldn't see myself moving out at eighteen." She described leaving her parents' home as a risk she wanted to avoid. Attempts to anticipate and confront uncertainty also showed up in her descriptions of everyday routines during college:

I have the whole thing just planned out in my planner. . . . That's a huge thing, so what I had started doing my sophomore year, I got a planner and at the beginning of the week, I just write down every single assignment I have, the due date—like if it's Thursday or Sunday—and just check it off as I go so that it slowly becomes less by the end of the week, and I know that I didn't miss anything. Just that preparedness aspect of it. . . . And I love checking things off, I love that. That's like my favorite part of the day. I'm like "oh, I've got this done, I've got this done." So, it's kind of like a reward system. I figured out what works for me.

As she mapped out deadlines and checked items off her to-do list, Emily tried to reduce uncertainty. When things went well, Sunday evening brought with it a completed list and an opportunity to begin again for the next week.

Some minimizers even described using a series of failsafe tactics to create guardrails for their plans. May, a White first-generation college student from a low-income family, spoke a lot about "responsibility." From her perspective, being responsible meant preparing for contingencies, including the possibility that she might forget to check one of her calendars and miss an important task. As she sat at her desk with an exuberant dog perched on her lap, May outlined her strategy for layering reminders:

I start in the planning mode, like "how am I going to handle this? What am I going to do? How is it going to affect this, this, and this?" [I'm] writing down everything. I have three different calendars. I put reminders in my phone when I can. . . . So, calendars, reminders, I have a planner, things like that, to just help me stay on course. . . . And then sometimes I'll put notes on my computer, because I'm always eventually on my computer. . . . I'll have a to-do list for the week.

As Emily and May's words make clear, day planners, calendars, electronic reminders, and to-do lists were crucial for minimizers and could be combined to provide additional security. Tools like these were ammunition against the uncertainties of their college journeys.

But minimizers' planning processes were about more than just coming up with a plan and sticking to it. These students thought about risk as something that needed to be actively managed through attentiveness to frequent changes in one's environment, recalibrating strategies when necessary. Trevor, a White LIFGWC student, discussed the importance of seeing uncertainty as "manageable" in order to deal with aspects of college life that felt unpredictable. But he acknowledged that even the best-laid plans sometimes had to be revised. "If [things don't go how] you expected, you just have to deal with it and alter the way you do things in order to counteract that unexpectedness."

These types of revisions and recalibrations could be aided by having backup plans ready. As Minh explained, "I guess I've always just been someone who hates uncertainty, so that naturally motivates me to want to come up with backup plans, just in case something doesn't work out." Developing multiple plans gave students the sense that they could manage uncertainty by choosing the safest route and having alternatives ready should something go wrong. Expanding on her previous point, Minh added, "And sometimes I'll have like multiple plans for like if I want to go one way or if I want to go a different way, so I can kind of compare those two plans side by side to see if one will like take longer, or be more difficult, or anything like that."

Of course, there were times when contingencies simply couldn't be anticipated, rendering backup plans less useful. A clear example could be seen in the ways minimizers dealt with the COVID-19 pandemic. Victoria acknowledged, "I like to plan, but I did not plan for a pandemic." Regardless, she intensified her efforts to stay on track for graduation. Because minimizers had no preexisting playbook for how to deal with this unprecedented situation, they doubled down on their organizational strategies. Having observed that "I feel like success in college is managing your time, managing your classes, having your plan and knowing what you're going to be doing with your classes," Pilar, a Latina LIFGWC student, proudly announced, "I have a COVID schedule now." She explained that her "COVID schedule" was a revised plan for managing her time day-to-day as she juggled deadlines for online courses with her new work schedule. While the pandemic represented a monumental risk, minimizers believed their capacity to develop and implement new risk-mitigating strategies could see them through difficult times. Emily summarized, "I think just that preparedness aspect [during the pandemic] kept me going."

MARGINALIZATION AS A RISK AMPLIFIER

Efforts to plan were sometimes guided by students' concerns about marginalization in their everyday interactions with others. In the instances when pioneers discussed their social location, they usually emphasized their status as LIFGWC students—and related material constraints or limited access to information—as affecting the insecurity they encountered in higher education. And they usually attributed these constraints to individual decisions or internal capacities, as described in the previous chapter. Some minimizers, by contrast, also described the impact of racism, sexism, ableism, and anti-immigrant sentiment as external factors amplifying insecurity. This recognition of other forms of marginalization guided their outlook on risk and their sense that it could come from a range of directions.

When reflecting on his efforts to minimize risk during college, Kaleb acknowledged that, "I would say there were times where I made different decisions than I would've done if I had a different ethnicity or a different position financially." He explained how his identity as a Black, low-income student from an immigrant family would "shape my experiences . . . [and] influence what I was able to choose." Kaleb often thought about the ways prejudice and exclusion affected his interactions with others. "It's difficult because you kind of feel out who around you is not accepting of you. Whether it's in school or the apartment that we live in, I kind of have to walk on eggshells, just trying not to run into any problems or anything like that."

Ellie offered another illustration of the ways encountering marginalization could inform efforts to minimize risk. She described how her perceptions of uncertainty were shaped by aspects of her identity, including

> my disability, being a woman, and because I'm Black. . . . And the reason I
> state those three things is because I went to work for a fast-food shop a couple
> of years back. . . . But because of my vision, he would not hire me. . . . And
> another thing I say being a woman . . . because some women don't tend to get
> certain jobs because they are women. Or women don't get to get equal pay as
> a man in the same position as them. And I say Black because—it's sad to say
> in this world—but I feel like not all but some Black people tend to get the end
> of the stick as far as like job placements or being in hierarchical positions and
> things like that.

54 CHAPTER THREE

After reflecting on the discrimination she'd encountered applying for jobs, Ellie described finding the same types of marginalization in higher education. She recalled,

> I experienced some forms of racism on my very first semester at CU. So, participation points was based on engagement in class, as stated in the syllabus. . . . I'm a student who likes to interact; I like to ask questions. If I don't know something, I like to ask questions. I like to give my answer. [The professor] called on people, stuff like that. I'm just like, interacting in class. . . . I had a [White] friend, she never participated in class—never spoke, literally—but she ended up with the A in participation points, and I ended up with a B.

That same semester, Ellie had a class with a professor who wasn't supportive of her learning accommodation. When she requested help finding an accessible version of an article with small font, the professor "was like, 'Oh, well that's not my problem.' . . . She literally had me in tears. . . . I just walked away and cried." Like other minimizers, Ellie worked diligently to counteract uncertainties at CU—in her case, by working to find inclusive classrooms. "I also do use Rate My Professor, honestly speaking, because after that very first semester, I do not want to go through that again." Poring over student reviews, Ellie tried to anticipate which professors would be welcoming and which should be avoided.

Using Community Cultural Wealth to Resist Insecurity

Minimizers' capacity to mitigate risk by planning for the future was facilitated by access to specific resources that set them apart from pioneers. While most LIFGWC students arrived in college without the forms of social, cultural, or economic capital expected by the university, minimizers had access to other kinds of assets that transferred into higher education in ways that helped them strategize about their paths through college. Perhaps the sharpest contrast between pioneers and minimizers came in the form of their access to familial resources, including encouragement and guidance from their parents. Where pioneers often described their parents as uninvolved or even opposed to their college attendance, minimizers spoke about the durable support they received. May recalled,

> It was always, from the beginning of high school, my dad was like, "So you're going to college, so make plans to go to college." My brother and I were always good students. It wasn't really a question if we wanted to go, but mostly because my dad was like, "I didn't go and I wish I had, so you need to go and at least get it done. I don't care what you do with it. I just want you to get it." . . .

My dad being so adamant about me going to college kind of also motivated me to be like, "I need to do well. I need to pass these classes." . . . That's been a really big thing for me. . . . It's just one of those things that's kind of kept me motivated, I guess.

For other minimizers, narratives of migration and opportunity were an important part of the way they thought about their family's influence on their educational progress. Marc, for instance, reflected on how "com[ing] from a family of immigrants . . . being a first-generation student has a lot of value to it. That was my motivation." And Minh emphasized the importance of her mother's immigration experience when she said,

I always knew that I wanted to go to college, because my parents always encouraged me to. . . . I definitely say my parents motivate me a lot, because especially my mom, since she emigrated from Vietnam. She's a very hard worker. She's been through a lot, so she definitely pushes me a lot to try and get through things. . . . So, when she lived back in Vietnam, she actually didn't really get the chance to attend school past maybe I think middle school because her family was really poor. So, she had to work instead of attending school to make money for her family. She also uses that sometimes to kind of motivate me. She's like "just take every chance you can to learn, because I wish that I could have."

While May, Marc, and Minh all described the influence of their families in shaping their "motivation," they also used these narratives of their parents' determination as inspiration to develop strategies for navigating higher education. Minh, for example, described how her mother worked to push through "language barriers," "get her GED," and complete certifications for various jobs. Similarly, Hannah, an Asian and White first-generation student from a low-income family, described herself as "close with both my parents," recalling how they encouraged her to use university resources to manage the "struggles" of college life. "I feel like I can go to all of my family members for different things. . . . I've definitely been open with them in all sorts of ways about challenges [in college]. . . . I was super transparent about [struggles] with my family because my parents taught me, raised me, to be open." In frequent communication with her parents and sister, she received guidance on strategies to navigate the challenges of college life. For instance, having heard from her family that she should be wary of relying solely on academic advisors to keep her on track for graduation, Hannah developed a proactive approach for engaging with CU resources:

I think although our advisors are humans and they deserve to be thanked, and I thank them, whenever I do have an advising appointment, I go in there

> knowing what I should or shouldn't be doing or what I have to take or what
> I don't have to take. And I ask my advisor about it, or I tell my advisor what I
> am or what I'm not taking and what I want to do. And my advisor just kind of
> sits there in silence and nods her head. She's like, "Yeah, that sounds great. You
> sound like you've got it covered."

Rather than risk getting incorrect or incomplete advice, Hannah approached her appointments with advisors having thoroughly researched her course requirements, employing them as a second check for her plans.

Learning from the ways their family members persevered in hostile climates and exclusive settings, minimizers used familial resources to resist insecurity. These resources—a subset of the forms of community cultural wealth described by Tara Yosso—provided a road map for approaching a university that was often unresponsive to their needs.[5] Cognizant of the fact that their parents, siblings, and other members of their family often had to resist the inequitable tendencies of various institutions, minimizers came to CU ready to do the same. In this way, community cultural wealth helped students to defy subordination and succeed in settings that tend to advantage middle- and upper-middle-class White students.[6]

Moreover, in addition to learning *how* to resist insecurity through detailed planning, these students learned that they *should* engage in such resistance. Whereas pioneers frequently felt uncomfortable pushing back against the norms of engagement at their university, minimizers were endowed by their parents—and occasionally by mentors or program involvement—with a sense that this was an appropriate thing to do. Lakshmi, a low-income and working-class Asian student, provided an example of this outlook when she exclaimed, "I'm not afraid to ask for help." She described her frustrations with staff members who "just transfer [students] to another person to get them off their back," recalling several experiences when "the counselors were no help." In one recent instance when she couldn't get her questions answered by academic advisors, Lakshmi recalled that "I actually went to one of my teachers." Regardless of the obstacles, she was determined to find guidance—a tendency she connected to lessons learned from her family about persistence and determination.

It's important to emphasize that the capacity to resist insecurity was not the automatic by-product of growing up in a working-class family, an immigrant family, or any other marginalized community. In fact, when we compare the sociodemographic characteristics of pioneers and minimizers, it's clear that these two groups were quite similar (see table 3.1). What typically distinguished minimizers from pioneers, giving them the resources to plan

TABLE 3.1. Pioneers' and minimizers' sociodemographic characteristics

Student characteristic	Precarious pioneers % (n)	Risk minimizers % (n)
Parental education		
First-generation college students	85 (23)	81 (21)
Continuing-generation college students	15 (4)	19 (5)
Family income		
Low income	78 (21)	73 (19)
Middle or high income	22 (6)	27 (7)
Social class background		
Working class	67 (18)	62 (16)
Lower-middle class	22 (6)	27 (7)
Middle or upper-middle class	11 (3)	12 (3)
Race/ethnicity		
Asian or Asian American	26 (7)	19 (5)
Black or African American	15 (4)	12 (3)
Hispanic or Latinx	22 (6)	31 (8)
White	30 (8)	27 (7)
Multiracial, other race/ethnicity	7 (2)	12 (3)
Family immigration		
Parents immigrated to the US	63 (17)	62 (16)
Parents born in the US	37 (10)	38 (10)
Gender		
Women	48 (13)	62 (16)
Men	52 (14)	35 (9)
Nonbinary or agender	0 (0)	4 (1)

for the future, was their sense of connection and alignment with their families. This is a factor that has been neglected in previous research on community cultural wealth, which often assumes that marginalized students receive similar types of benefits from supportive and encouraging families.[7] Emerging scholarship on college student experiences illuminates a diverse range of ways students may relate to their parents and home communities. While some tend to align with their families' views regarding educational, personal, and professional goals, other students see their own perspectives as irreconcilable with those of their family members.[8] Pioneers experienced tensions or limited engagement with their home communities that disrupted the flow of encouragement and strategies for resistance, leaving them to fend for themselves in an insecure environment. By contrast, minimizers found that the unwavering support of their families equipped them with some of the resources they needed to identify and circumvent the risks woven throughout higher education.

In addition to benefitting from supportive families, minimizers also sometimes found mentors or programs that contributed to their stock of community cultural wealth. Trevor credited his track and field coach with helping him navigate the complexities of university bureaucracy. Additionally, several minimizers were part of the University Honors Program (UHP), which diverged from the typical institutional arrangements at the university to provide proactive support services. Pilar, for instance, was involved in UHP. Her parents had no formal education beyond elementary school, and like many pioneers, she rarely spoke to them about college:

> They don't really understand it. I think they know what my major is, but besides that they don't really know anything. If I were to be like, "I can't help you this weekend, I have to study for an exam," they don't understand how exams make up the majority of your grade, exams are really long, exams are really time consuming and have a lot of concepts. That's something that they don't understand. . . . They feel like I'm talking back to them.

Yet Pilar acquired resources to resist insecurity thought her participation in UHP. In moments when she struggled to navigate college, staff members from the program stepped in to deliver support. This program provided the kinds of consistent guidance and encouragement that families provided for other minimizers.[9] In sum, minimizers traversed college with a team—of family and, in rarer cases, mentors or program staff—ready to support their resistance as they navigated an institution that wasn't built with students like them in mind. Having these resources made it possible to approach insecurity with the sense that one could head it off through careful planning.

Resisting Insecurity in the Do-It-Yourself University

When Sonia joined me for an interview one afternoon in early December, she looked tired—exhausted really. In a rush of papers and final exams, she'd carved out a couple hours to talk. While she was clearly busy, she was earnest and detailed in responding to my queries about her journey through higher education. With hands clasped thoughtfully beneath her chin as if in prayer, her methodical replies to each question echoed her methodical approach to college. A first-generation and low-income Latina student, Sonia was frustrated by many of the same elements of the do-it-yourself environment that stymied the pioneers from the previous chapter. She called out the ways CU resources were incomprehensibly organized and poorly advertised.

> I know that CU has so many resources, I just feel like they don't talk about them enough, or they don't have an easy way to access them. I've been looking at like counseling and stuff through CU, and I know CU offers it, but I have no idea where to go and look for it. . . . Their web page and stuff can sometimes be hard to maneuver. . . . It's frustrating.

Rather than be dissuaded by the opaque nature of university bureaucracy, Sonia remained certain that CU resources were essential to her success in college, and she was determined to access them. "I'll just spend hours, honestly, just going on [the university website] and trying to figure out where to go to find these things." Similarly, Minh recalled how she eventually connected with the Career Services Center when she was trying to finalize her decision about which major to pursue.

> I think I was actually just trying to find out if the university did have a resource [to help select majors], because I was thinking like I wish there was someone that I could like talk to about this, who is like knowledgeable and has experience with helping students choose their majors. So, I think I just Googled something like "CU career counseling" or something like that.

In this way minimizers pushed to access resources that were not well known and not integrated into the curriculum.[10] Though her persistence paid off, Minh noted that others were frequently unaware of the support CU's Career Services Center could provide with selecting a major connected to one's professional goals. "I've talked to friends who are struggling to find out their major. . . . I tell them about this, and it seems like a lot of people don't know about it."

After identifying a potential resource, minimizers would reach out to make contact. Sonia described working closely with an advisor to determine, "What classes I'm going to take, at what time, when they're going to be available, and when they're not." Though some offices were especially tough to navigate, she was resolute in locating the sources of information she needed, pushing through obstacles to create plans.

> There have been times in the year where I've had to go in three times in the financial aid office and be like "hey, why isn't this going through? The semester is about to start." And then they're like "oh, well you're missing this paperwork," and I'm like, "I was here two weeks ago, why didn't you give me this paperwork to fill out, or why didn't you tell me it was missing?" So, it's always a battle, but I'm used to it after five years.

Even when accessing these resources was "a battle," even if it meant approaching an office three times, minimizers believed that proactively resisting insecurity was a necessity.

Minimizers' approach to navigating the university wasn't just about discovering and using available resources; it was also about carefully assessing which of these resources were safe. Whereas guidance from an advisor or career counselor seemed helpful, engaging with some resources—the Study Abroad Office, student involvement, or other unpaid cocurricular opportunities, for instance—seemed risky. The caution with which minimizers approached university services could be seen in Marc's description of his encounters with the financial aid office. Like many LIFGWC students, he received recommendations to take out a mixture of federal and private loans to fund his education. But Marc was reluctant. Though he was willing to take on federal loans and had qualified for a private loan, he refused this offer, noting that the private loans "always seemed a little sketchy." Having learned to be skeptical of the default modes of operation in these offices, minimizers were cautious in their interactions. Chapter 6 more closely examines the normative institutional arrangements that complicated experiences for LIFGWC students. In this section, I focus on some of the specific strategies minimizers employed to deal with risk at the university.

FINDING "PRACTICAL" MAJORS

Minimizers dedicated substantial thought and energy to selecting the right major and putting themselves on a safe academic trajectory. To alleviate risk, they sought so-called practical fields of study, which they believed fit two main criteria. First, they looked for majors where they could succeed without much difficulty; in other words, these students searched for majors perceived to be less academically rigorous. Like Noah, who left electrical engineering in part to avoid having to retake courses, Minh explained, "I had my plan for the degree I wanted in the medical field, and then I was also like, 'well if those classes become too hard, here's how I can switch to a different degree.'" In a comparable way, Fran, an LIFGWC Asian student, recalled changing her major from nursing to information technology "after I was struggling with nursing . . . there was a lot of volume of information." Avoiding majors that seemed especially challenging, minimizers attempted to ward off academic failure.[11]

But efforts to be pragmatic went beyond choosing a field with manageable coursework. Minimizers also looked for fields of study that had solid employment prospects. Practical majors were thought to include fields that were relatively versatile, where the link between education and work seemed straightforward. This tendency could be seen in the experiences of May and Rick, who changed their majors from exercise science to business. Both students entered college with a passion for physical fitness and personal training. "I would have been very fulfilled if I did my exercise science degree," Rick observed, adding that, "I probably would have been really into what I was doing."

Though exercise science appealed to their personal interests, both students soon heard anecdotes from family and peers suggesting that business offered more secure employment prospects. After noting that, "I think [a business degree is] useful for almost everything," Rick recalled the moment when

> I was convinced not to [major in exercise science], since it's kind of like a little niche market. . . . So, I was kind of convinced not to, and to go with a more general degree, such as business management. . . . I was told I should probably go with something that has a little more applicable usage—or like it's more ubiquitous I guess, something like that.

As he pointed out, the fact that business seemed to have a range of job prospects—that it was "more ubiquitous," in his words—mattered a great deal to minimizers. Similarly, May described the business major:

> It was definitely something I could apply to real life. . . . It's definitely more inclusive, so I can do many things with it. . . . So, I changed my major. There are so many things you can do with a management degree. . . . I just did your basic job search, and I was like, "There's way more opportunities for this." . . . It's kind of universal in the business world. . . . That's kind of how I came to [realize] that there's probably more opportunities for me.

The result was that minimizers often found their way to applied fields with less extensive requirements for reading, writing, and math. In addition to the business major, criminology and technology were also popular among these students. Fran, for instance, described the appeal of information technology: "With tech stuff, I don't want to say you're guaranteed a job, but there's definitely a lot more opportunities and a lot more people trying to hire for that. I definitely like having backup upon backup." The sense that practical majors would offer safe routes to employment fortified minimizers' belief that their field of study could help to mitigate risk.

Minimizers often looked for cues from their families about which majors were most practical.[12] While they described their parents as broadly supportive, their financial circumstances often guided major choice. Kaleb recalled how his parents emphasized selecting a field where there were plenty of well-paying jobs.

> Right now, the financial situation that [my parents are] in, everything is tight on money. So, I don't think they'd take the risk to let me go into fields that are not pleasing in their eyes. . . . They really don't consider the social sciences

as something profitable and something to be proud of. I don't blame them. That's the society they lived in.

Although Kaleb attributed these tendencies to his family's cultural background ("I have Ethiopian parents"), the tendency to defer to parents' assessments of employability was shared by minimizers from a range of cultural contexts, including those whose parents grew up in the US.

When minimizers entered college in a field that they determined was "not practical," efforts to switch majors ensued. But in contrast to pioneers, who usually floundered when choosing and changing majors, minimizers leveraged the resources at their disposal to support a smoother transition. Their capacity to manage this transition was sometimes aided by their persistence seeking guidance from multiple academic advisors. In other cases, smooth transitions to a new major were informed by groundwork they laid earlier with detailed planning. Emily, for instance, had chosen CU because she "didn't want to get stuck" in the nursing major and knew the university offered two other degrees that she was considering. When she confirmed that the course of study for nursing was difficult, Emily transitioned to her second-choice major in health administration. This change was supported by the fact that health administration "fit really nicely into all of my classes that I'd already taken, so I didn't need any additional classes or to make up for anything. So, I was like 'okay, this is an easy transition, still health care.' . . . I won't have to do all the scary parts of nursing I was uncomfortable with." Though she had also considered teaching as a third possibility, the required course sequence diverged from the health majors, meaning that "If I'd done teaching, I would have been completely derailed. So, I ultimately ended up [in health administration], because if I had done teaching or something . . . I probably would not have gotten to graduate this semester." When declaring a new major was necessary, students like Emily tried to ensure it wouldn't delay degree completion.

Importantly, minimizers' detailed planning did not mean that changing majors was an effortless task. Their experiences were relatively smooth compared with pioneers, and yet fears of uncertainty made change—including making the switch to a new major—an alarming experience. For instance, Minh described how frightening it could be to switch fields of study. "I would definitely say I was very scared during that time just because I'm the type of person who always likes to have things planned out." While Minh had planned her transition to a new major in a careful and deliberate way, the stress of change was pronounced, nonetheless.

AVOIDING RISKY CLASSES, TRACKS, AND CONCENTRATIONS

Finding a practical major was far from the only task minimizers took on in attempting to avoid risk in their academic endeavors. Even after they settled into a major, these students remained on the lookout for hazards in their program of study. Challenging courses and difficult tracks or concentrations were seen as having the potential to amplify insecurity and were therefore navigated with care. The process of determining which classes were safe began anew every semester as students selected and tested a new course schedule. Patrice described the heightened uncertainty at the beginning of each term.

> I would say it's [most uncertain] at the start of the semester for me, when I'm starting new classes and every professor and every class is different—how they lecture, how they give assessments, how they grade. So, I would say honestly, that is the time I'm most unsure. After like the first test of a class, that's when you realize how things are going to go and how you need to study and all that.

One of Patrice's strategies was to sidestep or delay classes that might be especially difficult or where grading seemed arbitrary. "I don't enjoy feeling uncertain or nervous about a class," she explained, justifying her decision to postpone several math and science courses required for her major.

For minimizers, the assessment of whether a class was low risk was informed by close examination of course syllabi and cues from the instructor. Emily noted, "Some of these classes, like I had one coming into this semester, I read the syllabus and she said, prepare yourself for ten hours of work outside of the lectures and everything. And I was like 'yeah, I'm not doing that. I don't have time for that.'" Determining that this professor's expectations were too high, Emily withdrew from the class. Other minimizers described dropping a class after realizing it had too many or too few assignments. While a large number of assignments could be a sign that a course would be too time intensive, having just a few meant that risk was concentrated on a couple of high-stakes papers or exams. Minimizers tried to avoid both scenarios.

Moreover, these students paid close attention to the paths they were taking through their course of study, working to make sure they were following the most streamlined approach available. This meant that concentrations or tracks within majors that required additional investment were shunned. Kaleb told me about navigating the biology major. He entered CU on the predental track, which added a series of prerequisite courses to his program of study. Classes like anatomy and physiology, organic chemistry II, and statistics were recommended or required for predental students but not for the general bachelor of science in biology. Kaleb realized that he could complete his degree in a more streamlined fashion by leaving the predental track, describing this decision as a way to mitigate uncertainty.

> I would say continuing in a single, specific plan and trying to get to achieve that, most of the time it was uncertain, especially when I wanted to be a dentist. But what dentistry requires—the amount of classes and the amount of time and energy it requires—I'm not able to give that time.

He identified additional risks in being focused on a single career path:

> So, I would say uncertainty-wise, it's just choosing a major and continuing to a specific job feels just really hard. . . . I tried to make myself get used to being able to work in different job sectors so that I don't have to feel like my goal or my life is uncertain. Because this one plan could fail, and I won't be able to become something. So, I try to have this more of a wide, general thing, just graduating in biology and being able to join any certain sector.

The fact that predentistry paired challenging courses with what Kaleb perceived to be a narrow career route where there was greater potential for failure meant that abandoning this track seemed prudent. While he described the initial decision to leave the track as "emotionally draining," he noted that now, "I don't feel stressed as much as when I was in a single roadway."

STREAMLINED ENGAGEMENT AND FITTING
COLLEGE AROUND PAID EMPLOYMENT

Minimizers' tendency to avoid difficult courses or tracks in their field of study was part of a broader strategy to pursue streamlined engagement throughout their college journeys. In addition to looking for direct paths to completing their degrees, they shunned other types of college involvement that they perceived could be risky distractions from their goal to graduate in a timely manner. Like many schools, CU touted "high impact educational opportunities," including things like study abroad, student organization leadership, service learning, research experiences, internships, and other activities.[13] My field notes documented a litany of announcements, newsletters, and stories on the home page of the CU website that proclaimed the virtues of engagement beyond the traditional classroom. The next chapter will focus on a group of students who heeded advice to maximize involvement in college, but minimizers were wary of these opportunities. They worried that becoming overextended could elevate uncertainty and risk. Instead, they focused on using the resources at their disposal to winnow through the myriad opportunities at CU to find a direct path, maintaining a semblance of control in an insecure setting.

A succinct description of these tendencies was provided by Rick, who summed up his engagement on campus: "I'm kind of in and out. Like I said, I don't do any extracurriculars at CU." Lakshmi used similar words when she claimed, "my mentality is basically get in, get out, get a degree, start my life." She contrasted this perspective with people who "think about college as a way to make friends and like a social element to discover who you are." For minimizers, avoiding ancillary opportunities—especially unpaid extracurricular or cocurricular activities—in college was the result of a cautious approach to involvement. While some literature suggests that LIFGWC students are less involved on campus because they don't desire or recognize the value of engagement outside of traditional classroom settings, this was not typically the case for the students in my study. Pioneers were often involved in extracurricular activities, and while minimizers avoided engagement, this had to do with their assessment of feasibility and risk rather than disinterest.

Emily illustrated the tensions around college involvement when she said, "I'm happy to be graduating. I feel accomplished. . . . I should have probably done more clubs and things, but I didn't." Though she saw the potential value of involvement and attended an extracurricular fair early on in her time at CU, she felt "[college] was kind of overwhelming. . . . I wish I had just done more of those [extracurricular activities], but you're tunneled kind of, like you're just focused on getting through the semester." This sense that "getting through the semester" required vigilance made minimizers reluctant to engage beyond the classroom. Such concerns were exacerbated by ambiguity about what exactly was entailed in cocurricular or extracurricular involvement. With an emphasis on careful organization, minimizers were reluctant to commit to an activity when they were unclear about expectations. Emily explained,

> You have no idea like what the expectations are going to be going into the club. Like you don't know if they're gonna need you to show up two times a week or if it's just something casual. So that was another fear of mine, was I just didn't want to overcommit myself and then end up having to leave something I already said yes to.

Dedication to paid employment was another factor that informed minimizers' hesitations related to engagement outside of class. Sonia believed she could have been more involved in college if she wasn't working ("the majority of my college career, I've worked full-time and gone to school full-time"), but the modicum of stability provided by her job was important. When she reviewed her reasons for not participating in study abroad, internships, or research opportunities, Sonia pointed to work.

> It's been a little difficult because I have to maneuver around my work schedule as well. And that's the reason I've never done internships previously—because I can't, unless I'm getting paid, I can't justify not working. . . . There are certain internships that are obviously really good to have on your résumé, but again, I can't be like "oh yeah, well having this internship will be great on my résumé, but I can't put food on the table." Obviously, one is more important than the other.

Faced with choices between advantageous cocurricular opportunities and stable paid employment, minimizers opted for the latter. For most, work was their primary activity, supplemented by courses. In other words, rather than fit in work around college, minimizers tried to fit college around their work schedules.

Attempts to mold college engagement to prioritize employment showed up clearly in my interview with May, who like Sonia, noted that, "I also work full-time, so that's part of the reason I don't do many extracurriculars." As she elaborated on this point, the centrality of her job became clear. May began working at a fast-food restaurant in her final year of high school and transferred to the CU branch when she started college. Over the years, May had considered whether she should get more involved on campus. She described pressures to be a highly engaged student.

> There's a lot of pressure . . . because you see so many college students, and they're like, "I'm in this club. I do [another extracurricular activity]. I have straight As. I have this and that." Like, "What? Are you on crack? Are you okay?" Because college is hard. It's definitely like I feel the pressure to perform well and do well and be able to handle it all. . . . It makes me very nervous. Am I going to succeed?

In addition to coming from university representatives and from other students, May noted that some of this pressure emanated from popular images of college life. "And also, the media has a huge thing to do with it, making freshman year and your first year of college seem like it's so cool you don't really have to worry about anything. That's not true."

Though she felt pressure to become more involved beyond the classroom, May couldn't justify prioritizing this involvement over paid employment. Even the few paid cocurricular opportunities she'd found seemed less desirable when they were temporary or offered lower wages than her work at the restaurant. "I've applied for a couple internships here and there. . . . Some of them just honestly don't pay as much as [my fast-food job] does. So, it's not as appealing if they don't pay as much. Why would I leave my job for a job that pays me less?" She recalled a recent instance when she had to choose between her current job and an internship offer.

> I think it was last fall, right when COVID started. There was a virtual [internship]. They were like, "We'd like to go farther with it. Blah, blah, blah. Here are the benefits." And it's not as good as I thought it was going to be. If I leave [the restaurant] and then I want to come back, my benefits all reset, so I don't get all those benefits from tenure and bonuses and stuff. I was like, "I'm probably just going to stay where I'm at." . . . Yeah, I've definitely thought about [internships] a lot, but most of them don't pay as well, and I'm pretty comfortable where I'm at.

The job benefits May referenced were important in shaping her streamlined engagement in college. In addition to her hourly pay, she noted that "they reimburse tuition; they give you about $6,000 a year, and all you have to do is work. . . . That's been part of my reason for staying for so long." If she left the restaurant for a few months to work a temporary internship, her access to company benefits would reset.

At the end of the day, minimizers like May valued the stability of their current employment even if they weren't making direct use of the skills they acquired in college. She acknowledged that while others expected her to leave this job, her own plans put emphasis on continuity with work. "Everybody's like, 'When are you leaving [your fast-food job]?' It's like, 'I'm not leaving anytime soon.'" May explained that not having to worry about finances was worth sacrificing other opportunities: "Just having that stability from the start . . . was really nice, because it's something I don't have to worry about versus other people. So, I've been really grateful for that." Other students were in similar situations. Fran worked over thirty hours a week at an ice cream shop and a retail inventory position, and Lakshmi described herself as "kind of a workaholic," who usually held multiple jobs. When she began a new full-time position as a desk assistant, she stayed on in her part-time retail job on the weekends, explaining that "the reason I didn't let [my retail work] go was because of job security. I didn't know if [the new position] was secure enough for me to let go."

The Limitations of Minimizing Risk

Streamlining college involvement to emphasize practical majors and paid employment was helpful in some ways. It gave minimizers a sense that their college journeys would be safer and more stable. Equipped with resources that provided a tentative sense of agency, they felt capable of managing risk even if they recognized that heading it off completely was impossible. In short, minimizers' approach to navigating college gave them some peace of mind and meant they weren't as likely to be thrown off course as pioneers. There were also numerous examples of anecdotes shared by minimizers where it was clear that their thoughtful planning helped them to circumvent potentially catastrophic consequences. They avoided predatory loans, prejudiced classmates, indifferent or disengaged professors, and numerous distractions from academic progress. And yet seeking a safe route through higher education was not always advantageous.

Ulrich Beck observed that risk has a "virtual" component characterized by worries about events that have not yet occurred.[14] A focus on anticipating problems can create challenges of its own, and research demonstrates that taking risks can be advantageous in a society that rewards creativity and innovation.[15] The findings presented in this chapter show how similar patterns extend to higher education. Avoiding risk helped to address some of the liabilities of college attendance, but this strategy could also generate new ones in an environment that privileged students who embraced opportunities and flexibility.

Some of the limitations of minimizing risk related to the cognitive and emotional labor involved in these efforts. For instance, May reflected on the ways so much planning could be stressful. After claiming that creating detailed plans gave her some comfort, she also acknowledged that it occasionally made her feel "a little bit overwhelmed too. . . . Sometimes my worries weren't as much needed, I guess. I would say [I feel] overwhelmed, maybe a little bit of pressure going on there." Similarly, Victoria shared that "At some point, I was obsessing, you know, always when I have a spare moment my brain would just go to like, 'let's look at which classes I can take when and what I can do.'" As their words made clear, being vigilant about risk could be exhausting.

Minimizers' risk-evading strategies were also emotionally taxing in other ways. Their efforts to shoulder responsibility for managing insecurity corresponded with a tendency to engage in self-blame when challenges arose. Though these students sometimes acknowledged the impact of external sources of constraint (like when they talked about how prejudiced individuals could elevate the risks they encountered), they didn't usually extend this awareness to the way they thought about broader challenges in higher education. Like pioneers, they responded to the university's do-it-yourself environment by adopting a one-way honor system, blaming themselves for struggles. For instance, when Lucas described his most significant obstacles to success in college, he focused on two factors: "self-doubt and being my own worst enemy." These tendencies were often emotionally draining; chapter 7 explores their consequences in more detail.

In addition to the emotional toll of working to minimize risk, a great deal of time went into this detailed planning. Recall, for instance, Sonia's description of how she would "spend hours" on the university website "trying to figure out where to go to find [resources]." In effect, this meant that minimizers were dedicating more time trying to navigate CU than their more socioeconomically advantaged peers, whose access to dominant social and cultural capital made navigating the university a more straightforward process. Notably, though, the limitations of working to minimize risk went beyond the costs of additional time and emotional labor. Other drawbacks related to students' choice of majors, their selection of courses and tracks, and their emphasis on paid employment.

THE LIMITS OF AVOIDING ACADEMIC RISK

The sociology of education exposes some of the issues that can stem from selecting easy classes and "practical majors." As noted above, sometimes avoiding a class where faculty mistook excessive workloads or inflexible deadlines and grading policies for rigor could be an effective way of avoiding disruptions in one's academic progress. But in other cases, students may have missed out on influential challenges. In their study of learning in higher education, Richard Arum and Josipa Roksa found that students taking courses with faculty who held high expectations improved their capacities for critical thinking and complex reasoning significantly more than peers who reported that their faculty had lower expectations for course engagement.[16] Similarly, students who took courses where they read at least forty pages a week and wrote twenty pages or more over the course of the semester learned more in college and had improved college outcomes. Students who missed out on the types of learning that occurred in these rigorous classes were less likely to attend full-time master's and doctoral programs after graduation, and they were more likely to lose their jobs, be unemployed, or hold a position where a college education wasn't required.[17]

A few students in my study recognized potential drawbacks of pursuing less rigorous pathways through college. For instance, Emily reflected on her tendency to avoid "difficult" classes, confessing that she was "probably not [getting] the full extent of my education." Unfortunately, many other students seemed unaware of the potential downsides of selecting less rigorous courses. This trend is understandable given the ways colleges and universities frequently emphasize timely degree completion over the pursuit of academic rigor.[18]

Even when the avoidance of challenging classes was temporary, this strategy could still have negative consequences. Some students, for instance, put off required courses that they suspected would be especially demanding, waiting to take them later in their studies. This sometimes led to missing important course prerequisites and falling behind on progress toward their degree. Patrice provided a clear example. She had recently arrived at a point where she could not enroll in several required courses for her major because she first needed to complete foundational science courses that she'd been deferring. This caused significant anxiety. "And now I'm feeling scared again for when I have to start taking chemistry and physics and all that, because I know that will be difficult, because I'm not very great at math." Not only would Patrice still have to take these challenging courses, but she would probably have to take several in the same semester.[19]

Avoiding academic risks was sometimes taken to an extreme. Marc was apprehensive about succeeding in online classes, noting that he'd previously found distance learning to be a challenge. When he learned that many classes in his major would be offered virtually in the spring of 2021, he decided not to enroll that semester, rather than risk poor performance in his classes. In a similar way, Victoria noted that "obsessive" attention to doing well in each of her courses slowed down her progress to graduation.

> I wanted to make sure that if I take more classes, I would also continue to be able to study for them, because I have a few friends that also went to university, and they also did really well but didn't really care about having high grades or studying for all of their classes. So, they will make fun of me. They're like "just take five classes and get like Bs or Cs," and I'm like "no, that's not how this works."

Taking just two or three classes a semester allowed Victoria to feel in control, but it also meant that her progress to graduation was delayed by several years.

Other sociological research suggests that there may be drawbacks to gravitating toward "practical majors." For instance, sociologist Corey Moss-Pech argues that compared with practical arts graduates, liberal arts graduates are more likely to make use of the skills they develop in college, finding more engaging work where critical thinking, reading, writing, and analytical reasoning are key parts of their daily responsibilities.[20] Even graduates in business, who have fairly strong economic prospects, often end up in sales or clerical jobs where they use few skills from their majors.

Practical majors may also amplify inequality between students from different socioeconomic backgrounds. Low-income, first-generation, and working-class graduates may struggle to obtain jobs in fields like communications, recreation, journalism, public administration, tourism, or fashion, where an emphasis on social capital and elite styles of self-presentation creates barriers to entry.[21] Additionally, for some students, these majors may not have been a good fit for their desired career goals. Georgia, a Black student from a low-income family, switched her major from environmental science to environmental studies when she learned that the latter did not require as many math and science courses. She described her decision "to change to [environmental] studies, because I only have to take one math course. . . . It's easier for me. . . . Less math, and I had no physics and chemistry." Although the two majors had similar names, environmental *science* focused on the technical aspects of ecological systems and "fundamental techniques" related to practice in the field. Meanwhile, the environmental *studies* major was intended to prepare students for careers in the social sciences, policy, and environmental protection. Given her aspiration at the time to become a meteorologist, a science major probably would have been more advantageous for Georgia, but environmental studies seemed to promise a safer trajectory through college.

Finally, some students found that selecting a practical major meant giving up studying a topic they found more engaging for one that—despite the potential for safer job prospects—seemed less interesting. After describing his switch from exercise science to business, Rick recalled his struggles to connect with material in the business courses.

> I'm just in a bind because I'm in a degree I wasn't 100% on. Still, trying to make the best of it. . . . I mean some parts of the degree are still interesting. I try to make it as applicable to the stuff I like, but . . . I guess the subject matter, in general, I'd much rather learn about how biceps work than how perpetuity loans work, you know?

Similarly, Kaleb lamented that he wasn't able to major in the social and behavioral sciences or arts.

> I love psychology—even music, maybe I could've gone into music. I always wanted to be a piano player, but . . . I don't even think about them because that's not what I'm supposed to do. I always tell myself that I need to be focused on a biology degree. It is hard. The decisions you make are different when you're in a tight financial situation.

Notably, some of these decisions to move toward a "practical" field of study were probably prudent ones, given the specific challenges students were confronting. What is important here is that risk minimizers frequently found themselves in situations where their array of options for a major felt significantly more constrained than those available to their more socioeconomically advantaged peers. Chapter 6 explores the ways these constraints were amplified when the university failed to effectively pair resources and support with various pathways through college.

THE LIMITS OF STREAMLINED ENGAGEMENT AND CENTERING WORK

There were also potential limitations involved in streamlining college engagement and emphasizing paid employment. Fran recognized this challenge when she observed that "one thing I don't like about working is I'm kind of spreading myself out." She was a diligent student who wanted to succeed academically and earn a GPA that would allow her to gain acceptance to a graduate program in health sciences. "I want to do good; I want to get As. . . . In order to get accepted to graduate school, you should have good grades, so sometimes I'm like, 'should I quit [my job] right now to focus on learning?'" But leaving work did not seem like a viable option. She noted, "I think it would be best if I were to drop work, but then I wonder, where would I get funding?" Put simply, risk minimizers often had little choice but to devote themselves to work; the alternatives were extensive debt or leaving higher education. Here I highlight the consequences of streamlined engagement and centering work not so that students can be pushed toward other styles of engagement but so that scholars and higher education leaders can understand their causes and implications.

Employer policies sometimes incentivized a slower route through higher education. May, for instance, described how her job's tuition benefits led her to take longer completing college. She decided to enroll in just three or four classes a semester, rather than a full-time course load, in order to take full advantage of tuition reimbursement. "I get a solid twelve credits, and I work, and then I call it a day. It was definitely kind of like, 'Damn. I'm not going to graduate with my peers,' but in college, does that really matter?" While May was unsure whether taking additional time to complete her degree mattered, social science research suggests that it does. Extended time in college is associated with lower likelihood of completing a degree and with lower wages for those who do complete college.[22]

In addition to constraining their academic achievement or timely progress toward graduation, an emphasis on work meant that some students passed up valuable opportunities for professional development. As illustrated in the previous section, several participants noted that they'd turned down or deferred internship opportunities. Though they recognized, as Sonia stated clearly, that there were "certain internships that are obviously really good to have on your résumé," such opportunities seemed unrealistic if participating meant not being able to "put food on the table." For students who declined valuable internships and cocurricular opportunities to work low-wage jobs, there were also potential consequences for their future opportunities. Research shows that taking part in high-impact learning experiences in college helps students and graduates to secure career advantages. Experiences in internships, other cocurricular activities, and extracurricular involvement can be leveraged to signal social status and cultural similarity in job interviews, for example.[23] Without these types of experiences, minimizers may be at a disadvantage on the job market.

Moreover, because streamlined engagement left little time for extracurricular involvement, minimizers frequently struggled to form friendships in college. Of the four types of students described in this book, minimizers appeared to be the least connected to peers. Many described feeling marginal on campus. Sociologist Janice McCabe has shown that contrary to widespread beliefs that socializing represents a distraction from students' academic progress, college friendships can convey myriad benefits for students academically and professionally as they journey through higher education and life after graduation.[24] Such insights foreshadow some of the potential consequences minimizers may face as a result of dedicating less time to building social connections in college.

For some minimizers, the promise of financial security through full-time work was so great that it was tempting to leave college early to focus on paid employment. Marc described a recurring thought: "I wonder, what if I just entered the workforce right now and didn't stay in school?" Along similar lines, Kaleb claimed that, at the moment, he was determined to finish his degree,

> but there has been times, a couple of times, where I've been thinking, "oh, maybe I should pause on my education, work a few jobs, and come back to it." . . . There were times when I was thinking, maybe I should just stop my education and get a corporate job and work my way up. There were thoughts that I had in my mind, where I was thinking maybe education isn't what it is and stuff.

The impulse to forgo the insecurity of higher education for the appeal of full-time paid employment was difficult to resist.

Even for students who remained on track for graduation, strategies for minimizing risk seemed to carry over to their plans for transitioning out of college. This could often be observed in students' intentions to stay in their current jobs even after completing their degrees. Hannah, who sat down for her interview just days before graduation, acknowledged that "I don't have a job lined up, not in my field." Instead of leveraging her bachelor's degree to apply for a new position, she noted that "I'm probably going to stay at my retail job. . . . I want to pay my student debt off before I find a job that I'm not entirely certain of, if that makes sense." Like other minimizers, Hannah was apprehensive about repaying student loans and thought the safest way to accomplish this goal would be through sustained employment at her retail job, where paychecks seemed steady.

Other minimizers planned to pursue accessible jobs after graduation that didn't align with their interests or stated goals. Lucas, for instance, had hoped to work for a government agency after college, but he concluded that these opportunities might be a long shot. Instead, he decided to enlist in the military—an option he viewed as "safer" than straining to get his dream job. "Just because you have a four-year degree doesn't mean you're going to get a job. I know people who have the same degree as me and work at [a fast-food restaurant]." Similarly, although Georgia had been passionate about meteorology, she planned to go into teaching or a managerial position. She described how those jobs felt more accessible, even though she seemed unenthused about education or management.

Finally, some minimizers created so many backup plans for their future careers that they had trouble making progress toward a specific opportunity. Worried about "the competitiveness of the job market," Trevor developed a series of career goals for after graduation. His first preference was to start an entry-level job in finance, but he noted that "obviously I've also got my other thing," including going into alternative sectors, starting his own business, or going to graduate school. Though he was already well into his senior year, Trevor had little sense of which of these options he would end up pursuing. With so many career plans on the table, he found it difficult to channel his energy into any one of them.[25]

Rehearsal as Risk Mitigation

In his book *Homo Irrealis*, author André Aciman offers an account of the difference between ritual and rehearsal. "Rehearsal," he says, "is the act of repeating what has yet to happen." By contrast, ritual involves "repeating what has already happened."[26] This distinction is useful for conceptualizing the differences between the risk minimizers I've described in this chapter and the precarious pioneers from the previous one. Both groups, primarily composed of LIFGWC students, made repetition a part of their daily lives as they attempted to succeed in an insecure educational setting. But they were different in a crucial way. Where pioneers used personal resources to facilitate rituals of recovering from recurrent crises, minimizers were able to use other elements of community cultural wealth to rehearse for an uncertain future, fending off insecurity where they could.

The findings presented in this chapter complicate our notions about LIFGWC students and their experiences in college.[27] In contrast to assumptions that less socioeconomically advantaged students don't employ university services, some minimizers actually made frequent use of resources they believed would be safe and important to their success. Several participants regularly engaged academic advisors and financial aid officers, for example. Notably, however, they were usually wary of these resources and rarely felt comfortable relying on guidance from any one individual. Instead, they put in a great deal of effort to do their own research on majors, course requirements, and college funding.

This is not to say that minimizers were familiar with all university services. As prior studies have shown, there were important disparities in access to information, which meant LIFGWC students were often unaware of resources such as the Career Services Center, academic tutoring, the Center for Diversity and Inclusion, and the Office of Learning Services, among others.[28] Yet there were also times when minimizers did not take advantage of a resource or opportunity because they perceived it might be a risky way to invest their time. These students avoided the Study Abroad Office, student activities offices, and the Undergraduate Research Center. Such resources—as well as unpaid cocurricular and extracurricular involvement more generally—were seen as impractical ways to engage with the university. As these students noted, minimizers tried to be "in and out," focusing on their academics and a streamlined approach to completing their degrees. A clearer understanding of why some LIFGWC students pursued streamlined engagement in college (to be cautious rather than out of disinterest or a misunderstanding of the value of involvement) may help colleges and universities conceive of new approaches for helping students make the most of opportunities available without being derailed in their academic progress.

While we could critique minimizers for missing out on valuable learning and developmental opportunities, it is important to understand their strategies in context. Their approach to minimizing risk responds to a tendency in many contemporary universities to shift risk from the institution to individuals.[29] As I described in the first chapter, evidence of these patterns is present in the ways higher education is funded, marketed, and organized through complex bureaucracy.[30] Rather than accept this state of affairs, minimizers refused to take on risk whenever they could. Rebuffing the university's emphasis on complex programs of study, unpaid cocurricular activities, extensive extracurricular involvement, student loans, and other unstructured activities or resources, minimizers engaged in risk mitigation.

Both precarious pioneers and risk minimizers tried to make their way through an insecure setting that rarely recognized their needs as LIFGWC students. In doing so, they encountered arduous terrain and frequently struggled in their journeys.[31] Yet other students found more alignment between the policies and practices of the university and their own dispositions and resources. The next two chapters account for the experiences of these individuals.

4

Opportunity Maximizers:
Building an Enterprising Self

Brooke liked having choices and opportunities. The wall of her room in the CU residence halls featured an expansive collage. Posters and banners mingled with pictures and a student organization calendar, offering a snapshot of the elaborate life she'd built on campus. During our interview, she described how "being a successful college student" meant "being able to take advantage of the opportunities that you have." And she had done just that. An Asian continuing-generation college student from an upper-middle-class family, Brooke grinned as she described a strategic college-choice process. Having "always known" she'd pursue higher education, she looked for colleges that would help foster her passion for forensic biology. Seeking this specialized program of study brought Brooke hundreds of miles from home in the Midwest to CU's campus.

In college, she leveraged the opportunities available to pursue this unique major and pair it with a minor in psychology and law to further distinguish herself from peers. Moreover, she became highly involved, connecting with a range of student groups, professional organizations, leadership activities, and university resources. She built close relationships with staff members at the university's Career Services Center.

> I wanted to really get to know what career services had available. . . . The people there are so awesome. They've definitely helped me with professional development. . . . I've learned a lot for career development, and how to write a résumé. I knew how to do it, but just the little tiny details that you wouldn't think of, now I just know them off the top of my head.

While Brooke acknowledged that she already knew how to do things like craft a résumé, her connections at the Career Services Center supplemented this knowledge. With the support of their staff, she was currently looking into graduate school, seeking admission to several competitive programs.

In contrast to other students who sometimes felt lost at this big university, Brooke appreciated the choices available at CU. Reflecting on her experiences so far, she said,

> Being in college, I feel like there's so much that I've been able to do. There's so many things you can do in college. And I like to think that I've taken advantage of that, and gotten involved, and gotten to do tons of things that I want to do. Like I've been able to do a study abroad, which was kind of on my college checklist. I've been able to keep up with classes, graduate in four years. . . . In high school, it's more structured. So, it's like, "Oh, I'm doing this because I have to do it." Whereas in college you're choosing to do it, and you're putting energy to it. And sometimes after the end of a really busy week, you'll just be like, "I did that," and you feel accomplished.

As her words illustrate, Brooke's sense of accomplishment came in part from the way CU contrasted with her high school, where engagement was "more structured" and often mandatory. Because her extensive college involvement was optional—"you're choosing to do it"—she was able to highlight these activities as evidence of her own accomplishments. The items she marked off her "college checklist" became a series of achievements for the résumé she was strategically refining.

Students like Brooke encountered the college environment in a much different way from their LIFGWC peers. Seeing choice and the open buffet of university resources as desirable features, they channeled energy to extract valuable opportunities from CU. I refer to these students as *opportunity maximizers*. They had learned two of the lessons of privilege described by sociologist Shamus Khan: first, that "hierarchies are natural and they can be treated as ladders, not ceilings," and second, that "experiences matter" in attempts to climb these ladders.[1] Like the boarding school youth Khan studied, maximizers internalized and acted on both of these lessons. While pioneers struggled to stay afloat and minimizers cautiously planned for an uncertain future, these students worked to win at what they saw as a game of merit.

Coming from socioeconomically advantaged families with parents who had attended college themselves, the students featured in this chapter leveraged dominant social, cultural, and economic resources to gain a competitive edge in the insecure climate of public higher education. The very elements of this insecurity that frustrated or alarmed their LIFGWC peers—like abundant options and limited structure—provided the raw material for maximizers to curate a unique set of experiences that they used to position themselves as accomplished. Yet Khan also outlined a third lesson that maximizers did not have the luxury to learn, namely, that "privilege means being at ease, no matter what the context."[2] While these students were socioeconomically advantaged, they were intimately familiar with marginalization based on their gender, race, religion, immigration histories, sexual orientation, and ability. The intersections of these sociodemographic dimensions meant that maximizers experienced a confluence of advantages and constraints inhibiting their capacity to acquire ease as they navigated higher education. Their efforts to demonstrate merit may have been advantageous in many respects, but they were also stressful and sometimes exhausting.

Choosing CU for Opportunity

To understand maximizers, it helps to understand the way they arrived at CU. Their paths to higher education provided a stark contrast to those described by pioneers and minimizers. Janet, a White continuing-generation student from a middle-class family, described college as the assumed sequel to her K–12 education. "I decided to go to college in general just because it was the next thing to do after high school. That's just what I was brought up as. . . . I never considered anything else, just because I never thought about other options other than college." Walter, a Black continuing-generation student from an upper-middle-class family, noted that college wasn't so much a decision as an obvious next step. "I *had* to go to college . . . to increase my education level, and know more, and have more opportunities."[3]

For maximizers, attending a university fit with their disposition toward pursuing advantageous opportunities. Neville, a continuing-generation Asian student from a middle-class family, illustrated this point when he said that the main value of higher education was "the accolades from going to college." He expanded on this statement, noting that there were specific experiences that could only be accessed through college attendance.

> So, what I mean by that, the first one is in college you're not just paying for a degree and tuition, you're paying for an experience. You're paying for you to be integrated into an environment where . . . you're not just dropped on the streets and expected to do well, but you're not back in mom's house either. You have the flexibility to go out and explore and do things such as go abroad, or go do a job, or intern, or try to go on the subway by yourself.

Similarly, Felix, a continuing-generation Latino student from an upper-middle-class family, discussed how higher education facilitated access to resources and opportunities "that you wouldn't have anywhere else." Maximizers' perception of college as a set of opportunities they were "paying for" aligned with the customer-service model of higher education administration found at most postsecondary institutions today.[4] This model presents resources and opportunities in the form of an unstructured menu of options ("flexibility," in Neville's words) rather than requirements. Like diners at a buffet, these students arrived ready to feast from an extensive banquet.

Having grown up in families where going to college was familiar enough to be an expected part of the transition to adulthood rather than a luxury, maximizers focused not on whether they would attend college but on which one they would select. Acting on her preference for choices and flexibility, Felicia, a White continuing-generation student from a middle-class family, recounted choosing CU because "I also liked that there is a lot of options. It was a big school. I went to a tiny high school and didn't want to go to a school that was going to feel like very small and restricted." The kinds of opportunities students were thinking about when they described their college-choice process included the availability of unique academic programs, internships, extracurricular outlets, study abroad options, and research experience. Many of these opportunities were linked to one's field of study. Often completing high school with a specific white-collar career in mind, maximizers leveraged this knowledge to select a college that fit their goals. Walter said,

> I chose Commonwealth University because they had a great film program. I'm really passionate about being an executive producer one day, so I'm really into the program here. . . . I've always been super passionate about just film and the business side as well as the actual entertainment side. I came scouting colleges my sophomore year in high school. I came to this program; I just started studying the program. I started looking at some of the professors who are in the industry, like the cinematographer. I just started studying the program online, comparing the program, and I liked it.

Other maximizers chose CU because of its proximity to specific opportunities in a nearby city or because of its provision of certain extracurricular or cocurricular outlets. Regardless of their exact reasons, these students selected CU with intentionality, frequently traveling long distances and paying out-of-state tuition for the privilege.

Socioeconomic Advantage and Access to Capital

Maximizers' outlook on college was shaped in part by their access to middle- and upper-middle-class resources. Perhaps the most obvious thing that set them apart from pioneers and minimizers was their economic capital. Coming from relatively affluent families, these students entered college with a foundation of financial security. When I asked Walter whether he'd ever had concerns about affording college, he replied, "Not necessarily, I would say. I hate being that one kid that's like, 'Oh, wealthy this, wealthy that.' And I hate doing that, but I guess my parents, they've always tried to have my back. . . . As long as I have my focus on school, they're here to support me."

With a predictable flow of funds from their parents, maximizers rarely had to worry about money. Many of them did not even need to take out loans to afford college. Victor, a continuing-generation Latino student from an upper-middle-class family, displayed confidence in his family's financial situation as he explained, "I haven't had to take out any loans and I won't have to." His extensive involvement in high school and college also meant that Victor received several merit-based scholarships, awards that researchers have shown tend to advantage students from affluent families.[5] "I get one from the University Honors Program, I get one from the International Affairs Program, I get one from the humanities [scholarship fund]. There's always somebody that wants to give somebody else money for these types of things."

While Victor perceived that scholarships were plentiful, his experiences offered a sharp contrast with the LIFGWC students described in the preceding chapters. Where minimizers, for example, spent a great deal of time planning how they would afford each semester, maximizers rarely gave college costs much thought. Odessa, a continuing-generation Middle Eastern student from an upper-middle-class family, acknowledged that "I don't have a plan B for financials because everything is sort of handled."[6]

Maximizers' financial resources were compounded by their access to social capital and cultural capital in the form of *college knowledge*. In education research, this facet of cultural capital refers to one's familiarity with the contours—structure, norms, expectations, and procedures—of school settings.[7] Social capital refers to the benefits obtained through relationships with others that facilitate access to valuable information and opportunities.[8] While all students arrive in college with some configuration of cultural tools and social ties, those possessed by maximizers were of the sort that sociologist Pierre Bourdieu has described as "dominant" social and cultural capital.[9] In other words, their resources were recognized and rewarded by institutions like colleges and universities.

Maximizers grew up in households, neighborhoods, and schools surrounded by other socioeconomically advantaged individuals who equipped them with social and cultural capital. As they entered college, they understood how various majors connected with career opportunities, they recognized the nuances in different programs of study (e.g., which were more prestigious and advantageous), and they had a clear sense of the kinds of opportunities that would pay off as they made their way through higher education and eventually into postcollege life. Sociologists have shown how even general familiarity with the everyday, taken-for-granted elements of higher education, like how to use faculty office hours or how to build friendships on campus, can operate as cultural capital.[10]

Coming from continuing-generation families was an important part of this equation. In contrast to first-generation college students, whose parents or guardians had limited exposure to postsecondary educational settings, maximizers had parents with bachelor's and frequently graduate or professional degrees. With firsthand college experience, these parents were often directly involved in the ways students navigated higher education. For instance, Naomi, a Black continuing-generation student from a middle-class family, described receiving consistent guidance from her mother, father, and grandfather who were "constantly checking on me."[11]

In addition to direct parental involvement and intervention, maximizers also acquired college knowledge from observing the educational and career trajectories of family members. Walter drove this point home as he described the impact of his father:

> I guess the person I model every day is my father, because just seeing the work he puts in, and seeing his success afterwards, and seeing his attitude towards people. And professionally, and just everyday style, that's inspiring. So, seeing where he is, and seeing the route he took in college, that's a model I use every day.

Having knowledge about "the route" his father traveled through higher education, Walter was able to navigate college with an advantageous sense of familiarity.

Privilege and Vulnerability

With abundant resources, we might hypothesize that maximizers would be very comfortable in college, with few cares or concerns. But this was not usually the case. Shamus Khan proposes that *ease* be thought of as a central element of cultural capital, defining it as a privilege that manifests in the ability to feel "comfortable in just about any social situation."[12] In educational institutions, individuals who possess ease are able to engage fluidly in a range of settings, taking advantage of opportunities for self-development while "displaying the right corporeal marks of belonging."[13] Though ease may appear natural, Khan points out that it is the result of frequent practice that eventu-

OPPORTUNITY MAXIMIZERS 83

ally results in comfort with one's social position and surroundings. Students who embodied ease then would possess (or acquire) a sense of calm as they made their way through the twists and turns of their college journey. These students would be able to fully embrace the flexibility of contemporary higher education to maintain ease, even in moments of uncertainty. The next chapter describes a group of students who fit this description, but maximizers did not.

Although they arrived on campus with seemingly ample economic capital, social capital, and cultural capital in the form of college knowledge, these students also perceived liabilities linked to their social location. As table 4.1 illustrates, maximizers were a diverse group in terms of gender, race, and

TABLE 4.1. Maximizers' sociodemographic characteristics

Student characteristic	% (n)
Parental education	
First-generation college students	3 (1)
Continuing-generation college students	97 (36)
Family income	
Low income	3 (1)
Middle or high income	97 (36)
Social class background	
Working class	3 (1)
Lower-middle class	3 (1)
Middle class	32 (12)
Upper-middle class	62 (23)
Race/ethnicity	
Asian or Asian American	24 (9)
Black or African American	16 (6)
Hispanic or Latinx	11 (4)
White	27 (10)
Multiracial, other race/ethnicity	22 (8)
Family immigration	
Parents immigrated to the US	54 (20)
Parents born in the US	46 (17)
Intersections of race and gender	
Women of color	35 (13)
Men of color	35 (13)
Nonbinary or agender students of color	3 (1)
White women	24 (9)
White men	3 (1)
Nonbinary or agender White students	0 (0)

family immigration histories. Yet they shared something crucial in common: their unique intersectional social locations were characterized by an intermingling of privilege and vulnerability.[14] Only one of these students identified as a White man, with the remaining thirty-six identifying as students of color and/or as women. A sense of vulnerability to various kinds of marginalization and discrimination undermined their ability to navigate college and the broader transition to adulthood with ease. In other words, maximizers' intersectional identities meant they felt advantaged in some respects but marginalized in others. This tension informed the ways they leveraged economic, social, and cultural capital to maximize opportunities as a form of self-protection.

Caroline, a White continuing-generation student from an upper-middle-class family, offered a clear example of how this mixture of advantage and marginalization led students to use their resources as a form of protection from vulnerability. Throughout her interview, she acknowledged benefitting from elements of cultural capital, such as "knowing how to interact with people in the right ways and with the right 'professionalism,' quote unquote, and how to present, how to interact . . . because of the privileged experience [I've had] every day." She similarly acknowledged the impact of her racial identity:

> Being White, I feel like I have a strong advantage. Just last week . . . in Dr. Thompson's laboratory there are a good amount of us research assistants, and you know people under her, and I only realized when I had a training last Friday [led by a Black woman] that I had not once seen a Black female in the lab.

Nonetheless, Caroline did not believe that her racial privilege and middle-class cultural resources alone would be enough to propel her into middle-class adulthood. Instead, she felt pressure to maximize every available opportunity, a disposition she thought came in part from being a woman in a STEM field. She described frequently considering "how to be targeting [my efforts] and feeling like I might even have to target even more than like White guys who were able to just like stumble their way into the field and it worked for them. I'm like 'oh, I'm working my butt off and still feel like I'm not gonna [succeed in my field].'" In other words, Caroline's tendency to maximize opportunities was wrapped up with her sense that being a woman in STEM meant confronting systemic inequalities that might curtail her academic and professional success. She traced these concerns to experiences watching her mother's stalled career. "I was lucky enough to have a great role model of a mother, who has advanced her way up in her field, painstakingly so, with years upon years of undue credit and . . . doing her boss's work and not get-

OPPORTUNITY MAXIMIZERS 85

ting the credit for it. . . . But then a White guy came in above her." Caroline couldn't help wondering whether her mother's career struggles—feeling unrecognized and being passed over for promotions—foreshadowed her own future in STEM. While she couldn't ward off all forms of discrimination, she hoped that a stellar college record, full of accomplishments and valuable experiences, would buffer her from sexism.

Along similar lines, a multiracial, Black and White, continuing-generation student named Valerie reflected on how her upper-middle-class resources offered certain socioeconomic advantages. Yet she was also concerned about racism affecting her career trajectory.

> There is kind of this stigma of hair and professionalism. Because I do prefer to wear my hair in braids, I do know that there are existing stigmas about Black women and hair and what is professional and what isn't. It does concern me that even though I do keep myself well put together, that may not appear professional to some people. And that does concern me, and it's on my mind that others may be a little bit judgmental of that and may have an impression of me that's not necessarily true.

Valerie described how these widespread "stigmas"—which showed up even in workplace policies affecting Black women—informed her emphasis on securing skills and opportunities in college to increase her chances of being evaluated on the basis of her experience rather than racist stereotypes. "Ultimately I want to leave it to my skill set and my ability to perform the job at hand." With this in mind, she focused on

> being aware of the opportunities that are presented to me and preparing myself for those opportunities. . . . The focus on research and the environment here has definitely provided me with the mindset that I have a lot of opportunities. I'm very aware that there are a lot of possibilities, and I think that my experience [at CU] definitely has made that very apparent.

While Valerie felt like the university environment offered helpful opportunities to gain experiences that could offer some protection against racism, other students described becoming maximizers in part because of firsthand encounters with marginalization on campus. For instance, Kailyn, a continuing-generation Asian student from a middle-class family, described how her experiences at CU as a Muslim woman from an immigrant family taught her "not to put all your eggs in one basket." She elaborated:

> I've been in college for four years, and there has been a lot of stuff happening in the last four years. . . . I do feel vulnerable and [I encounter] a history that negatively impacts marginalized groups of people, including Muslim people. . . .

> And so sitting in class, hearing people talk about made-up terms that seek to
> further divide the Muslim community or terms that really isolate the Muslim
> identity and Islam as a religion, and just not feeling brave enough to speak out,
> or educated enough or just strong enough to, or just have the mental energy to
> give my stance on the topic. . . . Yeah, it's not all rainbows, there was definitely
> times where I just felt like it was a battle to be fought another day, so I just sat
> with that vulnerability and tried to channel it to something else.

She recognized that this "vulnerability" was shaped not just by prejudiced individuals but also by university policies and practices that affected the campus climate for students from marginalized groups. Efforts to "channel it into something else" informed Kailyn's attempts to capitalize on opportunities. By allocating effort to excel in a range of college settings, including in her classes, multiple internships, a religious community, a student governance group, and an international service organization, she hoped to provide some protection against marginalization within and beyond higher education. Maximizers' involvement patterns on campus aligned with the findings of other studies showing that socioeconomically advantaged students from marginalized groups often work to become engaged in a variety of activities and organizations in order to create a buffer from mistreatment (in Kailyn's words, by not putting "all your eggs in one basket").[15]

Finally, for some students, intersectional identities complicated their prospects of sustaining support from their middle- and upper-middle class families. As sociologist Jessi Streib explains in her book, *Privilege Lost*, it is important to recognize that not all parents convey their socioeconomic advantages to their offspring.[16] For a variety of reasons, some families may be unable or unwilling to allocate resources to support the transition to adulthood. Mills, a continuing-generation Asian and White student from a middle-class family, expressed fears of losing the support of his family, as he explained:

> I identify as bisexual, and that was hard; that's always been a dominating issue
> within my life because I grew up in a very conservative family background. . . .
> I had a very serious relationship my freshman year with another guy. And not
> being able to share that with my family and figure out how to navigate that was
> very difficult. I came out to everyone but my family in the fall semester of my
> freshman year, so that was a continuing struggle and challenge that created a
> lot of uncertainty for what my future would look like.

Mills described how concerns that his family might withdraw their support— not just emotionally but also financially—if they found out he was bisexual informed his efforts to maximize opportunity, pursuing a rigorous program of study and extensive involvement on the premedical track at CU. "I do think that [identifying as bisexual] played a role in me picking biology and the medical school route as a program to pursue, because I felt like I wanted to address that—the issues with coming out and the financial security concerns that come with that if your family doesn't accept you." If coming out to his family meant losing their support, he wanted to be prepared.

As the experiences of Caroline, Valerie, Kailyn, and Mills made clear, being a socioeconomically advantaged student did not mean one had the privilege of navigating college with ease. These students were acutely aware that reproducing their parents' socioeconomic status was not guaranteed.[17] Describing their identities as simultaneously conferring advantages and liabilities, maximizers worked diligently to use available resources to head off marginalization—from systemic inequalities, discrimination, and prejudice—by proactively leveraging the opportunities available at a large research university. Though their economic capital, social capital, and college knowledge could not give them a durable sense of ease, they did provide tools for pursuing success in college, equipping them with the capacity to navigate these opportunities.

The combination of socioeconomic advantage with marginalization based on gender, race, religion, immigration, sexual orientation, and ability informed the ways maximizers described the insecurity of their college environment. While they were not fully comfortable with all forms of uncertainty, they thought about options and choices as positive, in contrast to the LIFGWC students described in the previous two chapters. Grace, a continuing-generation Asian student from a middle-class family, acknowledged qualms with uncertainty, but she also noted,

> It's not always good if it's like too certain where it's like "Okay, do you have any other options? Do you have any other interests that you might want to do?" Like college gives you enough direction but it's not forcing you to go in a certain place—it still gives you room to decide. . . . I know that you're always worried about what might happen or what you might be missing that you need to graduate. I think it can sometimes bring out negative emotions, but in the long run, I don't think it's negative to have a little uncertainty. . . . It also gives you more options, rather than less options.

Grace made a distinction here between the types of uncertainty that might prevent one from graduating and the types that provide "options" rather than rigid structure. Even if the former was negative, she saw the latter as desirable. In short, maximizers viewed insecurity in complex ways. They worried that certain forms of insecurity could elevate their vulnerability as members of marginalized groups. And yet they also believed leveraging options in a strategic way could help to shield oneself from discrimination. When they looked at the abundance of choices for engagement in higher education, they saw a way to demonstrate merit and craft a specific kind of identity.[18]

Building an Enterprising Self

Melissa, a White continuing-generation student from an upper-middle-class family, described herself as a "hard worker and perfectionist." She thought about college in a very instrumental way. "You need to be able to sell yourself," she claimed, before elaborating on her decisions to study abroad, take part in a summer research program, and add an English minor to round out her environmental science degree. She described these choices as professionally advantageous, explaining that she hoped they would "set me up" to be "the most qualified" for future employment opportunities.

Even with these accolades, Melissa still worried. Should she have majored in biology instead of environmental science? Would employers view that degree as more prestigious? And what other experiences might she need? Reflecting on her time at CU so far, she expressed that perhaps she should have "done more research opportunities on campus, done more applicable jobs, been more of a leader." The anxiety in her voice was clear as she acknowledged, "I'm doing some of that stuff, but I definitely am pretty critical of myself. . . . It could always be better."

In college, maximizers embarked on a journey to be better. Better than their peers. Better than they were in high school. Better than they were the year, month, or week before. And for these students, the yardstick by which they measured being "better" was almost always their aptitude for labor market success. Having strategically chosen a big university with abundant choices and opportunities, they approached college in a way that was designed to optimize their transition to adulthood. Concerned about marginalization and discrimination, they used the resources at their disposal to craft an *enterprising self*, a concept that scholars have theorized, building on the work of philosopher Michel Foucault, as "a form of subjectivity that aligns with market needs."[19] More plainly, maximizers drew from the menu of opportunities provided by CU to strategically assemble a set of dispositions, experiences, and skills connected to their professional goals that would benefit them in a competitive labor market.

Wanda, an upper-middle-class, continuing-generation Latina student, described the transactional approach to college that was used to manufacture an enterprising self. "I've always thought of education as you get out of it what you put in." She depicted her vision of success in college as "getting something out of it that I wouldn't have found anywhere else" so that she could "do something I really like and be the best at it." The connection between experience and market needs was evident as Wanda justified her decision to study language in college. "Language has always been . . . commodified in the sense that language has always been something that could be useful in the future for my job and my career." Seen through this lens, going to college was an investment not just in marketable skills but more broadly in opportunities to craft a professional identity. Wanda used the word *cultivate* frequently in describing her efforts to build a specific kind of work-optimized self.

This orientation toward college necessitated intentional planning comparable to the detailed plans developed by minimizers. Janet illustrated this fact when she said, "I plan out my whole week, what I'm doing every day," and Victor noted, "I'm the kind of person who likes to have a plan of steps I'm going to follow." Yet whereas minimizers developed plans that streamlined a safe route to graduation, maximizers used detailed planning to partake extensively in the buffet of opportunities available at CU. Expanding on her previous point, Janet explained that a successful college student "is someone that takes advantage of the college experience, tries different things, and is involved in the campus. CU has a ton of amazing events that they put on to get people to be involved." She pointed to specific experiences and accomplishments—a high GPA and participation in university programs and student organizations—as evidence of merit.

For maximizers, the first step in building an enterprising self was the strategic selection of a field of study that aligned with a juncture they had identified between their personal interests and market needs. Shahid, a continuing-generation Asian student from a lower-middle-class family, offered a clear illustration of the ways participants wove together these interests and needs when he discussed his choice of the neuroscience major.

> You know, I've loved medicine my whole life. I love neuroscience, just because the field is so underdeveloped in a way. We're still researching about it, we're still finding nooks and crannies here and there, and so I just I love the fact that we don't know everything about it, and now we can research more, find out more. And it's such a delicate field, right, because it's the brain, and I want to do neurosurgery and medical school hopefully, fingers crossed. So, I feel like neuroscience is a good first step into that direction.

Identifying this connection between his love for medicine, his fascination with the brain, and the need for more knowledge in this field, Shahid declared a major in neuroscience. While many students who aspired to become doctors majored in biology or community health, choosing this major helped him to stand out. He explained his decision through an analogy to business.

> I like to challenge myself. . . . I've seen many people who've done everything right. Like they've got an MBA, they've gotten a bachelor's in business, they've done certain business fraternities and whatnot, and they still haven't gotten hired because they're too focused on just getting employed, and they don't go outside their comfort zone. I think as our world continues to grow and businesses out there expand their requirements, they want to see people with a broad perspective. They want to see people who have ventured out into other experiences as well and not just entirely like business focused or medicine focused. They have other things under their belt that they can contribute that will help them succeed in our workplaces. . . . They want somebody who can think outside the box. . . . I wanted to be a little bit more well rounded.

Desires like these—to show that one had "a broad perspective" and was "a little bit more well rounded"—informed the decisions students made about their field of study.

BEYOND A MAJOR: DOUBLE MAJORS, MINORS, CONCENTRATIONS, AND FELLOWSHIPS

In each of my interviews, I asked students how they'd chosen and whether they'd ever changed their majors. For pioneers and minimizers, these questions usually evoked discussions about the challenges of selecting the right field. For maximizers by contrast, such prompts were often seen as insufficient in that they didn't seem to provide an opportunity to expand on something they viewed as equally important: efforts to supplement their major with academic specializations.[20] Nonetheless, students managed to find ways to springboard from my questions to a depiction of their enhanced academic experiences. For instance, when asked whether he had ever changed majors, Neville replied,

> Changing, no. Adding on, yes. I would say that I never considered changing my base major from government, but I have considered adding on majors or at least minors, such as communication, due to the work I do—policy and debate, which are [minors] in the field of communication, and my interest in the study of Russian as a foreign language—I minor there too.

Neville's use of the phrase "base major" was illuminating. Maximizers saw the selection of a major as just the first step in a series of decisions about their academic engagement. Like consumers adding options to a base model car, they thought about enhancements, upgrades, and special features they could acquire.[21] Similarly, Wanda recalled a moment when she realized "I need to add other things. . . . I've been adding things on . . . that I can supplement my major with to help me with my career in the future." She provided specific examples, including a concentration within her major, a minor, and pursuing an accelerated master's degree that allowed her to combine graduate and undergraduate courses in her fourth year of study.

Maximizers treated minors and concentrations as weapons in an academic arms race. When I interviewed Rachel, a Black continuing-generation student from a middle-class family, she'd recently had a disagreement with friends about the value of her major in international affairs. Sitting in front of her whiteboard with an extensive to-do list committed to dry-erase marker, she described her frustration when, "they were like, 'Oh, well international affairs is kind of like a fluffy major.'" Although she was reluctant to change fields of study, Rachel sought to buttress her degree with a concentration in "human rights and social justice" and a minor in Spanish. At the time of our interview, she was also considering adding a second concentration along with an additional minor in nonprofit studies.

Declaring a concentration in one's major or a minor in a supplemental area of study could be used to signal unique skills and perspectives to various kinds of gatekeepers, including future employers and graduate admissions committees. Caroline added a computer science minor, recalling how "I felt lacking" and realized "how much of an asset it is to have those skills." Shahid admitted that he was planning to declare a minor in public policy to increase his chances of admission to a specialized medical school program. "I'm going to pursue a minor. I've actually applied to [another university's] early acceptance medical program with CU that they have. . . . So, if you get accepted to that, then you have to pursue a nonmedical- or [non]science-related major or minor." While it was unclear whether Shahid had much interest in public policy, he anticipated the potential payoff of incorporating this minor into his program of study.

The ways maximizers paired majors and minors allowed them to combine the prestige and versatility of a liberal arts field with the potential labor market benefits of documenting specialized skill sets.[22] In contrast to minimizers, who usually selected majors in applied fields like criminology or information technology, maximizers' social and cultural capital equipped them with knowledge about the ways different fields of study were perceived by various audiences. For instance, Carl, a multiracial Black and White continuing-generation student from a middle-class family, recalled his decision to major in sociology when "my [high school] teacher at the time, I told him I wanted

92   CHAPTER FOUR

to go to a criminal justice major. He was like, 'Don't choose it as your major. Make sure that's your minor.'" Coming to recognize that a liberal arts major would be viewed by many as more prestigious than a major in an applied field, Carl decided to take his advice. Others joined an applied major with a liberal arts minor to demonstrate that they were "well rounded." In the end, maximizers found their way to unique major-minor combinations, pairing film with business, foreign languages with environmental science, and psychology with health policy to name a few.

For some, academic fellowships provided another opportunity to set themselves apart. After emphasizing the importance of capitalizing on a range of opportunities, Janet described becoming involved in CU's environmental protection fellowship. These semester-long programs curated a series of academic courses and high-impact learning experiences.[23] Being a fellow conferred opportunities to specialize in one's program of study, access unique classes, and obtain other markers of academic achievement. Janet, for instance, observed that by "doing this program, I'll get a minor in environmental protection automatically. That was something that intrigued me to do this program." In a comparable way, Melissa noted that taking part in a fellowship program would "propel me" into other opportunities; for example, she claimed that completing a fellowship would "set me up for internships."

COCURRICULARS, EXTRACURRICULARS,
AND THE ENTERPRISING SELF

"You have to make the most out of your experience from college," Shahid claimed, adding that, "nobody can be perfect, but definitely maximize your college experience." When he offered this advice, I wondered what it would look like to maximize one's experience in higher education. As our conversation progressed, he provided a detailed illustration.

SHAHID. I'm part of CU Ambassadors, which we give tours around campus; I'm a part of the Religious Student Association; I'm a part of honor committee, as well as CU Rescue, which helps connect people interested in volunteering for the fire department . . . because I'm actually an EMT with the county fire rescue as well.

BRS. It sounds like you've been very involved so far in your two years here.

SHAHID. Yeah, I try to do everything I can. . . . Going into college, I knew that I needed to hit the ground running in terms of my involvement and like volunteering and shadowing and hours for premed clinical hours, volunteer hours for premed, as well as maintaining a very high GPA and

MCAT score. And so, with that in mind, my last year of high school, my senior year, I started volunteering for the fire department. . . . And so I've been doing the EMT for quite some time, but I also intern at the [nearby hospital]. . . . A couple other things as far as internships and stuff that just boost up my résumé, making myself seem like the [top] 1% as a medical school candidate.

While Shahid attributed his internship to his father's connections ("one of his clients actually works at [the hospital], and so it wasn't that difficult to connect"), he credited CU with supplying other opportunities, including his recent research experiences. "Providing you good opportunities for research, CU's really good with that. I mean, I've gotten one research project done, and I'm starting another one soon. . . . I think what they do with research is fantastic."

Beyond academic programs of study, maximizers worked to capitalize on the array of cocurricular and extracurricular opportunities available at CU. This often required highly strategic and transactional approaches to extracurricular engagement. During my interview with Rachel, I was shocked by how extensive her involvement was. As a sophomore, she'd already done a study abroad trip, taken part in two internships, and been engaged in innumerable programs and student organizations. When I expressed my surprise, she laughed. "I do a lot of things. All these things that we talked about today, I still do them all." She went on to explain how she worked to fit everything in, providing specific examples. "The thing with it though is that not everything is every day. Like the Mentor Club, me being a mentor, that's five hours a month. So, if I meet with my mentee just five times a month, that counts." Rachel's words illuminated the way maximizers thought of opportunities not necessarily for their holistic developmental potential but for the instrumental value of having something "count." Such an approach sometimes required moderating the amount of time dedicated to each activity so that they allocated just enough effort to receive credit for completion or participation.

Like collectors, these students thought carefully about which experiences they already had and which they still needed to fill their résumés. Grace illustrated this point: "I think study abroad has really been on my mind. . . . I have a few internships under my belt, but I don't really have any study abroad experience." Just as Melissa agonized over her résumé, Grace acknowledged the inadequacy maximizers felt when they were lacking an experience: "It definitely feels like I'm not getting as much done as I should be." To combat this inadequacy, they rarely passed on an opportunity. Victor reported, "If an opportunity comes up, I take advantage of it. I pursue it. I don't watch as it flies by." He explained that this approach would result in "building a nice web of things" and "getting more experiences under my belt."

The proliferation of opportunities for involvement beyond the classroom is often connected to students' desires to have fun in college and institutional efforts to treat students as consumers, fulfilling those desires for a social experience.[24] Yet for maximizers, cocurricular and extracurricular engagement were treated as additional tools for crafting enterprising selves. Troy, a continuing-generation Latino student from a middle-class family, was involved in multiple student organizations alongside several research opportunities. He explained, "I try to focus on things that will help out my résumé. . . . I don't party or do student organizations that are just for fun. I try to focus on more academic things."[25] And Neville was quick to describe how his involvement—especially his participation on the debate team—connected with his professional goals for a career in government. "My extracurricular activities, particularly in policy debate, have us talking about what theoretical actions may these actors take in relation to what we do as a nation in terms of policy or domestic policy."

Because of the ways maximizers worked to link their extensive involvement to the labor market, internships were prized. After noting that "I work hard and try to do the max that I can," Victor explained that "part of the benefit" of attending CU was access to "the opportunities that I knew CU would provide and has provided . . . especially with internships." As a sophomore, he'd completed an internship with a human rights organization in conjunction with a fellowship program at CU. He subsequently parlayed that experience to secure a second internship during his junior year with a federal government agency. The ways one internship could be leveraged for another were frequently highlighted by maximizers as they recounted their college journeys. For instance, Kailyn described taking part in multiple internships: "I've been interning alongside with my studies, since my sophomore year basically. I knew that I wanted to do an internship, but I didn't know I wanted to do so many at the time." By her senior year, Kailyn's first internship had morphed into several more, and she was surprised by how easy it had been to get additional ones after the first.[26]

Since about 2015, sociologists have begun to document the ways socioeconomically advantaged students use resources to stockpile opportunities within higher education.[27] The seeming abundance of internships described by maximizers provided a perfect illustration of this tendency in action. Internship opportunities are coveted by college students as a way to secure a smooth transition to full-time professional employment.[28] While pioneers and minimizers perceived that such opportunities—especially paid ones—

were few and far between, over the course of my interviews, it started to seem as if there were probably sufficient opportunities to go around at CU. Yet these internships had been concentrated among a smaller group of students who sometimes even had two internships at a time.

Socioeconomically advantaged participants were supported in their efforts to accumulate opportunities by family members, who frequently served as the spark for connecting with initial internships or extracurricular opportunities. Kailyn acknowledged, "My dad works [in a related field]. He just knows a lot of people here, and so . . . I do think it did impact my college career. I was able to talk to my dad's friends who are in the field, and my first internship was through a family friend." Other parents provided the resources to support an initial unpaid internship that later translated into paid opportunities.

Whereas nearly all LIFGWC students worked substantial hours—sometimes forty or more a week—at off-campus employment unrelated to their field of study (fast-food restaurants, grocery stores, or other retail jobs), maximizers seemed perplexed by how one might juggle that type of commitment with academic and extracurricular engagement. Janet, for instance, claimed, "I have not had a job at all in my life yet. . . . School is very busy for me. . . . So, how do people work and go to school at the same time? I don't know how that would work; I don't think it would work for me." Others were employed in more limited capacities until they transitioned to internships. This was the case for Walter, who had recently quit his part-time position to focus on applying for new opportunities, explaining that he hadn't really needed the money. Though he'd enjoyed spending time with his coworkers, leaving this job opened up more time for involvement geared toward his academic and professional success. Janet and Walter's experiences align with research showing that while more socioeconomically advantaged students spend less time working for pay during college, they're actually more likely to take part in internship opportunities.[29]

The COVID-19 pandemic seemed to amplify inequality in access to opportunities. This occurred in part because maximizers, with a stable financial foundation and greater familiarity with college, had an easier time than their LIFGWC peers navigating pandemic-related change. Zoey, for instance, recalled how distressed some of her peers were during the shift to online instruction in spring 2020, but she noted that, "I'm able to balance it all. I think it's kind of easier for me." When LIFGWC students were encountering new types of constraints during the early months of the pandemic, students like Kailyn and Walter managed to secure prestigious internships.

In contrast to pioneers and minimizers, who sometimes described the pandemic as undercutting their academic and professional experiences, maximizers were usually quick to highlight the ways they sustained high-quality opportunities. Victor, for instance, noted,

> Obviously, there was COVID and whatnot happening. So, I was certainly anxious about how that was going to affect my internship. . . . I figured, well, this is probably going to go virtual, so I should plan for that. . . . And yeah, it's been certainly weird, but it still hasn't at all I think diminished what I've gotten out of this internship so far. . . . It's still been really awesome.

Staking out this claim that COVID-19 hadn't "diminished" his internship experience, Victor worked to ensure that his accomplishments would still be viewed as substantial despite the limitations brought about by a global pandemic.

Of course, some of the effects of COVID-19 were beyond maximizers' control. Inevitably, some internship offers were retracted, study abroad trips were canceled, and other opportunities were lost. Maximizers were not fully insulated from these disappointments. But they did benefit from a capacity to identify and navigate other options. Leveraging social and cultural capital, they typically were able to pull together alternative experiences when needed. For instance, Naomi described becoming a teaching assistant when she struggled to find an internship during the pandemic.

> I'm applying to grad school, and I was like, "I have no experience," and I've been trying to find internships, but it's really hard to find internships. . . . It's like internships are very scarce. So, I was like, "I have to get some type of experience." And the teacher I'm a teaching assistant for, I've taken like three of his classes. Like, we talk all the time; he loves me. So, I was like, "Fingers crossed, he will let me be a TA for his class."

While Naomi had been involved in two professional associations, a cultural student organization, and a large research project, she wanted to ensure that she'd also have an intensive professional experience with a supervisor. "I don't really count [my research] as, like, major experience. So, that's why I really wanted to do something like being a TA to get some good experience and then get a closer connection with some of my teachers." By becoming a teaching assistant, Naomi was able to fill what she perceived as an important gap in her portfolio for admission to graduate school.

Leveraging the Do-It-Yourself Environment

Maximizers' ability to build an enterprising self was facilitated by the way their personal and family resources interacted with university resources. The previous chapters show how LIFGWC students struggled to navigate CU's do-it-yourself environment.[30] But in contrast to pioneers and minimizers, the socioeconomically advantaged maximizers were prepared to leverage this environment for their own advantage. The buffet of unstructured choices was exactly the type of setting these students believed would be beneficial for crafting a unique set of accomplishments, experiences, and skills. Having deliberately chosen a large research university, they gave CU credit for living up to their expectations. Rachel, for instance, summed up her affinity for the do-it-yourself environment when she proclaimed,

> I preach to everyone, like CU has a wealth of opportunities, like so much so that I can't even do all of them. . . . I think the university has been very helpful. Like if I need advising appointments or I need help from an advisor, it's really easy to get help, or if I'm looking for a study abroad program, it's easy. *You have to look though.* That's the thing. You can't just not ask for help or be looking for something. You have to go to those offices, or you have to look it up. . . . In college, you've got to find the people to help you. There's no one who's going to be like, "Hi, I'm here to help you." You have to make your appointment with your advisor. Your advisor's not going to send you an email saying, "Hey, I haven't met with you." They have hundreds of students they have to talk to. You have to find the people that can help you first and also be willing to ask them for help to even begin with. You'll be forced to advocate for yourself.

Maximizers believed they would be judged by what Natasha Warikoo describes as *calibrated merit*.[31] This framework posits that individuals should be evaluated based on their "accomplishments in the context of what opportunities they have had."[32] These contextualized determinations of merit presume that resources will be provided as optional to students, allowing those with the "best work ethic" to set themselves apart. Yet this assumes that all students have equal access the opportunities offered by their institution, an assumption that the two previous chapters clearly challenge. Just because resources are available at a university doesn't mean all students have the same chance to make use of them.[33]

In emphasizing the importance of advocating for oneself, Rachel acknowledged that the university was not structured to provide proactive support to students in need. While LIFGWC students recognized this as a problem, maximizers saw it as advantageous. "CU has all of the opportunities; you just have to take them," Rachel claimed, adding that, "They just have everything. They think of everything. It's great." She provided an example when discussing her experience applying for competitive fellowships. "I was looking for fellowships, and I feel like the fellowships office is not very publicized." Yet after reaching out to the office, Rachel recalled how a staff member "was telling me about all these different things that I can do that I've never heard of . . . and I was like 'okay, I'll be seeing you for the next four years, because I love those things!'" The fact that this office was known by few students meant that she received one-on-one guidance after making contact.

As Brooke showed in the opening of this chapter, the way university resources were offered on an optional basis appealed to maximizers. Not only did this mean that students could get personalized support from offices and centers that few others used but it also allowed maximizers to feature their engagement with various resources as evidence of their own dedication and determination. Neville emphasized this point when he described the value of "figuring out that you can . . . search out opportunities by your own initiative." He elaborated on this point to present an example. "College kind of shows you like, hey you don't have to attend this seminar with the US Supreme Court justice, but you could." In other words, the buffet-style presentation of opportunities allowed maximizers to frame their involvement as evidence that they were proactive and took "initiative."

In contrast to LIFGWC students, who often perceived that certain resources weren't for students like them, maximizers found ways to insert themselves into university programs and events even when these opportunities were geared toward other groups of students. Rachel recalled her first year at CU, when she attended a specialized career event that catered to juniors and seniors.

> As a freshman, all of [the employers] were saying like, "Oh, we're not looking for freshmen, but thanks for coming and take my card and call me in three years." I was like, "okay but I'm still here though." So, I met my [future internship supervisor]. She was like asking me some really interesting and thought-provoking questions. And she was like, "you know what, would you want to do an internship? I'm willing to take on one intern this year." And she offered me a job. That was a really great opportunity that I got, just by going to the fall career fair and like putting on a blazer and just showing up and having some copies of my résumé.

Rachel cringed, squeezing her eyes shut as she recalled the awkward moment of feeling out of place as a first-year student at this event. Yet her sense that she needed to pursue every opportunity overrode the discomfort of being at an event for juniors and seniors.

Maximizers were adept at identifying the types of resources that could help them succeed throughout their academic and professional endeavors. As prior research has illustrated, familial support was one of these resources.[34] Yet they also frequently found niche services provided by CU. For example, several maximizers talked about the university's writing center and library databases—resources that LIFGWC students hardly ever mentioned. Janet referenced both when she said, "I've used the writing center a lot. . . . I've used the library's online resources and databases; I always prefer actual resources over just Google," and Felix described his appreciation for

> all the resources CU has to offer, like the library databases, they have literally every study that you could possibly think of on their database. And they have a way that if you happen to find a study that's not on their website, you can fill out a form and they will find a way to get it for you. So, you have access to basically any knowledge base that you want to.

After recalling how "the writing center was really helpful," Grace also noted that CU had "just opened an economics tutoring department." She learned about and made use of this tutoring service before many other students were aware of its existence. Maximizers leveraged these types of resources to do well in their courses, overcome academic obstacles, complete thesis or capstone projects, and apply for scholarships and fellowships.

Even when employing the same types of resources, maximizers diverged from LIFGWC students in the way they used them to enhance their experiences. This could be observed clearly when students discussed meetings with academic advisors. Whereas minimizers met with advisors to engage in risk reduction, planning their course selection and trying to ensure they were taking the right classes to fulfill degree requirements, maximizers used these same resources to find unique opportunities. Instead of meeting with her advisor to avoid scheduling errors, Felecia, a continuing-generation White student from an upper-middle-class family, described using these meetings to plan for her career and connect with opportunities for informational interviews. Similarly, Melissa's self-described strategy of "sucking up" to professors who she hoped would one day write her letters of recommendation contrasted sharply with LIFGWC students who interacted with faculty in more limited ways, usually within the parameters of specific course assignments. Rachel summed up how such strategies linked to the ways maximizers thought about success: "I would say I've been very successful . . . in terms of advocating for myself. Most of the things I have on my résumé, I would not have them if I didn't put myself out there and meet someone to talk to at first."

Advantaged but Anxious

As they combined personal, family, and university resources to build an enterprising self, maximizers learned to narrate the opportunities they'd taken advantage of in order to frame themselves as meritorious. These participants illustrate how socioeconomically advantaged students can obtain benefits from an insecure environment, leveraging the abundant choices and flexibility that can be incapacitating for students who are less familiar with higher education. As sociologist Christopher Takacs has observed, "Access to the kinds of experiences that make for valuable stories, such as stories of leadership, international travel, and campus adventures is not equally available to all students."[35] While LIFGWC students often found themselves fighting to navigate the array of unstructured opportunities at CU, maximizers accumulated advantageous experiences and prepared to make the transition to white-collar careers.

The experiences of the students featured in this chapter contribute to literature on the dual impact of expanding choice.[36] As Allison Pugh shows, while options and flexibility have been celebrated by some who see these elements of insecurity culture as positive developments—"more freedom, more choice, more happiness"—it is also important to consider "the costs of all that flexibility," including "the uneven distribution of who can take advantage of it."[37] Though choice and a lack of structure can create valuable opportunities for some students, they also contribute to inequality, disadvantaging those who are not positioned to benefit from or leverage these options. As maximizers accumulated resources and opportunities, their LIFGWC peers struggled.

But the college experiences of maximizers weren't always easy. Though they had built impressive résumés, they remained anxious about the future. Their steadfast focus on opportunity led to frequent comparisons with others. Heather, a White continuing-generation student from an upper-middle-class family, summed up these stressors as she acknowledged, "I have these really high expectations for myself." She supplied an example:

> One of my best friends, he's getting the same major as me. And so, we take a lot of classes together. I think we go into it like, "okay let's study together. Let's do really well," but I'm a very competitive person. So, I'm like, "I have to do better than him on this exam because I want to win." It sounds really bad.

As she shared this anecdote, Heather acknowledged the stress linked to being "a very competitive person." Caroline described "unhealthy" worries of her own about whether she should have attended another school "like MIT or Stanford." Acknowledging some of the same concerns, Neville wondered whether he should transfer, and Valerie confessed, "My schedule is full. . . . It seems like I handle it pretty well, but there are times where it feels like my life is a mess."

As they anticipated life after graduation, maximizers expressed concern about things they "lacked," worrying that a missed opportunity could be the thing that prevented them from reproducing their parents' socioeconomic status. Melissa worried about "not finding a job or not being qualified enough," and Nancy had nagging thoughts about "if I'm a good fit for graduate school." For those who were in their final year of college, these concerns often grew. Pete explained, "I'd say I've been very anxious about [the future]. I don't even think it's exactly warranted anxiety; it's just, I think I have that fear of 'I need to be a full adult,' so to speak. . . . I've been applying to jobs now and I haven't heard anything back from any of them. It's like 'what's wrong with me?'" Though he recognized that his impressive record of achievements made it likely that he would eventually find a job, Pete couldn't dispel these thoughts.

Maximizers feared that despite their accomplishments, discrimination and systemic inequality would complicate their futures. As a Latino student from an immigrant family, Troy was anxious about a rise in racist attitudes and anti-immigrant sentiment in the US. As a Black woman, Naomi worried about "getting denied for loans." And as a nonbinary, agender, and queer-identified student, Ira described concerns about coming out after graduation: "Obviously, I plan to live as myself. . . . It's going to be very obvious who I am. I feel like that will definitely come in the way of relationships with relatives and family, and that is something that stresses me out about my future. I have to eventually face that."

In short, maximizers found that their sources of motivation were also sources of stress. This pattern aligns with findings presented by sociologist Yingyi Ma in her book *Ambitious and Anxious*, where she reports on a study of Chinese students attending college in the US.[38] Ma observed that many of these students were socioeconomically privileged, and they appreciated the choice, flexibility, and opportunity available in US higher education. But they also found that their college journeys evoked great anxiety. As they confronted prejudice and other sources of exclusion, her participants described the tense experiences created by the intermingling of ambition and anxiety. Maximizers show how similar trends emerge among socioeconomically advantaged students who face marginalization on the basis of an even broader array of sociodemographic dimensions, including their race, gender, immigration histories, ability, sexual orientation, and religion.

We might have expected that these experiences would lead maximizers to be critical of higher education or more sensitive to the constraints faced by their peers. But there was a paradox woven throughout their narratives. On the one hand, they claimed to recognize structural inequality, describing the ways encountering or anticipating discrimination shaped their efforts to capitalize on opportunities. Yet they also frequently adopted individualized explanations of the challenges encountered by others, emphasizing personal choice and responsibility. For instance, after cogently describing how an obscure "college language" could sometimes make higher education difficult to navigate, Brooke nonetheless claimed that "You have to choose to be a successful college student." I refer to this tendency to display awareness of systemic inequality in analyzing one's own life circumstances without doing the same for others as a *selectively sociological imagination*. This pattern fits with a broader trend uncovered in recent studies whereby efforts to help students contextualize the social, historical, and political dimensions of inequality sometimes counterintuitively lead to the reproduction of inequality and the perpetuation of individualistic understandings of the world.[39] The concept of a selectively sociological imagination is explored in greater detail in the final chapter.

By holding fast to individualized explanations of others' experiences, maximizers absolved the university of responsibility for the unequal experiences and outcomes of LIFGWC and socioeconomically advantaged students. Shahid explained, "if you're going through all this and paying so much and if you're not taking advantage of the resources and the events going on, then that's up to you." Victor similarly described success in college as the result of "becoming independent," adding that, "the onus is on *you*." Not only did maximizers seem to accept this explanation of student outcomes but their achievements helped CU to justify its buffet approach to resource allocation. By featuring the accomplishments of maximizers, the university could focus on these students as evidence of success, drawing attention away from contradictory evidence, such as low graduation rates, that could have called their approaches into question.

5

Insulated Explorers:
Flexibility and the Pursuit of Self-Discovery

It was a bright morning in early March when I met Brian. Shoots of uncombed blond hair suggested he'd just recently climbed out of the unmade bed beside his desk. With a sleepy smile he narrated his first three years of college, starting with a summary of how he approached college life. "I consider myself a pretty curious student. I think class is one of the highlights of my day. . . . I think that I've always approached school not as like a chore or like something I have to do but more as something that's a privilege."

A White continuing-generation student from an upper-middle-class family, Brian had many of the same socioeconomic advantages as the students described in the previous chapter. Yet his easygoing demeanor stood in sharp contrast to the often-anxious opportunity maximizers. Though he was a dedicated member of the CU lacrosse team, he made little effort to harness different forms of college engagement to build the type of enterprising self that maximizers cultivated. He seemed uninterested in discussing his résumé or specific plans for the future. Rather than valuing college primarily as a means to accumulate measurable accomplishments, Brian was grateful for the way it offered room for deep personal exploration. This was evident as he described his appreciation for uncertainty within and beyond college.

> I think uncertainty is a really positive thing, you know. I like not knowing what's going to happen to my life. Like, I have an outline for what I want to do in the next five to ten years, and I have goals, but I don't want to know how it's all going to go. If someone told me like "do you want to know exactly how your life goes?" of course I wouldn't. Like, I want to surprise myself, I want to struggle a lot, I want to fail, I want to hit some really low lows and then try and build myself out of it and see what I'm made of. I think that I really like uncertainty. I think it's pretty exciting.

Contrasting himself with peers who might be daunted by uncertainty, Brian added, "I think I felt unsatisfied with things that were certain." He went on to share examples of the ways his experiences in college offered occasions for personal development and self-discovery—the chance to "build myself" and "see what I'm made of." Summing up his journey through the university thus far, he announced, "I think I've grown tremendously since I've gotten to CU."

Brian turned out to be part of a fairly small group of participants who felt fully comfortable with the precarities of public higher education. He loved that CU was flexible.[1] The potential for struggle and failure in an insecure environment was alluring from his perspective. In other words, Brian had the type of ease described by Shamus Khan as emblematic of the elite.[2] It manifested internally in his durable sense of comfort as well as in the confidence he projected externally. It was this ease that informed his leisurely approach to college.

I refer to students like Brian as *insulated explorers*. They viewed college as a venue for an enjoyable and rewarding journey toward personal discovery buffered from the negative consequences of failure. Whereas maximizers saw their intersectional social locations—specifically their status as members of marginalized groups—as liabilities, explorers felt sheltered from harm. "I've had a very privileged life and I'm very aware of that," Brian explained. "I know I have all of these identifying traits like I'm White, I'm middle class, my parents are educated, I am out of state, I'm European heritage, you know, I have all these pieces that make me who I am." As maximizers worked hard leveraging resources to compete in a game of merit, explorers behaved as if they'd already won. Brian put it bluntly: "I'm going to be okay with whatever happens."

The three prior chapters have shown how the insecurity woven throughout contemporary higher education can make colleges and universities inhospitable places for many students. Pioneers encountered college as a series of unexpected hurdles, minimizers as a minefield of risk, and maximizers as an anxiety-evoking assembly line on which they tried to build a meritorious résumé. Students in each of these groups were familiar with feelings of alienation and anxiety as they navigated college. By contrast, explorers' focus on deep engagement with self-discovery was a close match with the ways colleges and universities talk about their missions.

Personal development and the acquisition of self-knowledge have long been emphasized by institutions of higher education. As Nancy Evans and her colleagues explain in their classic volume on *Student Development in College*, a focus on holistic personal growth can be traced back to the inception of the student affairs profession in the early part of the twentieth century.[3]

Corresponding theories address identity and psychological, intellectual, and ethical development, among other forms.[4] Commonwealth University's web page for its academic programs implored students to "discover who you are, and who you want to be," explaining that college is "a time to explore the unfamiliar, to visit new worlds, to find that your passion might be something you'd never imagined." The result was that explorers' understanding of higher education as an occasion for growth and development was affirmed by the university. They came to feel embraced and at home in the insecure college environment that alarmed so many of their peers.

Going to College for Self-Discovery

Explorers' sense of comfort with higher education became apparent early on in their interviews as they described their paths to CU. In contrast to the career-focused stories told by maximizers and the mobility-focused accounts of pioneers and minimizers, these students described searching for a developmental journey. Calvin, a continuing-generation White student from an upper-middle-class family, was earnest as he provided detailed responses to each of my questions. When I asked about his decision to go to college, he paused for a moment, adjusting his glasses before speaking.

> I sought out college more because I wanted that social-academic experience. I wanted that four-year space to grow as a person and as a student and to sort of like figure myself out independent of my home life. And to find new people that I wanted to meet and find new friends and like the looser, positive experiences of college. . . . I wanted—to say "the college experience" is very broad and vague, but I wanted that space to grow as a person before I entered the professional world.

As Calvin noted, explorers saw college as an experience. Laura, a middle-class continuing-generation Asian and White student, similarly described how her time at CU gave her a chance to get "that whole college experience . . . experiencing things, getting to know people, college life." While Calvin admitted this concept of a "college experience" could be vague, that was in some ways the point. Rather than viewing higher education as a route toward socioeconomic success or as a venue for the accumulation of accolades, explorers believed college should be enjoyed for its capacity to fuel personal growth.

These students bought into what Laura Hamilton refers to as the "hybridized experience" of higher education. This view of the purpose of going to college emphasizes broad kinds of developmental experiences that facilitate the transition to adulthood by cultivating autonomy.[5] Edith, a White continuing-generation student from an upper-middle-class family, joined Calvin in describing how the college experience would support growth in part by providing a bridge to early adulthood.

> Just to learn more about myself, I think that college is such a growing experience and has been a huge learning experience for me—being on your own and kind of figuring out who you are. I think these are the years when you don't have too many responsibilities yet, but you're also not a kid living at home. You get to make your own decisions, and I think it kind of tests your character a little bit . . . just learning things about myself that you can't learn at home, because I feel like you can't branch out as much and make your own decisions.

As Edith made clear, self-knowledge was seen as an important component of this trajectory toward greater autonomy. Notably though, it was the fact that this experience allowed for more independence than high school without too many responsibilities that these students most appreciated.

Explorers' eagerness to use college as a venue for self-discovery relied on a set of dispositions that differed considerably from those of their peers. As Brian's words illustrated in the opening of this chapter, they saw both uncertainty and flexibility as positive elements of higher education. A continuing-generation and upper-middle-class White student, Lewis offered a clear example when describing how he'd appreciated the opportunity to move between various fields of study. In fact, he explored three very different majors, switching from engineering to art and then to government. While other students would have found this process daunting, Lewis claimed that "introspection is important. . . . So my experience of questioning what I wanted to do, I think it was certainly beneficial."

Because of the way explorers saw uncertainty as a catalyst for introspection and other kinds of personal discovery, they claimed it was a crucial part of their developmental trajectories. Calvin underscored this point, stating, "If there's like some uncertainty in some parts of my life, I don't mind it. I think it can help me grow as a person who's sort of learning how to be an adult in this world." Likewise, a Black upper-middle-class and continuing-generation student named Devon said, "times of uncertainties are when I grow the most and when I have to develop new skills or learn something new." In short, explorers described a cause-and-effect relationship between the uncertainties woven throughout college life and the kinds of growth they believed were important for acquiring the self-knowledge and broad skills characteristic of adulthood.

There were a few explorers who recognized that the insecurity of higher education was experienced in negative ways by some of their classmates. Hayden, a White continuing-generation student from an upper-middle-class family, acknowledged that uncertainty could be difficult for others, but he quickly pivoted to make a contrasting case.

> There's the optimistic side that says it's a positive thing. That's what gives life joy, is not knowing everything that's going to happen. Because if you knew everything, then what's the point of experiencing it? . . . Uncertainty, in general, it is positive. . . . Like in sports, I love the uncertainty, because that's why we have [competitions]; that's why we show up to compete. That's why boxing matches aren't told ahead of time; that's why the Super Bowl, everyone watched, is because I want to know who's going to win. So, in that sense, the uncertainty can be great. . . . And I mean that's why my entire major is in the career field with finances, like what company is undervalued? And what are they going to do in the future? And what's the expected future cash flows of this? If you knew it, then there'd be no point having really smart people study a lot to understand what factors influence things. So, uncertainty is great, in a lot of senses, but I understand the other side of it too.

Using these analogies to sport and finance, Hayden explained his eagerness to soak up the unknown, unstructured, and open-ended experiences of higher education.

Insulation as a "Protective Blanket"

The value explorers placed on personal development in college and their related comfort with uncertainty stemmed from feeling insulated from precarity. Like maximizers, these students had long assumed they would attend college.[6] Shaun, a continuing-generation White student from a middle-class family, noted, "I think it was always expected of me to go to college. That was my parents' plan for me. So, there's never really a time where I didn't consider going to college. It's just like my future after high school." The durability of their plans was reinforced by having parents who could afford to provide a stable economic foundation for college attendance. When asked about how he funded college, Lewis replied, "one hundred percent, it's my dad. My dad pays for it. . . . I am happy for him to be blessed with a job that pays very well, and he always has guaranteed me that he can pay for it in full." Moreover, these students' access to dominant cultural capital in the form of college knowledge meant that they were generally familiar with the procedures, norms, and expectations of the university.[7] Having long known they'd go to college and that they could afford and navigate it, explorers had much in common with maximizers. They could dedicate attention to specific objectives for postsecondary education rather than decisions about whether or how to pursue it.

Where explorers diverged from maximizers was in their sense of ease within college. This broad feeling of comfort was informed by the way their social, cultural, and economic resources intersected with other sociodemographic characteristics—typically their race, gender, and/or sexual orientation—to shape their experiences. When asked how he would describe himself demographically, Adam said, "I'm pretty cookie-cutter, straight White male." In claiming to have a "cookie-cutter" identity, he illustrated the belief shared by many explorers that his social location was a normative one. In contrast to maximizers, who encountered prejudice and worried about future discrimination based on their race, gender, sexual orientation, immigration histories, ability, and other sociodemographic characteristics, explorers did not describe firsthand experience with marginalization.

As Brian demonstrated in the opening of this chapter, explorers believed that their intersectional social locations sheltered them from the dangers of insecurity in higher education, dangers that could have a negative impact on other students trying to navigate a large and often confusing bureaucracy. After Calvin observed that college life could be unpredictable, he also acknowledged, "Never was I at *personal* risk." I probed into this claim, asking him, "Are there any elements of your background or identity that have shaped your experiences around uncertainty?" His response was insightful.

> I think that there are a lot of aspects of my identity that provide me a blanket of protection around some of these uncertainties, and that comes from my family is sort of like upper-middle class, and I've never felt financially insecure. That comes from my race. . . . Like being a cis White man is sort of like a trifecta of privilege that I've learned about in the last couple of years, especially, but haven't experienced as like a hardship in my life. And that's not to say that I don't have unexpected moments, but I think they're made easier when I consistently have this privilege that comes through. . . . I am aware that my privilege makes my uncertainties less weighty.

As he described the "blanket of protection" he felt as a cisgender White man from an upper-middle-class family, Calvin offered a glimpse into the ways explorers came to feel sheltered from precarity with ample economic capital, social capital, college knowledge, and ease.

Shaun underscored how significant these resources could be in shaping students' lives. After describing the protection extended by his "family background," he highlighted the impact of being White: "I think definitely I'm a privileged person in society. I think there's probably definitely a lot less uncertainty that I feel than someone who might be in a completely different situation in terms of their ethnicity and identity. . . . I probably am less

INSULATED EXPLORERS

uncertain about [my future] because of that." Moments later, he provided a clear example.

SHAUN. I got arrested for drug possession my freshman year. . . . I had to go through court and everything, to the county court. That was very stressful my freshman year, because I had just gotten here. But it's been so long that now, I'm feeling like over that. . . . I was lucky enough to be able to hire a lawyer, so that helped a lot.
BRS. So, the lawyer could help you navigate the court stuff and things like that?
SHAUN. Yeah. Definitely like extremely overwhelming at first, because, like "oh my God I'm going to be on probation for a whole year," all this, this, and this. But I mean the court case got dismissed, so I didn't have to do any of that, which would have definitely added a lot of extra stress on to my schedule. So, I'm glad none of that happened.

This was exactly the type of event that could have thrown a pioneer off course. But as a White man whose family was able to afford to hire lawyer, Shaun moved past this incident without serious repercussions.

As Brian, Adam, Calvin, and Shaun illustrated, many explorers' abilities to embody ease were closely linked to the insulation they experienced as socio-economically advantaged White men. In fact, of the fourteen explorers iden-tified in this study, nine of them (64 percent) fit this description. Table 5.1 illustrates the sociodemographic characteristics of these students.

While White men were overrepresented among explorers, there were also a few socioeconomically advantaged women, students of color, and a nonbinary student. Despite being members of marginalized groups, these participants claimed not to have experienced discrimination and that they weren't anticipating it in the future. Laura, for instance, said she was aware of a history of prejudice against women in STEM fields but that she hadn't confronted any challenges thus far as an earth science major. "It could always happen," she conceded. Yet she felt buffered from marginalizing experiences at her institution. "CU does a good job of being open and accepting everyone. I never saw any discrimination or biases." Devon made a similar claim when he said, "I think CU does a good job of offering opportunities for minority students," adding that, "I've been fortunate, and I've been blessed."

These students also described how the "privileges" conferred by their identities outweighed what they sometimes referred to as "the drawbacks." Rebecca, a continuing-generation White student from an upper-middle-class family, described herself as "super privileged." She noted that "I identify as queer," and although she recognized the marginalization faced by LGBTQ+

TABLE 5.1. Explorers' sociodemographic characteristics

Student characteristic	% (n)
Parental education	
First-generation college students	0 (0)
Continuing-generation college students	100 (14)
Family income	
Low income	0 (0)
Middle or high income	100 (14)
Social class background	
Working class	0 (0)
Lower-middle class	0 (0)
Middle class	29 (4)
Upper-middle class	71 (10)
Race/ethnicity	
Asian or Asian American	0 (0)
Black or African American	7 (1)
Hispanic or Latinx	0 (0)
White	86 (12)
Multiracial, other race/ethnicity	7 (1)
Family immigration	
Parents immigrated to the US	21 (3)
Parents born in the US	79 (11)
Intersections of race and gender	
Women of color	7 (1)
Men of color	7 (1)
Nonbinary or agender students of color	0 (0)
White women	14 (2)
White men	64 (9)
Nonbinary or agender White students	7 (1)

individuals, she also professed, "I believe that the world is changing for the best, hopefully. So, I don't feel that my sexual identity would hinder my future." This sentiment was informed in part by the intersections of her race, socioeconomic status, and sexual orientation. She explained, "I would say that I, being a Caucasian, I definitely have the privilege not to worry about certain things, like I don't feel that I'm going to be insecure in an economic way or other ways." Similarly, a continuing-generation White student from an upper-middle-class family, Finley acknowledged that identifying as nonbinary could mean being marginalized in many settings. Yet when discussing their own experiences, Finley emphasized the role their "privilege" played as something that encourages a confident navigation of uncertainty. I definitely feel like that's a decent part of being able to express myself and have these choices [of what to do in college], where I'm not streamlined into being an accountant or a doctor or something. . . . I think in a lot of ways, I'm very fortunate in having these choices. I won't ever forget that I'm fortunate and I have that privilege. . . . I definitely think that there are a lot of aspects where, because of the position I am in as just White, American, middle-class, dad's this relatively rich White guy, I feel like I've received a lot of choices and freedom because that's the position I'm in. . . . There's an aspect to that where I have those choices, and that's helped me to navigate uncertainty.

As Rebecca and Finley show, having a sense of oneself as privileged made it possible to navigate the choices and flexibility of higher education in a more comfortable way. This informed how explorers used their resources as they approached college life.

Navigating College with Ease

Hayden seemed relaxed. He grinned often. He laughed frequently. And he spoke freely. During our nearly ninety-minute interview, he summed up his tendency to be easygoing—"I'm a pretty even keel person"—and "optimistic" about the future. Hayden discussed his passion for deep engagement with course material while also expressing frustration with higher education's emphasis on grades.

I love, I've always loved learning, but sometimes the grind and the bureaucracy of structuring any sort of educational endeavor will just lead to tough things. So, there's definitely parts about just college and high school—just grades in general make things tougher. . . . Within college, some things are annoying, but, in general, I love learning. I love trying my best. Like, I love the content; I'm very interested in all of it . . . but I'm definitely not a 4.0 student.

This emphasis on learning rather than grades represented a sharp departure from the philosophies of maximizers, who worked hard to produce quantifiable outcomes and impressive résumés. According to Hayden, learning and discovery should be prioritized even if that meant getting average grades. "I wouldn't say that I'm one who's committed to do anything to get an A. . . . I'm not like doing everything in the world to obtain the highest grade possible. I'm just interested in the material, in learning."[8] Summing up his thinking on the matter, Hayden said, "I try my best, wake up, do my tests, and then the results are what the results are."

Seemingly comfortable with wherever life might take them, explorers spent their time in college in ways that differed from their peers. They tried to achieve a sense of balance that they believed could foster personal development. Hayden illustrated this desire for balance when he summarized his approach to navigating daily college life.

> First off, you exercise regularly, you get good sleep, you eat good nutrition because that's going to balance your hormones and keep you in alignment or whatever. Aside from that, you have a good social network, so you're in constant contact with friends, loved ones—you're expanding your circle. Other than that, you take your courses, and they're stimulating enough to keep you engaged, but you don't worry about it too much that you're overstressed. Then you go ahead and you continually do introspection and understand where you are, where you've been, where you're going.

Like other explorers, Hayden was committed to frequent "introspection," and he believed it had the power to foster self-awareness. "So, you understand your path. . . . You also just are happy, and you enjoy life along the way, so that you don't regret the time you spent where you are now." These priorities guided his choices about allocating time each day. Rather than worry about grades or getting a prestigious internship, Hayden concentrated on three things: enjoying his classes, spending time with friends and family, and staying physically active as a member of the cross-country team.

Hayden's conviction that allocating time in prudent ways could foster the type of balance that supported self-discovery was shared by other explorers. Devon, for instance, claimed that it was crucial to be "using the time [in college] to grow and be a balanced person," and Brian said, "I think, to make a college student happy, it's all about finding the balance between extracurriculars, staying connected with other people, while reminding yourself what you're here for." They contrasted their approaches with students who were narrowly focused on academic achievement. Though explorers claimed to care deeply about learning, they worried that studying too much would mean missing out on enriching experiences. This led them to make distinctions between the types of academic engagement that were valuable and those that were tedious "busy work." Shaun explained,

> I don't think I'm a student that turns in work on time very well . . . but I think overall a pretty engaged student. I tend to care about learning in my academic classes. While I may not actually care about doing all the busy work required, I try to pay attention and do the reading in order to actually gain an understanding of things. I care less about my actual grade in the course, if that makes sense.

By separating worthwhile engagement that enhanced understanding from the mundane requirements to get good grades, explorers found ways to justify placing limits on how much they would study.

While some students may have worried that getting average—or below average—grades would hinder their progress toward professional goals, explorers dismissed this sort of thinking. Shaun explained, "I consider my growth here to be more of like a social growth." He advocated for "just trying to live and experience," cautioning that "you can't come into college and just expect life to find you." Edith similarly emphasized "being driven but not to the point where you feel like you have to study all day, every day." Instead, she recommended

> living your life, and experiencing things, and taking this time when we're young and able to be with people and have new experiences and go out and do things. . . . Like if you can have an experience today, why would you not? I think that a lot of people place a lot of self-worth in their grades . . . [but] in ten years, it's not going to matter. No one's ever going to ask you what grade you got on an exam.

By not worrying about grades, Edith claimed she was able to seek out everyday experiences as she worked to "live in the moment and have fun."

Moreover, the kind of perfection implied in being a "straight A student" with a "4.0 GPA" was anathema to explorers. By their logic, someone with perfect grades probably hadn't left sufficient room for growth and development. Roy, a continuing-generation White student from a middle-class family, described a successful college student:

> I think that you probably ended up making a few mistakes somewhere—in moderation, [not] too much or too little. . . . I think it's a big learning experience . . . and, you know, mistakes make you who you are. So, I think that's been a big part of it for me at least, in kind of shaping myself into the idea of the successful college student.

This was one of the reasons explorers claimed to appreciate the lack of structure of higher education, where there was room to try new things and sometimes make mistakes. Whereas some students' dispositions led them to engage in detailed planning, explorers' sense of insulation from the consequences of these "mistakes" meant they could take a much more leisurely approach to navigating college. They believed it was okay to dedicate themselves to deep engagement in a specific activity or to move from one experience to another without worrying about continuity or how these activities looked on their résumés. In short, they approached the college journey as an occasion to explore, discovering more about themselves, even if these discoveries might not have immediate payoffs in the labor market.

PASSION OVER CREDENTIALS

Explorers' laissez-faire approach to grades also translated to the ways they thought about majors. With few worries about the future, they placed little pressure on the economic implications of this decision. Instead, they emphasized the way a field of study should align with—or help to unearth—one's passion. Lewis, for example, said,

> I think when it comes to students who want to figure out what their purpose is in their life, and when they do go to like a four-year [college], they might change their path. . . . I think that for my experience, I wanted to do engineering and I wanted to do that for a bit, but I'm a terrible math student. So, I figured that's a waste of time, and then I wanted to do interior design, because I like art. . . . So, while in that debate about art, I was studying politics, and I was really inspired by my professor to do government, and so that's what I went with. . . . And I think when it comes to studying something, you should feel energized. So, I feel energized by politics.

Lewis's words highlight how explorers thought about majors as paths to self-discovery rather than to socioeconomic success. Instead of offering a defined route toward a specific job, majors were believed to produce certain kinds of emotive experiences—in this case, feeling "energized" by one's studies—that signaled the discovery of one's true passion. Other explorers talked about how their chosen field helped them to feel "a sense of purpose," "more engaged," and even "happier."

The economic, social, and cultural resources explorers possessed also allowed them to change majors more readily. For instance, Laura switched out of the geography major because she felt more passionate about earth science, even though "if I hadn't changed, I would have graduated faster." In fact, this revision to her field of study added more than a year onto her bachelor's degree, a delay she justified by repeating a familiar refrain: that college was "about getting experiences." While others may have thought such a decision was unwise, Laura pushed back:

> You know, even if you have those type of thoughts—like "is this right or not?"—it's like the right path is whatever path you take. Right? Whatever path you take, that's the one that you can improve, make better, or do anything. At the end of the day, that's just the truth. So, if you want to go with it, do it; if you don't, you don't want to do it. Either way, it's good.

INSULATED EXPLORERS

Like other explorers, Laura's sense of ease informed her decisions. Big changes were acceptable, even desirable, because they led to a broader swath of experiences and fed into one's trajectory of personal development.

Whereas maximizers layered majors, curricular tracks, minors, fellowships, and internships in their efforts to craft an enterprising self, explorers were less interested in these opportunities. Hayden recalled his decision not to not pursue a minor.

> I had considered Spanish, because the summer of my freshman year I went to Spain. I did a study abroad, and I took a few Spanish courses, but I didn't quite qualify for like 300-level courses. Because if I did, then I would have knocked out like two or three courses towards like a minor, and I would have just picked up a Spanish minor because I also love Spanish among everything. But since that didn't work out . . . it doesn't look like I'm going to have much time to fit another major or minor in, so I haven't thought about that.

Where a maximizer might have sought out additional opportunities to obtain the prerequisites for 300-level Spanish courses, Hayden perceived little urgency to complete a minor.

Along similar lines, when one of my research assistants asked Edith if she was interested in doing an internship during college, her response was casual. "I haven't like had one pop up for me yet, but if one could become available, then yes, of course." With little inclination to proactively apply for these opportunities, she was unlikely to intern unless an opportunity "popped up." Although my data did not speak to this possibility directly, the prospect of landing an internship without actively seeking one out was certainly more feasible for explorers than for their LIFGWC peers. Research shows that connections to internship opportunities are more readily available to socioeconomically advantaged students, who are likely to have peers, parents, or other relatives capable of facilitating offers.[9]

In some cases, explorers actively avoided additional curricular or co-curricular engagement. Finley, for instance, was dismissive of their friends' dedication to the premedical track for undergraduates. "My two best friends, Sarina and Priya, they are premed students. . . . I hear all of their complaining and help them study and all that. I understand where they're coming from, where they've been prepping for this since middle school." While all three of them shared a biology major, Finley grew tired of "my two best friends constantly being like, 'premed, premed, premed. I have one path and that's it.' I'm like, 'Jesus Christ, that's terrifying.'" Explorers believed having a singular focus would lead to missing meaningful experiences that were crucial for growth and development.

MAKING SPACE TO EXPLORE

Rather than focus on supplementing their degrees or crafting coherent résumés, these students tried to create room for exploration. One common way of doing this was by leveraging the flexibility available at CU to enroll in ample elective coursework. Finley, for instance, described seeking personal growth by taking new kinds of classes.

> I'm just doing what I can do. I think the best thing I have in terms of a strategy is that no matter what courses I have to take that semester, I will always, always, always try and save room for one course that I will take of my own volition. I'm just like, "Hey, this looks cool. I'm going to take this." . . . This semester with fourteen credits, I'm currently taking Japanese 202. . . . Then my choice course is screenwriting, because I want to do more of the [school of arts] stuff. But I always make sure that I have at least one course like that. Because I would drive myself mental if I didn't. . . . I try my best to at least make one class something that I genuinely really want to do as opposed to this is just something on the path to get me to a degree.

As Finley illustrated, these elective courses did not need to be even tangentially related to one's major or career plans to be perceived as valuable. In fact, the more distant they were from required courses, the better. Other explorers pursued similar kinds of experiences in cocurricular academic settings. Calvin, for example, discussed finding a speaker series he'd enjoyed attending as a way to "actively learn about a subject I don't know about."

Like changing majors, taking abundant electives sometimes delayed explorers' progress toward graduation. Yet they claimed it was worthwhile. Hayden, for instance, discussed the impact of exploring courses in a range of fields.

> The downside was it's not until my second semester my junior year that I'm finally taking like multiple classes [in my major] because I was so behind, because I was taking everything from international affairs to like whatever, and I didn't do the [pre]requisites. . . . So, I'm definitely glad I did that process, but it definitely came at the cost of being a little behind.

Though he would not be able to finish his bachelor's degree in four years, Hayden held firm to his belief that taking a broad range of electives was beneficial.

Similarly, when explorers became involved in extracurricular opportunities, they described doing so in pursuit of enjoyment or personal development, not professionalization. This could be observed through the levels and types of involvement they pursued. These students were typically part of just one or two activities, so they rarely felt overextended like maximizers.[10] Athletics were especially popular among this group. Brian's main extracurricular activity was lacrosse, Rebecca's was water polo, and Hayden's was cross country. Social organizations were also common outlets for explorers. Patrick, a White continuing-generation student from an upper-middle-class family, was a member of a fraternity. And Laura was "part of this K-pop dance club" that she described as "really fun." Explorers noted that deep engagement with these activities facilitated growth. Devon made this point when recalling how his involvement helped him to "kind of grow myself," becoming more comfortable in social settings. "I think I came into college as an introvert, and I still am, but I think I'm able to speak up more for myself and be more social with my classmates."

Lewis wasn't involved in any formal extracurricular activities, instead spending time socializing with his friend groups. Explorers appreciated this type of open-ended social engagement. Finley had gone as far as to earmark time for creative activities with friends—time when academic work was off limits. As we approached the end of our interview, their phone buzzed.

> I literally just got an alarm for eight o'clock; I have creative hour with my friends, where me and my friends get online, we write together or something like that.... [It's] something that came from me and [a friend], looking at each other and being like, "Hey, we should write," then never writing, then sitting down one day and being like, "Okay, this is our time. We can hang out. We can write something. We can bake something. Anything besides homework. No homework this hour, no academics this hour. This is our hour to do something creative." And that's expanded to everything. Last week I baked for that entire hour and complained about my dance team.

In this way, students found both formal and informal opportunities for self-discovery beyond the classroom.

Finally, explorers professed the value of growth through engagement with diversity and difference on campus. While students from marginalized groups sometimes described CU's diversity as comforting, explorers—as members of multiple advantaged groups, especially those who identified as White—framed diversity as a catalyst for personal development. In her book *The Diversity Bargain*, Natasha Warikoo shows how students who "view racial and ethnic groups as holding distinct cultures to be celebrated and engaged" hope that college will "ensure that they can learn from ethnic and racial diversity on campus."[11] Similar perceptions were prevalent among explorers. Lewis, for instance, claimed that "what I really enjoy about Commonwealth University is how diverse it is culturally, and there's so many different subcultures within them. . . . I love meeting new people who are quirky and full of different cultures." Brian discussed a similar appreciation for diversity at CU:

> That's what I love about CU so much is how diverse—but not even like diversity of ethnicity, but diversity of thought—like everybody at CU is coming from. . . . You can sit at a table and just like talk to some person that you would never normally meet in life, and they just have like this crazy story about like, how they have to work three jobs and they have a kid but they're putting themselves through online classes, because they have this dream. . . . That's so cool. That's what I love about it.

Students described how exposure to these forms of diversity helped expand their perspectives. Shaun claimed, "I think I've definitely become a lot more tolerant of other people and how they live their day-to-day lives. . . . I think I've definitely made a lot of growth with interacting with people, like socially." Notably though, his emphasis also exposes the ways explorers sought a very limited kind of engagement with difference in the form of what Lisa Nunn has referred to as "nice diversity."[12] This framework for approaching peers from a range of social locations focuses on conflict-free interactions that fail to alter the unequal distribution of power, as reflected in Shaun's claim to being "tolerant." Moreover, these students' words further illustrate the tendency of explorers to frame their own identities as normative while creating a spectacle of the identities of peers, whom Lewis and Brian characterized as "quirky" students with "different cultures" and "crazy stories."

GROWING THROUGH A PANDEMIC

Explorers even encountered the COVID-19 pandemic in different ways from their peers. These students' sense of insulation and their relaxed approach to navigating college made adapting to change easier. Roy, for instance, recalled the early weeks of the pandemic, noting that "I consider myself very lucky, because I know a lot of people didn't make it out smoothly in that transition." Finley explained why explorers tended to feel this way.

> Last year, last March [of 2020], we went to spring break, and all of my friends were back home. . . . Then one by one, their summer research got canceled, their internship got canceled, their job got canceled, because of COVID. I remember my friend Janelle complaining at the time—she's a statistician, super cool work, she's awesome—getting this really cool opportunity up in Vermont that was supposed to be last summer, them canceling it in March, and her being like, "That's so far out, what the heck?" Then the past year happened. The

thing is that throughout all of that, I didn't have a lot of plans. . . . I'm more of a go-with-the-flow kind of a person.

While some students—like Finley's friend Janelle—were devastated by the loss of opportunities during the start of the pandemic, explorers had few formal plans to be disrupted. Their "go with the flow" attitude made this precarious moment less difficult.

Not only did explorers find change easier to navigate; their focus on self-discovery meant that disruptions were often viewed in a positive light. Elaborating on his previous point, Roy observed that an "upside [of the pandemic] was more flexibility." This flexibility took many forms: class meetings and scheduled activities were canceled, deadlines were postponed, and grading policies were relaxed. With their preferences for limited structure and having room for exploration, students like Roy savored this moment. "I feel bad saying it," he confessed, "I thoroughly enjoyed quarantine. It was a unique experience."

Roy wasn't the only explorer to describe the pandemic as an occasion to have unique experiences. Calvin, for instance, described the start of COVID-19 as an opportunity to "slow down," noting that the disruption to daily routines "helped me to figure out what I enjoy doing and reminded me what designated free time felt like. I remembered free time is important." With this extra unstructured time, Calvin described finding "cool things I could do that would help me learn and grow as an adult." Similarly, Rebecca reluctantly admitted,

> I would say [the pandemic has been] a positive thing, because I feel that I have overcome all my challenges. And without like the unpredictability of certain things, such as the pandemic, I wouldn't be who I am today. . . . I would say that the pandemic has actually made me a better person, because I had a lot of time to myself. . . . So, I might as well start learning about myself and be comfortable with myself. I actually started meditating a lot in the last couple months, and that has made me more happy.

As Rebecca's story of acclimating to pandemic life illustrates, explorers thought about this as an occasion for self-discovery ("learning about myself") and growing as a person ("I wouldn't be who I am today").

This is not to say that all explorers were fully content with their experiences during the pandemic. Some of these students acknowledged frustrations when they seemed to be missing out on elements of the college experience that they valued. The disappointment in Edith's voice was apparent as she explained, "We're still taking classes and doing all that, but the experience wasn't quite there. So, it almost feels like something was kind of taken away—a little bit of that journey." She was especially disheartened that these changes had taken place during her first year of college. "I think your freshman year is kind of important to grow and like be on your own as a person, so I feel like some of that was taken away in the spring."

Several explorers expressed dissatisfaction with the quality of their online courses. Laura, for example, perceived that virtual classes placed an emphasis on grades over learning. "I feel like with this transition into online school, it's more about just getting that grade instead of learning. And I think that's really sad, because we're still paying the same amount of money . . . when we're not getting the same level—or I guess same type—of education." Brian recalled,

> I was unsure if online class is something I wanted to do. I think in the spring I really didn't enjoy the rest of my online classes. When I go to class, I like to have engaging debates and talk to people and ask questions of the professor, because most of them are doing pretty incredible research in their free time, and they're just interesting people to talk to. And I felt like over CU online class there was like this wall, and I felt like I was just checking off boxes on my degree [evaluation] page. I was like, "this isn't what I want to pay $30,000 to do."

Though he considered taking time off from college with the intent of returning once more classes were available on campus, he ultimately decided against this course of action. "I think that the inconvenience of taking two years off school and graduating when I'm like twenty-three. . . . It wasn't enough to outweigh the online classes." In the end, most explorers' sense of entitlement—the feeling that they (or their parents) were paying for a specific kind of experience—drove them to find alternative experiences. As they started meditating, joined fraternities or sororities, and scheduled time for creative activities with friends, they found ways to seek personal development even during a pandemic.

Open-Ended Futures

Explorers' preferences for flexibility and self-discovery were also evident as they looked toward life after graduation. In contrast to maximizers, who were focused on advancing toward specific white-collar careers, explorers intended to keep their futures more open ended. After stating, "I could never imagine being locked down into one thing," Finley elaborated.

> I'm not a very money-driven sort of person. I'm much more of a human-driven person, I suppose. I would be someone who's very content with, "Okay, I got a camera, I got WIFI, I got an RV or something like that, I'll be parked on the beach. Let me know if you need some freelance work." And that's it. If I even had to really work at all. I'm not a work-driven person; I'm an experience-driven person. I'm a make-others-happy and make-myself-happy kind of person.

In a comparable way, Calvin claimed, "I don't have a specific dream job that I want; I just have like a field that I'm interested in, and I know that I feel happy when I'm editing, or I feel happy when I'm working with the camera. . . . I find that fulfilling, so I'm sort of pursuing that feeling of fulfillment." These types of unstructured visions for the future were common among explorers, who prioritized happiness and fulfilling experiences rather than specific employment.

As they looked toward these open-ended futures, explorers were eager for the journeys ahead. Brian described his enthusiasm for the unknown.

> Where am I going to be in two years? Like, am I gonna be working? Am I going to be getting a master's degree, applying to law school? I don't know, and I think that's really exciting. I could be living anywhere in two years, and I think not knowing that really excites me a lot.

This laissez-faire attitude would seem especially impractical to minimizers, who worried about risk and sought safe paths toward adulthood. And explorers themselves sometimes acknowledged that their tendencies might mean being unemployed after graduation. Laura, however, argued that "It's important to do whatever you're passionate about, even if you won't get a job."

These students' sense of ease made unstructured futures comfortable. Brian's words, quoted at the opening of this chapter—"I'm going to be okay with whatever happens"—echoed in Shaun's speculation about life after graduation: "I know there's so many risks, but I think I'll be fine either way." Calvin similarly acknowledged, "I have like theoretical worries, but I'm not in a place where I know some of my friends are, where they need a job coming out of college, because they need to immediately start paying rent." He noted that his family's economic resources meant "I have that buffer."

Being at ease with an unplanned future sometimes required pushing back against widespread conceptions of success. For instance, Roy described his frustration with "the notion that there is a checklist for your life as a young adult . . . that you've got to keep up or you'll get left behind." Such perspectives are easy to identify not just in popular culture but also in scholarly literature on the transition to adulthood.[13] Yet Roy's view that "It's your story, your journey" led him to anticipate taking "a gap year" after college to do community service instead of getting a full-time job. Shaun made a comparable point.

> It's very easy to get caught up in a capitalist notion that "I must make more money in order to be successful," or like, "I'm going to have to reach the position of power in order to be more successful." But more thinking about it just as a person, if I'm successful, that means that I'm doing what I want and I'm content with my life.

Resisting traditional understandings of socioeconomic success, explorers emphasized continued growth and development. Roy underscored this point as he proclaimed the importance of "making sure you're still a dynamic person as you get older. You pick up new hobbies, meet new people, try new things, even a road trip."

The Advantages and Limits of Self-Discovery

As they ventured through higher education, enjoying the flexibility CU offered, explorers seemed to thrive. Of the four groups of participants in this study, they were the most satisfied with their college experience. This is perhaps unsurprising given the ways institutions of higher education cater to the desires of these socioeconomically advantaged students, especially those who identify as White men.[14] Though they accumulated few measurable accomplishments, they acquired a sense of themselves as emerging adults who were on a positive developmental trajectory. Patrick described the growth he'd observed in

> how I see myself really in general. Before you come out of high school—at least, I came out of high school [a] three-sport athlete . . . thinking I am like, the jock, that guy. And coming into college, I got humbled really quickly. I'm very happy I did, too, because I guess it made me like a bearable person to hang out with. . . . Looking back on myself, I was like, "God, I was a dick." Like, I could have been so much better. I've grown, like caring about my education a lot more, not taking it for granted. Um, let's see, what else? Socially, like actually caring about relationships and stuff like that. . . . A lot of things matured in me.

Journeys like the one Patrick described were broad; they weren't focused on making it to graduation efficiently or becoming well qualified for a specific career. These journeys were about coming to see themselves as more developed or educated individuals.

Along the way, they learned to speak a language about personal growth that differed from the students featured in the three previous chapters. Their story was not one of accumulating demonstrable accolades—minors, fellowships, internships, and so forth—but of personal discovery. Though they had few near-term plans to pursue high-paying white-collar jobs, if and when they eventually did, this capacity would likely prove useful. As research demonstrates, learning to tell a self-narrative of personal development is advantageous in a variety of settings, including in the labor market.[15]

Similarly, research conducted by Lauren Rivera shows the likely advantages of membership in the specific kinds of resource- and time-intensive

INSULATED EXPLORERS

extracurricular activities explorers took part in—those such as fraternities or intercollegiate athletics—that demonstrate cultural similarity to hiring authorities.[16] A student involved in a varsity sport, for example, may actually receive greater recognition in the hiring process than a student involved in multiple clubs or professional associations. Rivera reports,

> Across the board, [application evaluators] privileged activities that were motivated by "personal" rather than "professional" interest, even when activities were directly related to work within their industry (e.g., investing, consulting, legal clinic clubs), because the latter were believed to serve the instrumental purpose of "looking good" to recruiters and were suspected of being "resume filler" or "padding" rather than evidence of genuine "passion," "commitment," and "well-roundedness."[17]

Explorers' depth of engagement in activities that were sometimes far afield from their professional interests may, in other words, play a counterintuitive role in supporting their career success as well.

In some ways these students' focus on becoming better people was admirable. And they occasionally tried to link their growth to being able to make positive contributions to their communities, as Finley did when discussing being a "people-driven person" who would work to "make others happy." They talked about building healthy relationships, supporting well-being, and making a difference. And many claimed that their engagement with diversity and difference made them "more aware" of their privilege as members of advantaged groups.

Yet the ways explorers came to think and talk about higher education often served to justify the status quo. Like their peers, they emphasized individualistic understandings of others' successes or failures. For instance, when discussing how some of his classmates struggled in college, Adam said, "I think something people in general need to work on is discipline, personal responsibility," adding that, "I don't mean this to sound harsh, but people need to respect themselves enough to do what they have committed themselves to do." Similarly, Lewis noted,

> I think the biggest obstacle [to success] is oneself, because you have to—one of the words I used earlier was *tenacity* or *tenacious*. And you have to be tenacious to get what you want. . . . So, that's what I think someone's biggest obstacle might be. It could be—I'm generalizing—it could be someone thinking that maybe their skin color or their gender could get in their way. But from my perspective, it's not really that simple. It's not. I mean somebody might affect you externally, but I just say, "keep walking and keep your head up," you know. . . . It doesn't matter if you're purple or blue, I don't really look at it, as a race-specific or skin color–specific thing.

This type of perspective is representative of what sociologist Eduardo Bonilla-Silva calls "color-blind racism," a form of racial ideology that "explains contemporary racial inequality as the outcome of nonracial dynamics."[18] Notably, Lewis and other explorers extended this unwillingness to acknowledge the impact of racism to other kinds of prejudice and discrimination, including sexism, classism, homophobia, ableism, and xenophobia.

Dishearteningly, explorers connected these narrow perspectives on inequality to specific experiences they'd had in college. For instance, Brian described what he learned about individual success on a trip to Peru.

> I just like to hear people's ideas, and I think that's what I love about CU and that's kind of how I view myself, as like an open thinker. I don't care where you came from. I've interacted with people from every walk of life. You know, I was in Peru for about a month, working with people building little farms to give them a renewable source of income. And you just meet so many different people. I think that, through all of that, what I've learned is none of your background matters. Like all that matters is the ideas and how you think, and that's what I've kind of taken away from it.

The words of Adam, Lewis, and Brian provided additional illustrations of the selectively sociological imagination introduced in the previous chapter whereby students drew from their experiences in higher education to acknowledge some of the ways their own lives were shaped by social, historical, and political contexts but refused to extend similar sensitivity to recognize these contextual influences on the lived experiences of others. Though explorers came to rhetorically acknowledge their "privilege" and internalize a corresponding sense of insulation from harm, they failed to connect this privilege to the oppression of people in other social locations. The outcome, ironically, was that explorers were further advantaged by the discourse they encountered and participated in about privilege, benefitting from a durable sense of ease while refusing to extend that knowledge to combatting the marginalization of other social groups.[19]

In the end, although explorers seemed to put comparatively little effort into navigating higher education, they nonetheless secured enjoyable experiences for themselves and sustained many of the advantages that came with their background and sociodemographic characteristics. By creating a system that catered to advantaged youth, CU helped them to reproduce their advantages in the transition from adolescence to adulthood. The next chapter will delve into the specific institutional arrangements that accommodated these students while constraining their peers from other social locations.

6

Amplifying or Alleviating Insecurity:
The Role of Universities

Perusing the Commonwealth University website, a prospective student would find countless materials designed to represent the university to high schoolers, their parents, and guidance counselors. These web pages, videos, blogs, and brochures offered an illuminating glimpse of how the university presented itself to the outside world. Most were clearly designed to appeal to a sought-after group of socioeconomically advantaged (often out-of-state) students from families capable of affording full tuition. These materials described the university and its surrounding area as "vibrant," "active," "fun," "safe," and "customizable." They featured the endless opportunities available on campus. And they promised students "a college experience like no other" that would "help them grow" personally and professionally—in short, the types of assertions that would appeal to maximizers and explorers.

Such claims are so typical in college marketing materials that most of them felt generic and unremarkable.[1] But one item caught my attention: a video that described CU as "a university of strivers." When educators use the term *strivers*, they are usually referring to low-income, first-generation, and working-class (LIFGWC) students who are seeking upward mobility through higher education.[2] According to such a definition, one could easily argue that CU's claim was true; it was certainly a university of strivers. The institution enrolled large numbers of students who were part of the first generation in their family to attend college. Most received financial aid, including 30 percent who were eligible for Pell Grants. And many had parents who worked in blue-collar or low-wage service jobs. Unfortunately, while CU may have been a university *of* strivers, it was not a university *for* strivers.

As the preceding chapters make clear, students' journeys through the university were highly unequal. While explorers seemed to thrive navigating the flexibility of contemporary higher education with a sense of ease, their peers struggled in various ways. Pioneers worked tirelessly to be resilient in the face of pervasive insecurity, picking themselves up from myriad setbacks with little help from others. Minimizers relied on strategies of resistance with support from their families as they tried to push back against insecurity and alleviate risk, but in doing so they missed out on many of the opportunities available in higher education. And even maximizers, who shared explorers' socioeconomic advantages and engaged with abundant opportunities, were still deeply concerned about their futures and beset by the stressors of extensive involvement in so many arenas.

How did students have such drastically different experiences at the same institution? Why did some feel such affinity to CU while others felt alienated? And why did it seem that this university *of* strivers didn't work well *for* strivers? Such inequality resulted from the ways personal, family, and university resources came together to shape capacities to navigate insecurity in higher education. The previous chapters show how students' social locations informed how they encountered and dealt with this insecurity. Yet it is not a given that the identities and resources students bring with them to college would shape their experiences in such profound ways. We could also imagine more secure college environments where students were provided with the tools they needed to succeed, regardless of their social location. But this was not the case at CU.

This chapter seeks to expose the role of the university's *normative institutional arrangements*—the taken-for-granted organizational features that shape the college environment—not just in sustaining insecurity and corresponding forms of inequality but oftentimes in amplifying these problems. Sociologists including Rashawn Ray and Jenny Stuber have introduced a framework for employing this concept to understand inequality within higher education.[3] They note that normative institutional arrangements can include a wide range of features of the college environment, taking the form of housing policies, space allocation, reporting structures, or student affairs practices. These arrangements in turn structure students' journeys through college, dictating, for instance, whether educational pathways that emphasize partying or social mobility are more visible and accessible. By exploring normative institutional arrangements, it becomes possible to understand how rates of college completion have remained unequal across socioeconomic groups despite increasing rates of college access. While scholars frequently focus on student-level traits to explain this inequality, an analysis of institutional arrangements points our attention to features of the university itself.[4]

The Contemporary Public University

There was a time when US higher education was attended by a much smaller and more homogeneous set of individuals—typically affluent White men—who could use it as a predictable steppingstone to elite status and occupations.[5] But over the course of the twentieth century, colleges and universities changed in notable ways. There were demographic shifts that led to a more diverse student body on most campuses. More students of color enrolled in higher education.[6] Women surpassed men in college attendance rates.[7] And changes in financial aid policy and programs made it feasible for individuals from LIFGWC families to enroll.[8]

Yet at the same time that higher education was becoming more diverse, it was also becoming more insecure. This was no coincidence. As Laura Hamilton and Kelly Nielsen explain in their book *Broke: The Racial Consequences of Underfunding Public Universities*, as college student bodies diversified, legislatures simultaneously became less willing to dedicate public resources to fund those institutions. They describe the resulting "way that race and class, as systems of oppression, have recently intertwined in higher education—blocking access to postsecondary resources" for students of color and LIFGWC students by implementing fiscal austerity to "disadvantage the universities serving these students."[9]

Scholars often describe these trends as evidence of the impact of neoliberalism on higher education. The term *neoliberalism* is broad and sometimes applied in ways that make its meaning difficult to discern. When social scientists use this term, they are referring most directly to a set of social, political, and economic trends that result from a laissez-faire approach to the economy and an understanding of individuals as rational economic actors.[10] In higher education, neoliberalism specifically describes a context where notions of economic rationality undergird the policies and practices of postsecondary institutions. Eschewing traditional conceptions of higher education as a "public good," this model conceives of college as an investment made by individual consumers.[11] Students are viewed as "entrepreneurial learners" responsible for shaping the contours of their own education and ensuring their future labor market competitiveness.[12]

In this broader context, public universities today respond to new kinds of pressures. First, with limited funding, these institutions are forced to make difficult decisions about how to allocate scarce resources. This encourages colleges to reduce the provision of student support by creating an environment where most students do not use the resources available.[13] A common way to foster such a system is to make resources and opportunities optional and decoupled from the curriculum, thereby ensuring that few individuals will employ them.[14] As a result, the students most in need of support rarely receive it from their institutions.

This trend may seem to fly in the face of headlines about out-of-control spending in higher education. It is certainly true that ample data demonstrates administrative spending has grown over recent decades at most college and universities.[15] And yet such spending should not be conflated with a robust system of accessible student support. When researchers drill down to examine categories of spending, they frequently find divergence between the abundant funding dedicated to auxiliary services, student activities, and campus facilities, for instance, and the more limited funding for resources that directly support students' continued enrollment, academic success, and graduation.[16] Additionally, while aggregate trends are often the focus of general claims about postsecondary spending, broad-access public universities experience the fiscal landscape quite differently from more selective and elite institutions. For example, compared with their private four-year counterparts, which spend about 30 percent of their budgets—often significantly larger in per-student terms—on academic support and student services, public four-year institutions dedicate just 20 percent on average to these resources.[17]

Moreover, as I discussed in the first chapter, when universities cannot rely on state funding for day-to-day operations, they come to depend more heavily on tuition, and by proxy, the students and families capable of paying full tuition—especially those who pay out-of-state rates.[18] As my interviews with maximizers and explorers reveal, affluent students tend to place value on options, choice, and flexibility. They dislike too much structure, perceiving it as constraint. Recall, for instance, Hayden's complaints from the previous chapter about "the grind and the bureaucracy of structuring any sort of educational endeavor." Universities are sensitive to these preferences as they create policies and procedures that align with neoliberal sensibilities prioritizing consumer choice.[19]

While some take a positive view of this situation, arguing that the neoliberal environments of contemporary public universities support "innovation," most scholars suggest they contribute to inequality and undermine student success.[20] This inequality can be observed both in college experiences and outcomes. Though the college wage premium (the average pay advantage of college graduates compared to those with a high school diploma) has sustained itself—and even expanded—over time, there is significant variation in college outcomes.[21] And for those who leave college before finishing a degree, lasting debt can curtail opportunity. Because of this debt and opportunity cost, attending higher education itself has become a significant risk for many students.[22] In their book *Unequal Higher Education*, Barrett Taylor and Brendan Cantwell argue that while such patterns have become prevalent in a variety of institutional types, public colleges and universities like CU are increasingly "pairing high tuition prices with limited opportunity" in ways that undermine the success of less socioeconomically advantaged students.[23]

This chapter uncovers the specific mechanisms by which universities like CU foster an insecure environment. It does not attempt to provide an exhaustive account of all the micro-, meso-, and macrolevel factors contributing to the precarity encountered by college students today. Such an endeavor would require an encyclopedia. Rather, the coming pages will explore the specific normative institutional arrangements that amplified insecurity for students at CU. I show how fiscal constraints and a focus on affluent students led to four problematic normative institutional arrangements: (1) prioritizing choice and flexibility over structured guidance, (2) inadequate and invisible student support services, (3) reactive student support practices, and (4) decentralized and disconnected services. These features of the university amplified insecurity and corresponding inequality. Nonetheless, there are exceptional programs at many institutions that work against insecurity, providing a different model for student support that can reduce uncertainty. Commonwealth University had two such programs that are explored in the latter half of this chapter to illustrate how alternative approaches can combat precarity by boosting security.

Prioritizing Choice and Flexibility over Structured Guidance

In their efforts to appeal to more socioeconomically advantaged students, universities today offer a range of opportunities and parallel choices about which of those opportunities to pursue. At CU students navigated an array of options throughout their college journeys. When it was time to declare a field of study, they could select from over eighty majors, nearly two hundred minors, and innumerable concentrations and tracks within those curricula. For students who considered getting involved in extracurricular outlets, CU offered more than three hundred formally recognized student organizations, including thirty-four club sports teams, ten different dancing groups, and several clubs for students who wanted to play card and video games. There were hundreds of study abroad programs each year and countless university-sponsored events each week. Living on campus came with options, including approximately thirty theme-based learning communities that students could apply to join. And living off campus came with options, including a dozen different student parking permits for decks and lots with varying proximity to campus buildings. There were even extensive choices about where to eat, with more than twenty-five dining locations available on the main campus.

More socioeconomically advantaged students discussed these options with enthusiasm. Maximizers appreciated the chance to be extensively involved. Rachel was pleased that "CU has a wealth of opportunities, like so much so that I can't even do all of them." Explorers were also eager for unique opportunities. They described how such abundance was valuable for promoting broad kinds of personal development. For instance, Calvin reflected that "there are a lot of opportunities that I've found," which he believed had helped him with "professional growth," "interpersonal learning," and "soft skills" development.

The ability to make choices also appealed to socioeconomically advantaged students, who found rigid pathways frustrating. Adam (an explorer) explained his preference for flexibility by contrasting his ideal vision of universities—as "institutions of learning, of knowledge, of research"—with his experience at a highly structured community college before transferring to CU. "It is, I might argue, a factory where anyone could go in and get a degree and then get out. The quality of the instruction, the quality of that institution has decreased. . . . I'm trying to think of a way to communicate this well. You almost feel like a cog in a machine." Adam's words echoed Hayden's frustrations with "structuring any sort of educational endeavor." His aversion to feeling like a "cog in a machine" led him to express appreciation for flexibility and individualized choices.

With socioeconomically advantaged students being so eager to have choices, it is perhaps unsurprising that this type of flexibility was woven throughout the university. Though opportunities for engagement abounded—from study abroad and internships to curricular tracks and fellowships to other university programs, events, and extracurricular activities—very few were required or integrated into students' everyday experiences. Instead, CU employed a do-it-yourself model of higher education administration where courses, programs, resources, and other opportunities were offered as a buffet of choices. Even the web page listing CU's majors began with a reminder that in addition to having programs in dozens of fields, CU also offered opportunities to "craft your own course of study" with a create-your-own-degree option. If none of the thousands of major-minor combinations available fit one's needs, the university encouraged students to "design their own" major in the form of an "individualized interdisciplinary program of study." By limiting requirements and expanding choice, CU doubled down on efforts to treat students as consumers.[24]

As a result of the way it prioritized flexibility, the university was less effective at offering clear guidance on how to navigate college. Commonwealth

University's do-it-yourself model was the opposite of a guided pathways model, where structured resources are integrated into the curriculum to foster the success of students who may not be familiar with navigating large bureaucracies generally or higher education specifically.[25] The issue with providing such a broad and flexible menu of options was that it departed from the ways many students learned to navigate previous educational settings and created an environment in which it was easy to make costly mistakes.[26] Flynn (a pioneer) illustrated this point when he contrasted his experiences in high school and college.

> As a college student, you have so much more freedom than when you were in high school. Because high school, there are a lot of requirements. You had to be here at this time. You have to do this at this time. For college, you get to decide that for yourself, and then that's when you really have to start trusting yourself, relying on yourself to do certain things and not to do certain things.

Juxtaposing the "freedom" of college with the "requirements" of high school, he depicted a crucial distinction between his previous educational institutions and CU, where he described needing to "build up that diligence" and "do things myself." These observations are supported by scholars who have documented the myriad ways K–12 education in the US has become highly structured over the course of recent decades. Following the emergence of standardization around state-level minimum competency exams in the latter part of the twentieth century, passage of the federal-level No Child Left Behind Act in 2001 and the launch of Race to the Top grants in 2009 accelerated the adoption of common educational standards and related means of assessment.[27] Today, the notion that children's and adolescents' paths from elementary through high school should be formulaic is usually taken for granted.

Flynn's sense that "relying on yourself" was crucial in the much less structured college setting was shared by other students, including Rachel, who noted that programs and resources were available but not always visible. "*You have to look though.* That's the thing. . . . You have to go to those offices, or you have to look it up." Like Flynn, she summed up the resulting importance of self-reliance. "You have to find the people that can help you first and also be willing to ask them for help to even begin with. You'll be forced to advocate for yourself." In this way, CU's do-it-yourself model fostered an environment where students understood that it was up to them to navigate the array of optional services and opportunities.[28]

This environment amplified insecurity for students who were not equipped with dominant forms of social and cultural capital. Recall the words of Daniel (a pioneer) from the prologue, when he described his desire for a university that was "a lot less flexible," noting that many individuals "have this idea that flexibility is a great thing, but in some ways, it can be a choke point. It's information overload." The stories of other LIFGWC students underscored the veracity of Daniel's claim. Alvin (a pioneer) recalled experiences of "feel[ing] like I'm helpless" while trying to navigate the university. "I don't have the information. I don't have anything I can do to help or mitigate some of this." He'd wrestled with the flexibility of CU on multiple occasions, struggling to choose a major, find academic support, negotiate with university offices, and recover from mishaps like taking a science course that he later found out didn't meet the requirements for his major. Throughout their college journeys, pioneers and minimizers struggled to access the guidance they needed about how to succeed in college.

At such a large university, there were many instances where LIFGWC students felt lost without resources integrated into their programs of study. A lack of specific guidance about how to navigate college led students to engage in what many described as a "trial and error" process. Flynn recalled, "It was a lot of trial and error. And even now, I'm still getting used to it." While we might hypothesize that these experimental approaches would eventually lead to a workable knowledge of how to navigate the university, this was not usually the case. Sonia (a minimizer) explained, "The longer you're at the university, your needs for different resources change." In her fifth year of study, she recalled semesters where she'd searched for academic advising, mental health counseling, financial aid, and other sources of support. Now, as she approached graduation, Sonia struggled to figure out which resources were available for career guidance: "I know they're trying to use [a website] for that, but I think it's super complicated." In short, discovering one resource did not mean that same resource would also be able to support a student through their next challenge.

Another way that a lack of clear guidance and structure amplified insecurity was by creating circumstances in which students were unsure of whether seeking out resources was appropriate. Lucas (a minimizer) explained how limited guidance affected him as a first-generation student: "Sometimes you don't know where to go, just because you can't go to your parents. Sometimes there's times where I don't even know if I should go to someone. I don't even know, like, 'is this right, is this how it should feel?' The fact that you're the first one to go down this path, it gets scary sometimes." Though Lucas had a close relationship with his family, he acknowledged that they were often unsure about what steps he needed to take to address specific challenges in college. When LIFGWC students had doubts about whether seeking out a resource was appropriate, they were much less likely to do so. These students' experiences illustrate a pattern described by social scientist Richard Settersten, who noted that when individuals traverse paths that are "not reinforced and protected in institutions or policies, they may lose important sources of support and find their pathways prone to breakdown."[29] In other words, the problem with prioritizing flexibility while providing little structured guidance is that it can set students up for failure when unexpected challenges arise.

In contrast to their LIFGWC peers, socioeconomically advantaged students felt capable of navigating the flexible buffet of opportunities and resources presented by CU. Hayden (an explorer) summed up the ways these students thought about the do-it-yourself environment when he argued that

> the way I would say CU is, is whatever you put in you get out, which is great. . . . All that matters is the harder you try, the more you get, the more resources you'll find, the more help you'll find, the more availability there is. It's a huge university. You can make it as big or as small as you want, so that's the pro—that's definitely one of the upsides.

In a comparable way, Shahid (a maximizer) claimed that "I have a mindset that's different than most others: I think [success in college comes from] however much you put into it. Like I said, it's your initiative." Providing an example of his own attempts to leverage university resources, Shahid went on to talk about his experience becoming involved in research at CU. Concluding this discussion, he added, "because if you're going through all this and paying so much and if you're not taking advantage of the resources and the events going on, then that's up to you." While Hayden and Shahid believed that their efforts would lead to success navigating the university, what they failed to recognize was that this was in part due to the familiarity socioeconomically advantaged students had with higher education. Being able to take advantage of a "huge university" that one could make "as big or as small as you want" was a direct result of their access to dominant forms of social and cultural capital.[30]

Inadequate and Invisible Student Support Services

In addition to a dearth of clear guidance on how to navigate the university, CU also provided inadequate student support services. There is a tendency to lump all student affairs work under the umbrella of "student support," but here I want to focus on a specific subset of this work. Commonwealth University employed a range of student affairs personnel to maintain the abundant amenities and opportunities offered by the institution. There were scores of recreation staff who ran the campus gymnasiums, facilitated intramural sports, and led "outdoor adventure" trips. There were a dozen student activities personnel responsible for extracurricular involvement in clubs, fraternities, sororities, and student government. There were nearly fifty full-time staff who worked in university housing. And there were twenty in charge of student events and related entertainment. Publicly available data indicated that each of these offices received substantial funding.[31]

In short, it was readily apparent that CU invested in certain types of student affairs work. But I am not referring to these kinds of services here. Rather, I use the phrase "student support services" to designate resources like academic advising, centers for underrepresented students, mental health counseling, and other resource offices designed to assist individuals in navigating the challenges of college life—challenges that do not affect all students equally.[32] These are the services that ostensibly provide assistance to LIFGWC students, students of color, and students who are members of other marginalized groups. At CU, support services were understaffed, which made it difficult for many offices to provide adequate resources or get the word out about the kinds of services they were intended to provide.

By creating an unstructured menu of opportunities, CU ensured that many students would only be aware of the most visible options on that menu. Interviews suggested that LIFGWC students frequently remained unfamiliar with less visible resources. For instance, chapter 2 introduced Kwang (a pioneer), who wished he had guidance on coming out to his parents but didn't realize CU had an LGBTQ+ center that could help. Even when LIFGWC students had a sense that the university offered a specific form of support, finding it was no small task. Sonia described her frustrations with the university when she noted, "I know that CU has so many resources. I just feel like they don't talk about them enough, or they don't have an easy way to access them." She gave several examples, including an instance mentioned in chapter 3, when she was trying to find mental health counseling.

> I've been looking at like counseling and stuff through CU, and I know CU offers it, but I have no idea where to go and look for it. . . . Their web page and stuff can sometimes be hard to maneuver. . . . It's frustrating. The first thing I always do when I'm looking for something is go to the college page. But there are so many levels, I get lost on CU's page all the time because they have a lot of resources for incoming students and applications and stuff like that. . . . But when it comes to once you're a student and you're trying to find a specific phone number or email or something like that, it can be a lot more difficult. I'll just spend hours honestly just going on [the university website] and trying to figure out where to go to find these things.

The result of this labyrinth of web pages was that crucial support services sometimes remained invisible to students like Sonia.

In other cases, LIFGWC students discovered a support service but not until late in their undergraduate studies. For instance, May (a minimizer) worked to navigate the impact of attention deficit disorder throughout college but only found out about the university's Office for Learning Services in her fourth year, when another student described academic accommodations he received through the office. She recalled,

> I do have my learning disability, so that does make [my courses] very challenging, and I only just this semester found out that Learning Services accommodates ADD, which was pretty exciting for me. . . . It was actually a friend who mentioned it to me, because he also has ADD. . . . I was like, "That's a thing?" He was like, "Yeah. You should do it. I'm surprised you didn't." Because we both have similar struggles with learning and staying focused and getting stuff done. He was very surprised I hadn't heard about it, so he actually told me what to do and stuff.

May emphasized how thankful she was to have finally discovered this resource through the suggestion of her friend. "Otherwise, I probably wouldn't have found out about it." Nonetheless, navigating her first three years in college without such support had consequences for her academic progress. She'd failed a required course three times and had a C average overall. As the examples shared by Kwang, Sonia, and May illustrate, a lack of visibility for support services had pronounced impacts on students whose social locations were multiply marginalized based on the intersections of their LIFGWC status with other marginalized identities, such as being LGBTQ+ or being a student with a disability.

It wasn't just LIFGWC students who were negatively affected by inadequate and invisible support services. Students of color, including those from socioeconomically advantaged families, found little support from CU as they confronted racial marginalization. This was clear as students described encounters with various forms of discrimination and prejudice in their daily lives on campus. Hugh (a maximizer) said, "I remember there was one time where my roommate and his friend were drunk, and they were joking around. They were all like, 'Ha-ha, we'll say the N-word. What are you going to do?' I was like, 'I don't care how drunk you are, that's racist,'" and Pete (another maximizer) struggled to find help dealing with a roommate who "said racist things a lot." Despite approaching multiple housing staff for assistance, they weren't able to find anyone who would intervene. Pete recalled, "It was just like, 'Well, we can't do anything. We can't really transfer you anywhere.'" With no one willing to address the other student's racism or facilitate a room transfer, he was left in "a hostile living environment."

Students of color encountered similar challenges in the academic realm. Lucas had a fear of speaking in his classes. "Sometimes I'm like, 'uh it's a lot of people.' And you wonder what people can be thinking about you when you're standing up in front of all them." Describing the way he thought about his identity as a Latino man in the classroom and its impact on his concerns, Lucas noted that there were some "bad apples" who expressed biases and prejudice, "you know because I'm a male Latino." He expanded, noting that

> there has been moments in class—either a class or like a room—where I've been the only Latino person. Part of me is like "hey, you know I'm representing my culture here," but part of it is also I might be looked at differently as a human, or at least being me, I can be self-conscious. Maybe they might not take me seriously, maybe they have something against me that I don't even know. Sometimes, it is in the back of my head.

These experiences of feeling as if he were a representative for all Latinos created significant obstacles to academic success, but Lucas dealt with them on his own, without support from the university.

In situations like these, students of color could have benefitted from robust support services—in the form of advisors, counselors, faculty mentors, and other university personnel—to proactively address racism and mitigate racial and ethnic marginalization. Unfortunately, this did not usually occur. A clear trend emerged across interviews with students of color: while encounters with racism were commonplace, few students reported receiving tangible support from the university. This applied to LIFGWC students like Lucas, but also to more socioeconomically advantaged students like Hugh and Pete. In other words, the lack of support services for students of color at CU was a problem that even dominant social and cultural capital could not overcome.

The patterns these students describe have been documented as widespread in higher education. Although most colleges and universities today profess their support for diversity and inclusion, there is a long history of failure to translate words into action.[33] Moreover, sociological research on "diversity initiatives" shows how these efforts frequently fall short of—or even work against—their stated goals. Such initiatives often focus on performing or celebrating differences in superficial ways and individualize students' experiences with hostile campus climates.[34] The result, as W. Carson Byrd shows in his book *Behind the Diversity Numbers*, is that many organizations extract status and prestige from their efforts to quantify the diversity of their campuses while simultaneously perpetuating racism and racial inequality.[35]

Sociologist Veronica Lerma and her colleagues found that a lack of structured support for students of color often means they must engage in uncompensated work to address racial and ethnic marginalization on college campuses.[36] Commonwealth University differed from the site studied by Lerma in that it had an established Center for Diversity and Inclusion that was responsible for supporting marginalized student groups, especially students of color. And yet, the same patterns were prevalent. The Center for Diversity and Inclusion had changed names and structure at least three times over the previous decade, making it difficult for students to find information about the center or approach its staff for support. Significant turnover and a lack of investment in new hires left just two full-time employees to serve a university of nearly forty thousand students. Perhaps unsurprisingly, few participants described receiving any support from the Center for Diversity and Inclusion.

The result was that students of color usually worked on their own or with informal groups of peers to manage instances of prejudice, discrimination, and other forms of marginalization. Some, like Ellie (a minimizer) from chapter 3, did independent research to find out which classes, settings, and individuals at CU would be inclusive of students of color. While she used professor review websites to try to identify and avoid prejudiced faculty, other students shared information through informal peer networks. These strategies provided some relief, but they were no substitute for robust university support. Corey (a minimizer) drove home this point as he discussed concerns about "my race, because as of right now, there's Asian hate crimes going on and all of that. That's basically causing me like a little bit of insecurity and everything." He dedicated time to thinking about strategies for keeping himself and his family safe. Unfortunately, dealing with these stressors on his own had cognitive costs that Corey noted, "impaired me a little bit on my education towards me graduating."

In a few cases, students of color came to rely on individual faculty members for support. Alvin, for instance, provided an example when he shared his experience as a Black student navigating the pain of encounters with racism, both those he experienced firsthand and those he discussed in various courses.

> Last semester really challenged me, not just academically, but also emotionally as well. [Some of my classes involved] talking about things that were really, really tough. . . . We're talking about police brutality but also the mistreatment of African Americans in our country. And how a lot of the things that we do is rooted in systemic racism, so having to understand that and deal with that, especially seeing the pictures of it, too, it took me a long time—it took me a minute to basically be able to be at peace with it, because it was so

tough. . . . It was mainly the lack of care that certain people had, especially around my friend group. There was someone from my college who took an African American literature class with me but still didn't understand why did Black people do the stuff they do. After that class, it made me extremely reconsider the friends that I made. I didn't want to make friends anymore who were making insensitive jokes.

When asked if he had received any support from university offices or services, Alvin said no. Yet he did find support from a Black professor, whom he described as "very kind," noting that, "she gave me help with . . . just how to navigate through the pain." Though finding helpful faculty could be beneficial for students, scholars of higher education remind us that the emotional labor of these faculty members is often uncompensated, unrecognized, and comes from the generosity of individuals rather than intentional support created and sustained by the university itself.[37] Moreover, as Alvin's example illustrated, this work often falls inequitably to faculty of color.

Reactive Student Support Practices

Other support services failed to adequately meet needs not because students were unaware of them but because offices were not engaging in proactive outreach. Higher education research demonstrates that this type of intrusive support is crucial to student success, especially for historically underserved and marginalized populations.[38] Yet participants' words made clear that CU's support services rarely offered this kind of proactive outreach. Instead, they were typically reactive, waiting for students to request help before engaging with them. Recall, for instance, in chapter 4 when Rachel explained,

> In college, you've got to find the people to help you. There's no one who's going to be like, "Hi, I'm here to help you." You have to make your appointment with your advisor. Your advisor's not going to send you an email saying, "Hey, I haven't met with you." They have hundreds of students they have to talk to.

Her claims aligned with details about academic advising shared in other interviews where students gave voice to a sense that university advisors were stretched thin with unreasonably high caseloads.

I decided to explore this topic myself. Comparing website descriptions of advising resources in each department with publicly available data on the number of CU students enrolled in each major, I calculated advisor-to-student ratios. It didn't take long to confirm Rachel's assertion: most advising caseloads far exceeded the national average of 296 students per advisor.[39] Equally alarming, as I tried to collect this information, there were multiple

AMPLIFYING OR ALLEVIATING INSECURITY   139

majors where I was unable to find contact information for specific advisors online. Rather, several departments listed a general email address for advising queries. This helped explain the experiences of students like Jonah (a pioneer), who had never met his advisor. Despite being in his third year at CU, the only advising he'd received was in the form of brief correspondence from a general department email account.

Students' interviews gave clues about how CU advisors handled being overextended with excessive caseloads. A clear example came from Pete, who noted that, "I would have appreciated more thorough advice, really, from my academic advisor. Because I went my second semester, and she gave me a sheet, and she was like, 'Let's just go over your four-year plan.'" He read between the lines of this encounter, determining that the implication of presenting a four-year plan of study during a first-year advising appointment was that "you don't need to come back." When he tried to return with a question about internships, his advisor again directed him to this four-year plan. "It was sort of a dismissal. It wasn't as much like shutting down or forbidding talk about [internships], but it was, 'Are you doing [the four-year plan]? All right, well that's great.'" Feeling brushed off, Pete rarely returned to his advisor's office, which eventually created problems.

> There was even a semester where I went into a class that the [four-year plan] had recommended, and then I got an email two weeks in saying, "You don't need to be in this course, because it doesn't count towards your major." That was really frustrating. It was just like, "Well, I think this would've been more helpful if we had been talking more frequently."

As a continuing-generation student from an upper-middle-class family, Pete was able to draw from college knowledge to trace this issue to a specific change in the university catalog that hadn't been reflected in his initial four-year plan document. With this information, he dropped the class, received a full refund, and registered for the correct course the following semester. In this way, he remained on track for graduation and didn't incur financial penalties. But other students who received reactive advising were not as fortunate.

As prior research has shown, less socioeconomically advantaged students were sometimes uncomfortable initiating meetings to ask for help from university resources.[40] And even when pioneers and minimizers made efforts to reach out to support services, more socioeconomically advantaged students' own efforts to accumulate opportunities sometimes had a stifling impact.[41] For instance, Lance (a pioneer) felt crowded out by students who were quicker to obtain resources. Concluding his interview, he told me about how he'd come to realize that "knowing how to self-advocate" was essential at CU, adding that "I wish I could go back and tell myself that my first semester. . . . As you can imagine, being in a big school, if you don't speak up, you will be drowned out by others who do."

Relying on reactive rather than proactive approaches, understaffed offices were often unsuccessful at providing LIFGWC students with the support they needed. Other participants talked about waiting in long lines, dealing with electronic forms instead of people, and having emails go unanswered or calls be unreturned. These signals that their presence was a burden dissuaded students—especially those who were LIFGWC—from approaching these resources again.

By contrast, many socioeconomically advantaged students' comfort with seeking help paid off when they obtained support from university staff. Brian (an explorer) was effusive as he claimed, "I think CU definitely has good services. . . . I've only had good experiences." He knew how to locate and extract what limited support was available, even from services that weren't well publicized. In other instances, socioeconomically advantaged students realized it was necessary to forgo or at least supplement university resources with family resources to make up for limited capacity.[42] In a moment of honest self-reflection, Jimmy (a maximizer) noted that if he'd needed to rely on academic advisors rather than parental knowledge, "I probably would have been here for another year" before completing a degree. Being able to lean on family resources was a luxury that allowed advantaged students to succeed despite reactive student support practices.

Decentralized and Disconnected Services

On top of being invisible and reactive, CU's student support services were decentralized across a multitude of disconnected offices, which amplified the insecurity of navigating college. Pilar (a minimizer) explained how the decentralization of various services led to challenges finding guidance at the university.

> I have these questions and I don't know who to ask because every department is different, and separated, and their own entity. . . . Departments don't really talk to each other. If I'm talking to one, then they send me to the other one, then I go to that one and they're like, "you have to go to this one," and I'm like "thanks, but that doesn't really help me."

Spreading various services across distinct offices with little coordination of responsibilities is a common normative institutional arrangement in contemporary higher education, so much so that it is often taken for granted as a best

AMPLIFYING OR ALLEVIATING INSECURITY   141

practice.[43] Yet the participants in this study illuminated how decentralization coupled with CU's size created an environment that felt impossible to navigate.

April (a pioneer), whom we met in chapter 2, recalled struggles to find her way around so many disconnected offices and resources after transferring to CU. She described how this process became "a little bit overwhelming" when she called one office where a receptionist "gave me about twenty different things that I needed to get in touch with." She explained why having resources available was not the same as having resources that were centrally organized and interconnected.

> For me, sometimes having a huge amount of different resources that you have to check each different one and you've got to go through different offices and call different phone numbers and really hope that you don't get put on hold or that someone answers your email, can be as difficult as having no resources. It's not a simple system. . . . It was one more stress on my plate at a time when there was a lot of stress. So, the resources are there; the work to get the resources is a little bit taxing. . . . There are a few different suborganizations. It's not like there's one cohesive part of CU that is there to help.

April's observation that "having a huge amount of different resources . . . can be as difficult as having no resources" was illuminating. When I asked how these two scenarios were comparable, she responded bluntly: "the end result is the same." In other words, having resources that were incomprehensibly arranged meant that they were unlikely to be accessed by LIFGWC students.

Commonwealth University's complex organization of services meant that April's experience of calling myriad offices only to be placed on hold or transferred was common. Dee (a pioneer) recalled that, "whenever I call the student offices . . . they're like 'I don't know. Here, I'll transfer you to somebody else,' and by the time thirty minutes have passed, I've already been transferred through fifteen people." Similarly, Lakshmi (a minimizer) shared her perception that many offices responded to students' calls by "just transferring them to another person to get them off their back." She expanded with an experience of her own. "A huge problem in college is that no one knows, no one is willing to help you. They're willing to transfer you. . . . I did have that experience when I was trying to get my financial aid back." While she first approached the financial aid office to discuss a scholarship that was missing from her aid package, counselors there indicated that her funding was the jurisdiction of another office. At that point, Lakshmi recalled,

> I mentioned it to [my academic advisor], and she also tried to talk to financial aid and stuff, but then she transferred me to [another program] coordinator,

then the coordinator who was in charge of all the scholarships. . . . Unfortunately, when we were actually getting to the bottom of things, the [scholarships] coordinator, I guess quit or something. So, everything got lost in translation, and then I had to talk to [staff in another office]. It was just a whole hassle.

Though students hoped that offices like financial aid would offer a hub where support for specific challenges—in this case, financing college—could be addressed in one location, they often discovered that each challenge had multiple components, responsibility for which was spread across multiple units.

In this way, efforts to find resources often morphed into scavenger hunts for LIFGWC students. Amal (a pioneer) gave an example from his own struggle to find academic support. When he went in search of tutoring, he had not expected to embark on a difficult quest, but he discovered that tutoring services were decentralized across dozens of departments at CU.

Most classes, they have like a certain spot where you can go for support, but it's not like a support center where there's multiple people ready to jump onto your question and help you. . . . Most of my classes they had [online] forums or places where you can ask questions. . . . You just have to refer to your professor.

Tutoring for math courses was housed in the math department, and economics tutoring could be found in the economics department. But some academic units lacked formal tutoring entirely. A few opted for a class-by-class approach, like the one Amal described, where professors posted general resources to their course web pages. Others provided vague recommendations to seek support through separate organizations and offices. For instance, to receive tutoring for a finance or management course, students were directed to peers in various student organizations. Ironically, the same web page where the business school claimed to have "a strong commitment" to student success also provided generic advice that students in need of academic support "check with each student club" and with the Office of Learning Services "to see if tutoring is available," and if so, "what hours are provided."

Students' struggles on these scavenger hunts made apparent that the absence of centralized academic support created a litany of challenges for LIFGWC students. Amal was especially frustrated by the fact that the solution to these challenges seemed so obvious. He remarked, "If you have a support center [that includes] every single class, that would be better." Unfortunately, centralized support services like a tutoring center were not the norm at CU.

This type of decentralization has consequences that go well beyond creating barriers to accessing resources. Scholars of organizations and institutional change show that when there is an absence of centralized oversight of specific functions within a college or university, it can be especially difficult to improve practices in ways that would support student success. For instance, in his book *Diversity Regimes*, sociologist James Thomas shows that when the work of supporting marginalized students is spread across departments and divisions with little coordination between them, it is rarely feasible to make changes in how authority, resources, or support are distributed.[44] In other words, decentralization was a problematic normative institutional arrangement that sustained other problematic normative institutional arrangements by making them difficult to correct.

Though LIFGWC students found it daunting to navigate decentralized and disconnected offices, socioeconomically advantaged students again experienced this institutional arrangement differently. They occasionally found CU's organization of departments cumbersome, but maximizers and explorers benefitted from the ways their dominant social and cultural capital helped them to strategically piece together the support they desired. The fact that services were decentralized was less burdensome for these students, whose families were familiar with where to look for various kinds of assistance.

Moreover, socioeconomically advantaged students appreciated the duplication of resources that sometimes accompanied decentralization, when multiple offices were endowed with comparable kinds of knowledge, influence, and authority. Several acknowledged that a benefit of having multiple staff doing the same types of work in disconnected offices was that they could go shopping for a desired outcome or response. Debbie (a maximizer) explained, "I just email who I think would give the best answer." Though I initially interpreted this statement to mean that she tried to reach out to whomever would give the most accurate or comprehensive information, it turned out that "the best answer" referred to Debbie's preferred response. She clarified by providing a recent example of when she sought an exception to a college policy about course credit transfers. Though her initial request for the exception was denied, she eventually found a staff member in another office who was willing to approve it. In this way, Debbie was able to use the decentralization of CU to obtain a unique allowance that many of her peers were unlikely to receive.

Other socioeconomically advantaged students used this context to shop around for staff resources they perceived to be more lenient, more knowledgeable, or more competent. In this way, decentralization was concordant with these students' preference for flexibility and choices. If a maximizer or explorer was unenthused about the reception they received with a resource in one office, they could sometimes find a comparable resource in another office.

Alternative Institutional Arrangements

The preceding pages of this chapter present a critique of the organization, practices, and priorities of CU, highlighting how various normative institutional arrangements serve to amplify insecurity and corresponding forms of inequality between students. Such a critique begs the question of what a better model might look like. How could a university alleviate, rather than amplify, insecurity? To find alternatives to the arrangements described so far, we don't need to imagine a utopian college with boundless resources and perfect systems. Rather, we can observe the contours of a better model within CU itself.

The university was home to two programs that offered a vision for what higher education could look like if universities shifted from focusing primarily on affluent students to creating new organizational arrangements that support a broader range of students by bolstering security. The first of these programs, the Linked Pathways partnership, shows how a university can provide structured guidance and a manageable number of focused choices. The second, the University Honors Program, presents a model for organizing student support services in visible, proactive, and interconnected ways. Both programs provide insights for how to combat insecurity and reduce inequality in higher education.

THE LINKED PATHWAYS PARTNERSHIP: STRUCTURED GUIDANCE AND FOCUSED CHOICES

In 2019, CU won a national award for its Linked Pathways partnership with Regional Community College (RCC). This new program, designed to connect the two institutions and facilitate transfers, was credited with generating a "seamless pathway" to a bachelor's degree. The press release for the award touted the way Linked Pathways had "radically transformed the internal practices at CU and the way they collaborate with colleagues at RCC." To say the program represented radical transformation may sound overly generous, but there was a ring of truth to this statement. Linked Pathways was radical in that it required a significant departure from the university's deeply entrenched emphasis on flexibility and boundless choice in order to provide clearly structured guidance.

This partnership had several unique features. First, students who participated in the Linked Pathways program were treated as part of two integrated institutions. They had access to shared resources, including events, programs, and services at both institutions. Additionally, the fact that they were coen-rolled at RCC and CU meant that students could take classes at both schools simultaneously, and they did not need to complete a separate application process to continue through a bachelor's degree at CU after finishing their associate degree. Andre (a pioneer) described how Linked Pathways alleviated his concerns about starting higher education at a community college. "I did not have stress at all, because I knew I was going to be accepted into CU as long as I was doing what I do," he explained, adding that the anxiety he'd anticipated having about transitioning from RCC to CU "was really eliminated by that guaranteed admission part. . . . I was fortunate not to have that uncertainty."

Perhaps most importantly, students in the Linked Pathways program were provided a student success coach who guided them through a clearly laid out plan for an associate degree that would translate directly to CU without having to take additional general education credits. Not only did the partnership specify which courses to take but it did so with scaffolded "milestones" and limited choices. When options were available, they were presented as focused decisions between a small number of equivalent courses (usually just two to four) clearly bracketed within a specific category. And every RCC course in Linked Pathways mapped onto a specific course at CU to ensure there were no "wasted credits." Layne (a minimizer) described the benefits of this structured pathway, where "a lot of advising was done through the lens of how this will apply to a bachelor's degree at CU, so it didn't feel like I was doing my associate's in a vacuum."

Before the implementation of this partnership, students often struggled when transferring from RCC, finding that several of the courses they took at the community college didn't count toward a bachelor's degree. My interview with Ingrid (a minimizer) provided a clear example. When we met, I learned that Ingrid had transferred from RCC to CU several years before the Linked Pathways partnership launched. She described her experience.

> I found it was very hard to navigate RCC. I'd have one person telling me something and then another one telling me something else. . . . I took a lot of classes that I didn't need to, and . . . I wasn't really aware that you could take just general education requirements and kind of figure [your major] out when you transfer to a four-year degree—what you want to declare. I thought freshman year at RCC I had to know right then and there what I'm going to be doing for the rest of my life, and I just didn't really realize that you still have time to decide. . . . I wasn't really aware of that at RCC. I met with many different guidance counselors who kind of told me something different each time, and that got really confusing, so I just tried to figure it out myself. And I ended up taking a lot of classes I didn't need to. I think I have about twenty unused credits.

146   CHAPTER SIX

Ingrid's frustration was clear as she described the confusion that came with receiving contradictory advice about how to find courses that would smooth her transfer process. She recalled how disheartening it was to learn that so many of her RCC courses hadn't counted toward her degree requirements at CU.

> I found that out at CU when I initially did all the transfer and I met with my one advisor, and we looked at what came over and what didn't. It's just frustrating, because I felt like I wasn't given a road map, or I wasn't even given the information to be able to make educated decisions. So, I just kind of winged it. And it cost money, and it costs time, so it's a little frustrating.

Ingrid's sense that she had been navigating college without "a road map" was shared by RCC transfers who came to CU before the Linked Pathways partnership as well as students who transferred from other community colleges without such partnerships in place. And it was exactly this road map that Linked Pathways tried to construct for students.

Participants who had transitioned from RCC to CU more recently described very different outcomes. Victoria (a minimizer) recalled her experiences in Linked Pathways with enthusiasm. "Oh, it was so easy. It was really great. So, I finished [my RCC credits], and I was already . . . accepted. There was no interruption whatsoever, which made it really, really good." Linked Pathways students often characterized their transfer process as "simple." For example, Carl (a maximizer) recalled that transferring from RCC to CU "was pretty simple; the Linked Pathways coaches were very helpful." And Patrice (a minimizer) noted that, "there was a whole plan outlined [in Linked Pathways] . . . of what to do and how to do it, and so I found it simple to transfer." The result was a program that many students, especially those who were LIFGWC, found to be beneficial. In contrast to other CU resources, Linked Pathways was well publicized so that students usually learned about the program well before they began their associate degree. Lakshmi, for instance, recalled that "I'd been trying to go for the Linked Pathways program since high school."

This partnership made clear that CU had the capacity to create structured guidance to alleviate insecurity. It was unfortunate that the same approach wasn't extended to students outside of the program. In fact a limitation of Linked Pathways was that it didn't continue once students began the upper-division coursework in their major. Despite the program's aspirations to create continuity, students acknowledged that the guidance they'd received usually dropped off after they completed their associate degree. Sonia, for instance, recalled that after a straightforward transfer process, her experiences became "overwhelming" upon transitioning into her upper-division classes at CU. She described struggles finding the correct courses, advising, financial aid, and guidance on the seemingly endless stream of "paperwork." Similarly, Andre recalled how he came to feel like "just a number" after finishing the program. While Linked Pathways helped to structure part of these students' paths through higher education, it stopped short of guiding them through the completion of their four-year degree.

THE UNIVERSITY HONORS PROGRAM:
VISIBLE, PROACTIVE, AND INTERCONNECTED SUPPORT

The University Honors Program (UHP) stood out in my interviews with students and in my ethnographic field notes. Like Linked Pathways, it represented a significant departure from the usual modes of operation at CU. Specifically, it provided visible, proactive, and interconnected support that stood in sharp contrast to the invisible, reactive, and disconnected services offered elsewhere at the university. This program was built around a compressed, multidisciplinary alternative to the general education requirements. Students from any major at the university could participate in UHP, taking part in an "inquiry-driven curriculum" that built high-impact learning such as research opportunities, leadership experiences, and various community-engaged projects into required coursework. The program accepted approximately 12 percent of each incoming first-year class, with additional students joining in their second or third year of study or after transferring from another institution.

The University Honors Program's robust student support services included an honors advisor, who was not a substitute for the student's major advisor but an additional resource. The program website described the role as a dynamic one, noting that this individual was a "lifeline" who would provide specific kinds of guidance "throughout your undergraduate career." Students confirmed this in interviews, where they frequently gushed about their honors advisors, describing them as "really caring," "the one to help me, tell me how to navigate everything," "always very helpful," "knowledgeable and passionate about what they do," and "this steady person throughout my entire college career." In short, honors advisors were lauded by students as highly effective and highly visible forms of support.

In contrast to students like Pete, who felt like a burden when approaching advisors in their major, UHP students described getting a very different impression from their honors advisors. For instance, Barry (a minimizer) said,

When I have any doubts about anything academic, I immediately scheduled an appointment with my [UHP] advisor. . . . I go to my University Honors

Program advisor, and I'm always relying heavily on those people. . . . We would always discuss like clinical opportunities, research opportunities, and volunteer work and things like that. It was always something that we would talk about because I am premed, and my advisor knew that, so she would sometimes contact people who knew more about that stuff and helped me in that way. . . . She said, "Oh, I know a professor who probably could use someone in her lab."

Since his UHP advisor made this fortuitous connection, Barry had begun conducting research with the faculty member who eventually served as a mentor for his undergraduate research project. In this way, he became one of the only minimizers in the study to have such a significant high-impact learning experience and to sustain aspirations to attend medical school. Barry acknowledged that he was not initially inclined to become involved beyond the classroom; however, his advisor encouraged him to think about involvement differently, focusing on how it would affect his chances of medical school admission.

And through [conversations with my UHP advisor], I've learned a lot about networking and the importance of that. Because, especially when you're looking to apply to medical school, they need all these hours for research and clinical and all that. But you also need letters of recommendation, and it's so hard to get letters of recommendation from people—it's impossible to get them from people you don't know. . . . I've always been good just taking the course and doing the work, and I've never had any problems. And for a lot of classes, I've done it that way, and I barely even know the professor. But through [my UHP advisor], I've realized that a better way of establishing those connections is through stuff you don't necessarily do in the classroom, like some stuff that you do outside of the classroom like research, which is extracurricular, I guess. I mean it's a little academic, but you're not getting a grade for it.

By going beyond offering a plan of study, this honors advisor worked with Barry's dispositions as a minimizer to understand his goals and connect specific cocurricular involvement—in this case, research experience—to those goals.

Additionally, UHP provided students with two other crucial student support services in the form of peer mentors and a student success coordinator. Peer mentors were more senior UHP students who received training through a peer mentorship course to provide proactive support during students' first-year transitions. They offered one-on-one guidance that was integrated into the college's required first-semester "research and inquiry" course. In this way peer mentors were able to be both visible and proactive in large part because they were connected directly to the curriculum.[45]

The UHP's student success coordinator was employed to help students work through specific academic and social challenges and "connect [students] to campus resources that will support [their] success" in order to facilitate retention. In other words, this staff member worked to combat the decentralization of CU by helping students navigate a big university. The coordinator relied on UHP's early intervention system to identify and provide resources to students in need without students themselves having to reach out to request support. This system prompted faculty members, advisors, and other staff to submit an early outreach request for students who might be "facing barriers" to success as signaled by missing an assignment, being absent from multiple class meetings, earning a low grade, or other signs of distress.

Collectively, UHP advisors, peer mentors, the student success coordinator, and the faculty they collaborated with created a student support structure that was visible, proactive, and interconnected—the very opposite of the support services that existed across other departments and programs at CU. This model was valuable for students from a range of social locations, especially those who were LIFGWC. As with many other honors programs in the US, UHP was not as diverse as the university overall.[46] According to an article written about the program the year before my study, first-generation and Pell-eligible students were slightly underrepresented compared with their presence in the full undergraduate student body. However, the program did enroll a substantial number of LIFGWC students—for comparison, at much higher rates than the state's flagship university. And in fact, 37 percent of the UHP students who took part in this study were low-income, first-generation, and/or working class. Some of these students, like Pilar, introduced in chapter 3, were minimizers despite the fact that they received little family support for navigating higher education. The collective impact of UHP's student support services provided them with the resources they needed to resist insecurity as they made their way through college. And a few, like Barry, were exceptional among the minimizers because they came to have a sustained high-impact learning experience, such as research with a faculty mentor, leadership in a CU organization, or an internship—experiences that were otherwise rare for minimizers.

In sum, UHP's approach to organizing and administering student support services was unique. By pushing back against tendencies to make services invisible, reactive, and decentralized, this program helped alleviate the insecurity students encountered and mitigate related inequality between LIFGWC students and their socioeconomically advantaged peers. However, it is important to emphasize that this program was only able to affect a relatively small portion of CU students. Moreover, because it existed as just one part of a large university, UHP couldn't fully counteract the limitations of other facets of the university and its do-it-yourself environment. Pilar, for instance, described the ways that other offices at CU, such as financial aid, remained difficult to navigate. University Honors Program advisors sometimes stepped in to help students negotiate with other units, but some students were reluctant to ask UHP staff for guidance with problems that they perceived might be outside of the program's jurisdiction. In the end, UHP was able to provide important support but not complete security.

Trading Insecurity Amplifiers for Security Boosters

The problematic normative institutional arrangements described in the first part of this chapter are often thought of as disconnected elements without consideration for their cumulative impact on students. This is a problem for scholars and practitioners in higher education. I propose we recognize these arrangements as *insecurity amplifiers*—policies, procedures, and practices that serve to privilege already advantaged students who are able to navigate complex bureaucracy and take risks while disadvantaging students for whom insecurity poses a more immediate and pressing danger. These are the types of arrangements that Elizabeth Lee and Jacob Harris have shown frequently require LIFGWC students to create their own "services that augment or replace . . . advising, networking, and even funding."[47] Though such strategies represent a creative form of resistance, the need for them places an unfair burden on students to overcome the shortcomings of the university.

The stories shared by participants in this study expose the ways insecurity amplifiers were woven throughout CU. They could be found in some of the most prominent features of the university, including the proliferation of choices and flexibility as well as in the lack of structured guidance, invisible student support services, reactive practices, and decentralized organization of offices. As research on neoliberal trends in public higher education illustrates, these arrangements do not occur by coincidence or accident but instead are the product of fiscal austerity.[48] By catering to students who would find these arrangements appealing, the university fostered a do-it-yourself environment that compounded the uncertainties confronted by LIFGWC students, students of color, and other marginalized populations.

But institutions like CU also deserve credit for the ways they sometimes succeed in creating more equitable institutional arrangements. By exploring the Linked Pathways partnership and the University Honors Program, this chapter featured two promising alternatives to the insecurity amplifiers that abounded elsewhere at the university. These programs illustrate how structured guidance, focused choices, and visible, proactive, and interconnected support can provide much-needed stability for students as they navigate college. Such organizational arrangements can be thought of as *security boosters*, structures and practices that mitigate insecurity in order to foster success for broader groups of students. The final chapter of this book turns to consider the lessons learned in this study, including specific lessons for how universities can draw from these insights to reduce insecurity and inequality. In doing so, public postsecondary institutions can go beyond being universities *of* strivers to become universities *for* strivers.

7

The Lessons of Precarity

The students in this book told their stories over the course of an academic year. They shared accounts of the challenges they'd faced, of the victories they'd won. They shared the things they worried about and the things they wished there was time to worry about. They shared ideas, frustrations, and questions. And they shared their sense of what it was like to be a student at a college where insecurity was inescapable. Though it was clear that this insecurity was experienced very differently by students based on their intersectional social locations, it had a profound impact on the ways each of them traversed higher education.

When the end of the year arrived, I spent time reflecting on what might be learned from these stories. As I dug through the pages of interview transcripts and field notes, it became clear that they illuminated a series of important lessons. These weren't the lessons we might learn from youth attending the elite, highly resourced institutions that are so often the focus of social science research on higher education.[1] They were lessons of precarity. This chapter is about those insights, which can be examined from three sets of perspectives, namely, those of students, those of scholars, and those of higher education leaders.

First, we'll consider the lessons students themselves learned at a precarious university. While participants often saw utility in these lessons, they are perhaps not the primary insights we'd hope young people would take with them from college. And they are certainly not the lessons that universities profess to teach. Commonwealth University's mission, like that of so many other colleges, emphasized cultivating "engaged citizens" who were socially aware and committed to building just communities. But as I'll explain, many of the notions that students took away from their college experiences ran counter to these goals.

The second section explores what scholars can learn from students' stories about insecurity in higher education. Chapters 2 through 5 illuminated new ways of thinking about inequality by accounting for the manner in which personal, family, and institutional resources came together to shape the experiences of four different groups of students. The resulting insights complicate understandings of cultural capital and community cultural wealth, providing a more comprehensive picture of the resource configurations students rely on and their role in reproducing inequality at the intersections of socioeconomic status, race, gender, and other sociodemographic dimensions.

Finally, we'll examine the lessons university faculty, staff, administrators, and policymakers could learn about how to create less insecure and more equitable universities. Building from the literature on normative institutional arrangements, I've identified two types of arrangements that dictate the uncertainty and instability college students encounter, namely, insecurity amplifiers and security boosters. When higher education leaders are cognizant of the lessons of precarity, it becomes possible to work toward eliminating the former and expanding the latter. This requires moving beyond a tendency to focus primarily on affluent students to recognize the experiences and needs of a diverse range of students. I suggest specific policies and practices that can support this work. Though powerful forces work against change, the findings presented in this book offer avenues for making real progress.

The (Problematic) Lessons Students Learned

What do young people learn in a precarious university? We could speculate about the insights and capacities students might acquire through encounters with an insecure environment. Perhaps in a context of instability and uncertainty it might be difficult to learn much of anything. After all, studies have demonstrated that many college students today aren't making significant gains in various measures of academic skills or cognitive development.[2] Alternatively though, maybe their encounters with a large public university provide students with broader lessons that are more difficult to quantify. Could they develop a critical perspective on society or form new questions about old ideas of merit? Might they learn the importance of community? What about patience? Empathy? Compassion? Generosity?

Or maybe students could come to better understand how people's lives are shaped by broad social, historical, and political contexts. Perhaps experience in this insecure setting equips young people with what C. Wright Mills termed the *sociological imagination*. Having identified a common failure of individuals to understand "the troubles they endure in terms of historical change and institutional contradiction," Mills proposed that a sociological imagination should help people recognize "the intricate connection between the patterns of their own lives and the course of world history."[3]

This capacity can be observed when individuals are able to link "personal troubles" with "the public issues of social structure."[4] Mills defined personal troubles in this sense to include events and experiences that relate to everyday interactions with others, experiences that many therefore interpret to be personal or private. By contrast, "public issues," he explains, "have to do with matters that transcend these local environments of the individual and the range of his inner life," matters that relate to "the larger structure of social and historical life."[5] A sociological imagination has many benefits for individuals as well as communities. It can combat loneliness and isolation while cultivating feelings of connection and an understanding of the complexity of the social world.[6] Similarly, it can foster critical thinking, empathy, civic engagement, social responsibility, and positive social change.[7]

An emphasis on the development of capacities to contextualize individual experience can also be found in other fields across the social sciences and humanities. Faculty teaching college history courses, for example, often focus on helping students "situate themselves in a larger context and stream of time" as a way of developing capacities for "perspective taking and empathy."[8] In a similar fashion, those in communication have learning objectives directed toward fostering students' abilities to recognize how perspectival differences are informed by the ways individuals exist within broader contexts. Beyond specific disciplines, overarching goals to assist students in making connections between individual experience and social, political, and historical contexts are common in articulations of the purpose of general education requirements.[9] Commonwealth University's general education core, for example, had a requirement that students take a course that would equip them to "explain how individuals . . . are influenced by contextual factors," which could be filled by taking any of a number of designated courses in sociology, anthropology, education, psychology, economics, government, history, or international affairs. Furthermore, these capacities are emphasized by student affairs practitioners as the result of active engagement beyond the classroom.[10]

As they encountered a range of new experiences and perspectives in college, we might hope that students would acquire this appreciation for the

THE LESSONS OF PRECARITY

interwoven nature of biography and broader contexts, recognizing how individuals are shaped by social, historical, and political forces. Unfortunately, there was little evidence that this was the case. In fact, the converse often appeared to be true, as many students seemed to have developed individualistic perspectives. Others acquired what I refer to as a *selectively sociological imagination.* Although these two perspectives were distinct from one another, neither conveyed the full range of personal and community benefits attributed to the sociological imagination, and both had problematic results.

LIFGWC STUDENTS AND INDIVIDUALISTIC PERSPECTIVES

Near the end of each interview, I asked students to reflect on the things they'd learned or the ways they'd grown and developed during college. When presented with this prompt, LIFGWC students articulated individualistic perspectives that emphasized the independence of personal troubles from social structure. They cited self-reliance and individual effort as the most important variables influencing success or failure. Such perceptions often encouraged students to engage in self-blame for the challenges they encountered in college.

These individualistic perspectives were clear throughout my interview with Miguel. Over the course of our conversation, we discussed myriad obstacles he'd encountered during college. Given Miguel's social location as an LIFGWC student who had emigrated from Mexico along with his family when he was seven years old, one could hypothesize about the various social, legal, economic, historical, and political factors that may have shaped his journey.[11] Yet he didn't describe broad structural forces or even mesolevel organizational features of the university as the root of his troubles. When I asked what his biggest barriers to success had been, he responded simply, "just myself." This individualistic explanation of his experiences was closely linked to the lessons he claimed to have learned in college. As we reached the end of the interview, I asked Miguel about the ways he'd grown or developed in higher education. He told me that he'd learned to be "very independent," characterizing his time at CU as "a very independentizing experience." He elaborated.

> I don't think it's a word, *independentizing,* [but college was] a very independentizing experience—I don't know if I just made it up—it's just a lot of independence on yourself. . . . Relying on yourself without relying on others is a

very good thing I learned here. . . . Because if you don't have anyone around to rely on, it's basically yourself. I survived, I guess. Barely.

The type of self-blame that showed up in Miguel's interview proved to be common among LIFGWC students, including both pioneers and minimizers. As noted in chapter 3, when asked about his biggest obstacles to success in college, Lucas (a minimizer) cited "self-doubt and being my own worst enemy." Andre (a pioneer) similarly responded, "Honestly, nothing except me. 'Me' is my biggest challenge to myself. That would be the only thing I can say, my inability to—like not performing the best, those things. This is my main hurdle. . . . I have been lazy or did not want to do things." These responses were concerning, not just because of the pain they clearly evoked for Miguel, Lucas, and Andre but also because of the way they seemed to misrepresent their experiences. These students had worked diligently throughout their college journeys despite encountering innumerable structural barriers, and yet they were quick to blame themselves for times when they'd fallen short of their goals.

Notably, minimizers sometimes identified external sources of insecurity in the form of prejudiced peers, faculty, staff, or employers. Their descriptions of these individuals, featured in chapter 3, shed light on their concerns about discrimination on the basis of race, gender, ability, immigration histories, and other sociodemographic characteristics. Yet it's important to note that these concerns were not usually articulated as an awareness of structural inequalities or systemic racism, sexism, ableism, or xenophobia.[12] Rather, they emphasized that others might occasionally harbor prejudice or discriminatory tendencies that needed to be monitored (recall, for instance, Lucas's discussion of "bad apples" in the previous chapter). Additionally, they managed these concerns with the same types of individualistic approaches—working to shelter themselves from prejudiced individuals—and blamed themselves when things went badly.

Students described individualistic understandings of their experiences not as beliefs they'd always ascribed to but specifically as ways of thinking that they'd acquired in college. Ingrid (a minimizer) remembered how early on in college she often felt like the deck was stacked against her. Yet she described having "a progressive mind shift" until

> I just I had this realization that like there's no excuse—there's really no excuse, except you're not doing it right—and that the only barrier is myself. Everything else will eventually fall into place if you do the things that you need to do. Again, if there's a problem, I try not to instantly forget about it. I just say, "you know, how can we approach this differently?"

Though Ingrid described this moment as a notable "realization" that reshaped her thinking, it could just as easily be viewed as an attempt to conform to the types of individualistic ("no excuses") explanations students felt obligated to adopt in college.[13] Flynn (a pioneer) made a similar point when he recalled experiences pushing through obstacles in college as moments when he'd learned "to really build up that diligence, to know what's best for myself, and not only know what's best for myself, but to actually put those words into actions to really do those things myself." Quotes such as these illustrate how LIFGWC students' individualistic perspectives were often inextricable from the insecurity culture and the do-it-yourself environment they encountered at CU.[14]

In addition to fostering self-blame, individualistic perspectives also made college an isolating experience for some LIFGWC students. Recall, for instance, April's description from chapter 2 of the ways she was an "atypical" student. Without a clear explanation of how her lived experiences—and many of her peers'—were shaped by structural inequality and a history of the intergenerational transmission of such inequality, she perceived herself to be unusual. Feeling like an exception to the norm, students like April often absolved the university of responsibility for providing necessary guidance and support.

To point out the problematic nature of these lessons is not to say that developing aspects of independence in college is a bad thing. As the previous chapters show, for some students, adopting an individualistic explanation of personal success or failure could be empowering. Focusing on individual agency gave some the sense that they were prepared to overcome great odds. And we certainly hope that young people will learn how to do new things for themselves in college.[15] Being able to "self-advocate" in the way Lance (a pioneer) described in chapter 2 was valuable in certain moments. Moreover, as Miguel noted, becoming independent can be a perfectly reasonable strategy to "survive" in an insecure environment.

Nonetheless, it is clearly undesirable that painful self-blame accompanied these lessons. And research shows that there are real limitations to the effectiveness of self-reliance, especially in educational settings where students who seek help are often rewarded with additional support.[16] Individualistic perspectives inhibited students' willingness to seek help from university resources. For instance, when I asked about whether he'd found sources of support from the university, Lucas seemed almost surprised. "It's up to me to make sure I graduate on time," he explained. Put simply, the individualism fostered by CU caused a great deal of anguish and left students with few tools for critiquing their institution or pursuing broader structural change.

SOCIOECONOMICALLY ADVANTAGED STUDENTS
AND THE SELECTIVELY SOCIOLOGICAL IMAGINATION

Socioeconomically advantaged students came to interpret their experiences in somewhat different ways, ways that could not be described as purely individualistic. Rather, these students developed what we might refer to as a "selectively sociological imagination." This could be observed through differences in how participants discussed their own lived experiences. As described above, LIFGWC students engaged in self-blame for the challenges they encountered, and in the rarer cases when they discussed external obstacles (as minimizers sometimes did), they were usually in the form of prejudiced individuals who they drew from their own resources and strategies to avoid. By contrast, socioeconomically advantaged students discussed the impact of systemic racism, sexism, homophobia, and other forms of structural inequality in shaping their firsthand experiences.

These understandings of one's lived experiences could be observed in two main forms. Maximizers displayed a capacity to explain their own experiences of marginalization in relation to structural inequality, and explorers typically described having experiences of privilege. Such capacities seemed to offer glimmers of the sociological imagination described by Mills. And yet it wouldn't be fair to credit these students with displaying it consistently. I refer to theirs as a *selectively* sociological imagination because, although they used structural explanations to describe their lived experiences, they quickly reverted to individualistic explanations when discussing the troubles of others.

A clear example of these patterns was presented in chapter 5, where Brian (an explorer) acknowledged his "very privileged life" as a "White . . . middle class" individual of "European heritage," only to later claim that "what I've learned is none of your background matters" when discussing the obstacles encountered by others. Similarly, Grace (a maximizer) spoke in detail about how her social location as an Asian American student from an immigrant family shaped her experiences with uncertainty in higher education, highlighting broad differences in the cultural norms, opportunity structures, and societal constraints of her family's preimmigration context in Thailand and those found in the US. Yet moments later, Grace claimed to be baffled by how anyone would struggle at CU. "Another aspect of being a successful college student is to make sure . . . you explore opportunities . . . because CU has so many resources, there should really be no reason that you should fail any class."

Just as individualistic perceptions of personal responsibility led LIFGWC students to absolve the university of blame for inequality, socioeconomically advantaged students frequently used their selectively sociological imaginations to do the same. Shahid (a maximizer) drove this point home. After describing how widespread stereotypes of Muslim students and stereotypes of immigrants had affected his college experiences, he used a very different explanation to account for the factors that influenced other students' experiences.

> I have a mindset that's different than most others. I think it's however much you put into it. Like I said, it's your initiative. I mean, the institutions' job, CU's job, is to provide you with classes and professors and material to study and whatnot. And so, it's what you do and what you decide to do with those materials that's going to make the difference. So, you can choose to study for an hour or two and then blame the institution for not preparing you as much, but you can also study for four or five hours and then not blame the institution.

Later in our conversation, Shahid chastised individuals who didn't take full advantage of university resources, declaring that "if you're going through all this and paying so much and if you're not taking advantage of the resources and the events going on, then that's up to you."

Because socioeconomically advantaged students used individualistic explanations of others' experiences, they usually laid blame for negative outcomes at the feet of their peers rather than the institution. The only exceptions occurred when a feature of the university negatively affected their own journeys through college. As previous chapters described, in those moments, maximizers and explorers were often able to draw on their dominant social and cultural capital to make the university work for them. In this way, adopting a selectively sociological imagination served to perpetuate inequality. For instance, while maximizers used insights about systemic inequality to inform their approaches to navigating college, positioning themselves to reproduce their parents' socioeconomic advantages, they were usually unwilling to leverage these understandings on behalf of their peers.

We might wonder, however, why socioeconomically advantaged White men (who were typically explorers) acknowledged their privilege rather than denying its existence to maintain advantages. As chapter 5 noted, for some explorers, talking about privilege seemed to contribute to their sense of ease, reaffirming the belief that they were insulated from external threats. Additionally, research suggests this tendency might be indicative of the ways students are learning to talk about their social location in order to be successful in various middle- and upper-middle-class contexts.[17] For instance, studies show that "diversity statements" and elements of interviews focusing on racial and gender privilege are becoming more common in hiring processes. In this way, socioeconomically advantaged White men's discussion of their privilege does not necessarily indicate progress toward greater equality; rather, it may actually be a way to reproduce their advantages in the transition from higher education to white-collar jobs. In the end, they managed to pay lip service to privilege without acknowledging oppression, thereby leaving their own social positions unchanged.[18]

But why was it that socioeconomically advantaged students developed sociological explanations of their experiences while LIFGWC students did not? Though my data offered no definitive answers, it did provide some clues. First, the selectively sociological imagination may have been the result of socio-economically advantaged students' more extensive involvement in certain extracurricular outlets and cocurricular opportunities.[19] For instance, Calvin described how "being a cis[gender] White man" was "a privilege that I've sort of learned more about as I've been a CU student," particularly through a training he took part in for peer leaders. Others spoke of student organization activities that explored privilege.

Second, it is important to remember that in the aggregate, LIFGWC and socioeconomically advantaged students tend to sort into different types of majors.[20] The arts, humanities, and social sciences, where approximately half of the socioeconomically advantaged students majored, were more likely to involve classes where these concepts (e.g., structural inequality and systemic racism, sexism, homophobia, etc.) were extensively engaged. This contrasts with the STEM and applied fields, where nearly 80 percent of LIFGWC students majored. A few students suggested as much when they talked about discussing social issues in classes with the history, film, English, and sociology programs.

Finally, it may be that these students' structural explanations of their experiences were reinforced by parents whose firsthand experiences in higher education and white-collar jobs equipped them with similar ways of thinking about the histories and present realities of racism, sexism, and other forms of structural inequality. As I discussed in chapter 4, for example, Caroline (a maximizer) described how her mother's encounters with institutionalized sexism at work informed her own concerns about gender-based discrimination in STEM fields. Regardless of how socioeconomically advantaged students developed sociological accounts of their own lived experiences, these accounts need to be examined with a critical lens. By failing to extend such perspectives to understand the experiences of peers who were marginalized in other ways, students perpetuated inequality.

Individualistic perspectives and selectively sociological imaginations were problematic in many respects. They contributed to self-blame, isolation, and the reproduction of inequality. Moreover, it was unfortunate that so many students' primary takeaway from going to college was an emphasis on independence. In this place, where people from a range of social locations come together to learn alongside one another, it would seem preferrable for students to learn interdependence, to build and be part of strong communities that provide mutual support.[21] The lessons for universities, described in the third section of this chapter, offer some possibilities for working in that direction.

LESSONS SCHOLARS CAN LEARN ABOUT INSECURITY AND INEQUALITY

The insights that come from studying students' journeys through a precarious university can teach scholars new things about how to understand insecurity, inequality, and their connections to one another. These insights have value for those working across the social sciences, including in sociology, anthropology, education, social psychology, and many other fields. When we examine the stories of individuals who are bombarded by precarity, we learn about what they do in moments where resources are stretched thin—moments when they must rely on the full capacities of their personal, familial, and institutional assets. The opportunity to see these three types of resources interacting can illuminate crucial dynamics of inequality and their reproduction through higher education.

Examining personal, family, and institutional resources simultaneously is easier said than done. The limitations of various methods, small samples, and other logistical constraints often mean that scholars must focus on a single resource type. Moreover, some sources of support generally receive less consideration in studies of higher education. For instance, while scholars often pay close attention to personal resources in the form of cultural capital, the impact of family resources—including parental economic, social, and cultural capital—tends to be conflated with personal resources or neglected entirely.[22] Laura Hamilton notes that although "there is a rich literature on how parents influence the educational experiences of younger youth" in K–12 education, consideration of family resources "often stops at the college gates" because "college students are thought to be mostly autonomous actors and parents are perceived as distant funders."[23] Moreover, it has only been within the past decade that sociologists brought sustained focus to the study of inequality in student experiences within higher education. These studies, with a few notable exceptions, have paid less attention to the influence of specific institutional resources and normative institutional arrangements.[24]

The ethnographic interviews that inform this book therefore provide a unique opportunity to generate more comprehensive understandings of the tools students bring to bear on navigating higher education. By considering personal, family, and university resources among a sufficiently large sample—104 students in total—we can see how students' experiences at the intersections of socioeconomic status, race, gender, and other sociodemographic dimensions shape the resource configurations they come to rely on for dealing with insecurity in college.

Recognizing the influence of each of these resource configurations can help scholars move beyond simplistic notions that some groups of students have or lack a single consequential resource. In the literature on community cultural wealth, there is often an essentialist assumption that students from marginalized backgrounds will always possess community wealth endowed by their supportive families. This literature typically lacks attention to variation in familial support. Similarly, many studies in the cultural capital tradition place emphasis on whether students possess dominant forms of capital without considering variation in their elements, exercise, or impact.[25] The findings presented in *Degrees of Risk* offer a corrective to both tendencies. Put simply, the students who took part in this study showed that rather than access to resources being all-or-nothing, individuals often have differential access to specific facets of social and cultural resources based on how they're positioned in relation to family, the institution, and society more broadly.

COMPLICATING THEORIES OF COMMUNITY CULTURAL WEALTH

My findings help expand understandings of the complexity of community cultural wealth. To begin with, not all LIFGWC students benefit from the full array of cultural wealth described by Tara Yosso.[26] Though Yosso herself did not claim that the forms of wealth were a package deal, many who have employed her framework have built this assumption into their conceptualization of resources. The result is that scholars frequently rely on essentialist understandings of LIFGWC students, students of color, and students from immigrant families. Yet the differences I have documented between pioneers and minimizers make clear that students' access to the dimensions of community cultural wealth is highly variable.

This variability stems from inequality in the degree to which LIFGWC students enter college with familial support.[27] On the one hand, pioneers reported receiving little support from their families. Strained relationships or limited interactions with parents, siblings, and other relatives meant that they often felt on their own in higher education. With few of the dominant social, cultural, or economic resources expected by the university, they usually had to rely on their personal capacities to recover from crises, exercising resilience to move forward from setbacks. By contrast, most minimizers received encouragement and insight from parents and other relatives. With this support they learned from the ways their family members persisted in unwelcoming institutions to resist many of the inequitable tendencies of the university, pushing back against the insecurity that abounded at CU. The painstaking efforts they made to leverage elements of community cultural wealth and chart a smooth path through college meant that they did not need to rely on personal resilience to the same degree as pioneers.

By moving beyond the assumption that all LIFGWC students have supportive families, we can begin to distinguish between the types of capital these students bring with them to higher education, better understanding the impact of various resource configurations. Recognizing that some students have the familial support to generate proactive strategies for resisting insecurity while others may need to employ personal capacities for resilience helps to illuminate how consequential inequalities emerge between students who are otherwise similar in terms of background and sociodemographic characteristics. This can equip scholars to push back against simplistic explanations of these inequalities—like differences in "motivation" or "talent"—that too often take center stage not just in popular culture and media but also in policy and practice surrounding education.[28]

Future research should more closely explore how and when variation in familial support emerges. While my data were not able to speak to this dimension of inequality, the findings of other studies offer hints about where we might look. For instance, Josipa Roksa and her colleagues show how the presence of older siblings who attended college can shape the ways cultural resources move through families by lubricating pathways for sharing information, encouragement, and other kinds of support.[29] Similarly, other scholars show that the cultural norms of certain educational settings can create friction between students and their families.[30]

Understanding how these variables inform access to familial support can facilitate deeper accounts of how inequality emerges among LIFGWC students. Building knowledge in this direction requires that scholars move away from notions that this group is monolithic. As sociologists Janel Benson and Elizabeth Lee note in their book *Geographies of Campus Inequality*, less socioeconomically advantaged students "have a wide range of experiences at college" that relate to "significant and meaningful differences" in students'

164 CHAPTER SEVEN

broader college journeys.[31] Acknowledging variation in access to familial support and related elements of community cultural wealth can further explain these differences.

COMPLICATING THEORIES OF CULTURAL CAPITAL

The lessons of precarity also add important nuance to theories of cultural capital. First, they underscore that not all socioeconomically advantaged students possess every dimension of cultural capital theorized by Bourdieu and those who have followed this tradition. Over the years, understandings of cultural capital in research on education have grown broad and sometimes ambiguous, encapsulating knowledge, practices, and a series of related dispositions.[32] But recently, some scholars have become more precise in articulating its specific dimensions. For instance, sociologist Denise Deutschlander illuminates how cultural capital manifests as both general and specific information—what scholars of higher education sometimes refer to as "college knowledge"—that comes from familiarity with a setting acquired through parents or specific kinds of lived experiences.[33] She suggests that these general and specific dimensions should be considered separately in research because of the ways they play different roles in reproducing inequality across generations. Separate from information, Shamus Khan described another key dimension of cultural capital in the form of "ease," a sense of comfort that can be especially advantageous in elite educational settings.[34]

This book contributes to that conversation, showing how even socioeconomically advantaged students have unequal access to ease. Though maximizers and explorers alike had similar information about navigating higher education, divergent understandings of their intersectional social locations meant that they had very different feelings about their security within and beyond college. Socioeconomically advantaged White men often possessed large stocks of economic, social, and cultural capital, including both college knowledge and ease. They felt buffered from the dangers of uncertainty and came to navigate college as explorers. Meanwhile, socioeconomically advantaged participants who identified as students of color, women, members of marginalized religious communities, immigrants, LGBTQ+, and individuals with disabilities did not usually have the luxury of ease. Their encounters with prejudice and discrimination elevated anxieties about the future, and they often leveraged a combination of economic capital, social capital, and college knowledge to demonstrate merit and build a résumé that they hoped would shelter them from marginalization.

These patterns underscore the ways an intersectional lens is crucial for

THE LESSONS OF PRECARITY   165

understanding disparities that emerge within the demographic categories used to understand inequality. Only accounting for typical dimensions of socio-economic status—such as parental income, education, or occupation—would miss the meaningful differences between maximizers and explorers. Even a study that considered socioeconomic status and one other sociodemographic characteristic (like race or gender) would probably have failed to observe the pronounced differences between affluent White men and their peers from the same socioeconomic backgrounds who experienced marginalization on the basis of race, gender, religion, immigration histories, ability, and sexual orientation. This attention to intersectional variation exposes how social location doesn't just inform access to money and information but also shapes whether students experience their identities as a privilege or a liability—and by proxy, whether socioeconomically advantaged individuals embody ease.

In addition to appreciating this variation in the impact of cultural capital *within* socioeconomic groups, the findings presented in this book teach us something important about inequality *between* such groups. Specifically, the lessons of precarity show that one's level of college knowledge is an insuffi-cient (not inaccurate, but incomplete) explanation of how inequality emerges between LIFGWC students and their socioeconomically advantaged peers. Most previous research explains socioeconomic differences in college en-gagement as the result of differential access to information, emphasizing the role of "knowledge gaps" in producing inequality.[35] Though access to infor-mation is certainly important, it is not the sole force driving inequality in higher education. Rather, it is also apparent that students make different deci-sions about college engagement based on the ways their personal and family resources position them in relation to institutional resources. The result is that some students select or avoid certain types of engagement based on self-protective strategies that have less to do with information than with the fact that universities structure opportunities for involvement in ways that align or conflict with their dispositions.[36]

This could be seen most clearly in the case of minimizers, who avoided certain types of college opportunities (such as extracurricular activities, study abroad, unpaid internships, and even certain kinds of financial aid) because they recognized that engaging with them could be risky. Cognizant that their university wasn't providing all of the institutional resources needed to make these opportunities safe, they opted out of participation. In this way, mini-mizers shouldn't be viewed as passive individuals who simply lacked infor-mation but as strategic social actors who used community cultural wealth to avoid becoming derailed by insecurity.

Similarly, most LIFGWC students, including pioneers, took note of when university resources were limited (e.g., meetings with advisors who had large caseloads or office hours with overworked contingent faculty) and sometimes avoided engaging with these resources not out of lack of awareness but because they were trying to be sensitive to the circumstances of these overextended employees. Furthermore, maximizers and explorers showed clear differences in the quantity of opportunities with which they engaged; these differences were about ease and anxiety rather than information. By shifting beyond a focus on college knowledge as the primary manifestation of cultural capital, scholars can begin to pay greater attention to dispositions and related practices that contribute to inequality in student experiences and outcomes.

Collectively, the lessons this book offers to scholars can help foster awareness of the diverse configurations of personal, family, and institutional resources that interact with students' social location to inform their encounters with insecurity in college. The preceding chapters show that doing so requires stepping out of scholarly camps and integrating various conceptions of resources to more fully account for the impact of both agency and structure.[37] All students bring certain assets to higher education, and these assets contribute in unique ways to their efforts to achieve social mobility or social reproduction. And yet personal and family resources cannot place students on an even playing field because the structure of the university positions them unequally.

Despite abstract praise for "resilience," CU failed to reward pioneers' diligence. In a similar fashion, minimizers' careful planning and focus on academic progress was framed as insufficient engagement, and the university's emphasis on self-discovery extended recognition to explorers in a way that it did not for maximizers. In sum, inequality between groups of students isn't simply about having or lacking resources; it is driven by the degree of alignment between available resources, social location, and the insecurity culture that pervades higher education. This observation underscores the crucial role that could be played by university faculty, staff, administrators, and policymakers in combatting insecurity and inequality. That is the direction to which I turn next in the third and final segment of this chapter.

Lessons for Universities to Alleviate Insecurity

The insecurity that saturates higher education today is a problem—one that needs to be addressed. The previous chapters depict the hardship confronted by many students when their college journeys are unpredictable and uncertain. This insecurity undermines their ability to meet goals and prepare for the future. It amplifies inequalities among students and teaches them problematic lessons about the world. To deal with these issues, higher education leaders—faculty, staff, administrators, and policymakers alike—must work against insecurity, building postsecondary institutions that provide the stability students need to succeed in college.

The findings presented in the previous chapter offered a framework for distinguishing between two types of institutional arrangements: *insecurity amplifiers* and *security boosters*. To become more equitable, colleges and universities must revise policies and practices in order to remove insecurity amplifiers. These normative institutional arrangements benefit students who are comfortable navigating complex bureaucracies and taking risks while undermining those who are not, thereby exacerbating inequality between students with different capacities for dealing with uncertainty. This book documents four main insecurity amplifiers in the form of (1) pervasive choice and flexibility, (2) invisible student support services, (3) reactive support practices, and (4) decentralized organization of services.

Though these arrangements are taken for granted at many institutions, they are not the only options available. How could colleges and universities move past them to offer something different? I argue that such change would require that universities replace each of the insecurity amplifiers outlined above with security boosters, such as (1) structured guidance, (2) visible student support, (3) proactive practices, and (4) integrated services. Here I propose several strategies for making this type of progress.

SERVE A BROADER GROUP OF STUDENTS, NOT "CUSTOMERS"

The affluent out-of-state student cannot remain the primary focus of public universities. Higher education leaders must recognize a broader range of student experiences, backgrounds, and resources. This requires responding to the needs of a much more diverse student population. As the previous chapters show, such change involves working against powerful forces, both internal and external to the university. For instance, leaders must confront institutional isomorphism, or the tendency for organizations to become increasingly similar over time.[38] When schools like CU seek to mimic other colleges and universities—especially elite ones—they adopt policies and practices that fail to recognize the unique characteristics and needs of their own students.[39]

It's not difficult to understand why so many administrators feel obliged to focus their attention on affluent students and treat them like customers. They rely on the tuition payments made by wealthy families in order to stay afloat.[40]

In other words, as the first chapter of this book explained, the fiscal pressures institutions encounter drive tendencies to design universities for a particular kind of affluent student. It is crucial that federal and state policymakers recognize the problems with this dynamic and fund higher education. Without ample funding, it will remain difficult for institutions to adequately serve students, especially those who are LIFGWC and those who are marginalized on the basis of race, gender, and other sociodemographic characteristics. Fortunately, scholars have offered a range of promising strategies for improving the financial situations of public postsecondary institutions.[41]

Increased funding is essential. But higher education leaders cannot wait for a change in government appropriations to begin their efforts to serve a more diverse group of students. With the resources currently at their disposal, colleges and universities need to prioritize robust student support services— academic advising, tutoring, mental health counseling, and other resources designed to help students navigate the challenges of college life. Additionally, higher education leaders need to reconsider the ways they frame what a successful "college experience" looks like. In this book we saw how the types of self-actualization that appealed to socioeconomically advantaged students did not usually seem feasible or safe to their less advantaged peers.[42] When universities extol the virtues of engagement beyond the classroom in the form of extracurricular activities or unpaid internships, for example, they prop up the types of involvement that are most accessible to the affluent, leaving unacknowledged the commitments—to academic priorities, skill development, paid employment, and family—that are central to the lives of many LIFGWC students.

This was especially clear when juxtaposing the experiences of minimizers and maximizers. For instance, whereas Rachel (a maximizer) scooped up "a wealth of opportunities" to be part of clubs, internships, and community service, minimizers were unnerved by CU's emphasis on cocurricular and extracurricular engagement. The way the university framed these opportunities as "achievement," without making them accessible to a broad range of students, proved to be especially frustrating.[43] Near the end of her interview, Hannah (a minimizer) recalled filling out a university survey that inquired about her "biggest accomplishment at CU." She suspected that the question was inquiring about experiences such as internships, study abroad, campus leadership, and other extracurricular engagement. The frustration in her voice was obvious as she recalled, "I pretty much said, the fact that I did the damn thing. The fact that I came here and got a degree was my biggest accomplishment, because that's all that I really came to college for was to get a degree and gain skills." Even as she completed the final credits for her degree, Hannah continued to feel like her dedication to making academic progress while working full-time was not recognized or appreciated at CU.[44]

Moreover, by allowing uncertainty to run rampant and praising open-ended self-discovery, universities cater most directly to dispositions that this book shows are found primarily among affluent White men. Recall, for instance, how Brian "felt unsatisfied with things that were certain" and appreciated the university's emphasis on unstructured opportunities for personal growth. While he and other socioeconomically advantaged White men embraced insecurity, most of their peers found it to be daunting. This included the socioeconomically advantaged maximizers who experienced marginalization on the basis of race, gender, sexual orientation, immigration histories, religion, and ability. As Kaylin (a maximizer) described in chapter 4, for these students, open-ended trajectories through higher education seemed impractical. Instead, she tried to confront the "vulnerability" she felt as a Muslim woman from an immigrant family and "channel it to something else" by becoming engaged in myriad outlets to avoid putting "all your eggs in one basket." These findings align with other research showing that universities often assume a White student body and create environments that advantage men even when demographic change in higher education means that the majority of students on many campuses are students of color and women.[45]

Finally, universities should not simply replace one imagined customer with another. Instead, institutions need to stop treating students as consumers altogether. Students are many things. They are learners; they are scholars and researchers; they are family members and neighbors; they are professionals in training; and they are certainly important members of the university community. But they are not customers. Nonetheless, so many social, economic, and political changes in the US have made them feel like consumers in educational settings, and universities have contributed to this sense in a variety of ways.[46]

The outcomes of the customer-service model of higher education have been alarming. Research shows that it fosters campus environments that prioritize partying, detract from academic rigor, and undermine learning.[47] This occurs in part because of the pressures placed on faculty and staff to ensure satisfaction, make college easier, and inflate grades.[48] Moreover, this model perpetuates inequality. Studies, including this one, expose the ways a customer-service approach advantages middle- and upper-middle-class students—who tend to be more comfortable being positioned as customers— over their working-class peers.[49]

Moreover, I argue that treating college students as customers undermines their abilities to develop a sociological imagination. By encouraging students to see themselves as consumers investing in an individual good, universities effectively obscure the connections between individuals, their communities, and the broader social forces that shape their lives. These tendencies foster the specific approaches to understanding life circumstances that show up in the individualistic perspectives and selectively sociological imaginations described in the first section of this chapter.

In short, building a more secure and equitable university means working with students as students, not customers. And when higher education leaders think of the individuals who enroll in their institutions, they need to do so in ways that recognize a diverse range of social locations, experiences, and needs. Rather than having a single idea of the type of student who goes to college, institutions must constantly consider their policies and practices from a range of perspectives, examining their impact on a diverse student body.

BUILD A GUIDED PATH, NOT A BUFFET

Once higher education leaders move beyond a customer-service model to consider the needs of a broader group of students, they can build universities that are different. To do so, faculty, staff, and administrators need to develop clearly structured pathways through college, rethinking the emphasis on choice and limited structure in higher education. Where possible, choices should be focused. The students I spoke with over the course of this study were confronted with an avalanche of consequential decisions: which residence hall to live in, where to seek out tutoring, which semester to take a foreign language class, whether to sign up for an optional meeting with an advisor, which office to ask for approval of transfer credits, or whether to declare a concentration in one's major. For students who had little familiarity with higher education, each of these choices represented an opportunity for miscalculation.

Of course, students have to make certain choices, such as selecting a field of study, for instance. Given that choice is frequently necessary, options should be organized in clear ways that support easy navigation and minimize costly mistakes. Even Grace, a socioeconomically advantaged maximizer who saw options as desirable, acknowledged that "when you have more options, it's more uncertainty about what's going to happen, what are we going to choose?" In other words, the insecurity brought on by choice is obvious to students who navigate our colleges day in and day out. But higher education leaders need to spend more time understanding the implications of this point.

Thinking about choice and flexibility in more critical ways provides an opportunity to foster student experiences that feel less like navigating an expansive buffet and more like a guided meal at the chef's counter—or at least much closer to the latter than the former. Students will still make choices, but the overarching structure is designed to lessen the risk of becoming lost. As chapter 6 showed, the focused choices between a few options in the Linked Pathways program were helpful for many students. Weaving similar structures throughout higher education—in the curriculum, cocurriculum, and extracurriculum alike—could have positive impacts.

Though this work will require pushing back against an emphasis on consumer choice, flexibility does not have to be eradicated to make a better university. In fact some forms of flexibility can be widely beneficial. A clear example can be found in curricular policies. Creating clearly laid out plans of study that don't penalize missteps or reasonable exploration could help individuals regardless of socioeconomic background. For example, a student who wants to explore a class in art history could receive approval to substitute the class for their recommended studio art course. The point is that rather than starting from a sea of options, students could begin with a clearly illustrated path and modify it as circumstances require.

Similarly, expanding certain types of flexibility at the K–12 level, especially in high schools, could provide students with opportunities to practice navigating focused choices with ample guidance before college enrollment. Many of the participants in this study emphasized that the ease of becoming lost or overwhelmed in college was in part due to the drastic change in the amount of structure students encountered in high school compared with college. The accumulation of state- and federal-level policies promoting common educational standards in the late twentieth and early twenty-first century made contemporary K–12 education highly structured.[50] As Daniel noted in the prologue, "It was structured in high school. . . . But when we got to university, it's like, 'look, we're not going to tell you how to do anything. Everything you do is up to you.' . . . At the end of the day, every decision you make is on you." This disjuncture could be smoothed by pairing guided pathways in college with greater opportunity to practice navigating choices in high school.

Part of building guided pathways in higher education is making student support services visible. This can happen in myriad ways. First, it can occur when there is enough funding to allow offices to hire adequate staffing. Commonwealth University's Center for Diversity and Inclusion was visible to few students in part because, with just two full-time staff members, it was unlikely that students would learn about this office or encounter its representatives at campus events or programs. Well-funded student support offices can engage in the types of communication needed to be an active presence in students' lives.

Second, the visibility of student support services can be fostered by pairing resources with students' curricular experiences. A second-year business major shouldn't have to go searching for tutoring in finance or for a career counselor to help with finding an internship. These resources could be integrated within the curriculum to match challenges with support.[51] In this way, resources could become a built-in part of students' programs of study rather than an array of options.[52] Such an approach means that many resources would become opt out rather than opt in, so that students are no longer assumed to have preexisting knowledge of how to navigate complex bureaucracies or dispositions toward engaging with extensive opportunities.

Finally, a guided pathway with visible support becomes most feasible when university resources are centralized and interconnected. This requires reducing the decentralization that amplifies insecurity on college campuses so that instead of having resources scattered across a range of disjointed offices, universities bring them together in ways that are more intuitive for students. Such goals can be furthered by considering the spatial configuration of resources (how are they organized across a campus), the distribution of various responsibilities, as well as the policies and practices that shape how staff interface with one another to support students. In addition to making services visible, centralized resources are also easier to use, requiring less movement back and forth between offices.

Collectively, these strategies can promote new normative institutional arrangements that act as security boosters, reducing the uncertainties students encounter along their journeys through college. The University Honors Program, for example, provided an illustrative contrast to the tendencies observed elsewhere at CU. By integrating support (like peer mentors) into the curriculum and creating practices that brought together a cohesive support network (faculty, advisors, and a student success coordinator), the program ensured that resources for students were visible and connected in ways that made them widely accessible. Scaling these types of arrangements across universities could bring similar benefits to larger groups of students.

THINK SMALL, NOT JUST BIG

Many of the strategies described above are large in scale. They require changes in state and federal policymaking, university structure, and campus culture. Yet there are also strategies that can be implemented within specific offices and everyday practices. Though they may be smaller in scale, they can accumulate to have a substantial impact. Perhaps the most important of these is the adoption of proactive outreach strategies for student support services units. Reactive practices that wait for students to identify a need and find an individual capable of providing help are the norm in most offices.[53] But this does not have to be the case.

Faculty, staff, and administrators can work to create practices that bring resources directly to students without them having to ask. The previous section highlighted the value of integrating resources into the curriculum. Though some of these efforts will occur at the level of university-wide curricular design, others can be initiated by smaller groups of faculty and staff. A professor and career counselor might partner to bring a workshop on developing résumés and cover letters to students enrolled in an upper-division anthropology course. In a similar way, a faculty member teaching a research class might partner with the campus writing center to provide additional support with composition.

Other resources may not be as easy to link with a specific class but could be targeted more effectively to specific students with the support of data. For instance, an early intervention system, like the one employed by the University Honors Program, could use information on absences and students' first exams or assignment scores in each of their classes to proactively identify individuals in need of support. Additionally, surveys that capture interests and goals could be used to introduce students to tailored opportunities offered by specific offices or practitioners. For example, a student who indicates interest in going to law school could be connected with a prelaw advisor early in their program of study.

I want to emphasize that these practices cannot rely on individual faculty or staff to overextend themselves. When university personnel are themselves overwhelmed by precarity, it is nearly impossible to foster stability for students.[54] Universities and policymakers must make it feasible to initiate proactive support by providing the funding and structures described in the previous section. Additionally, faculty, staff, and administrators must ensure that the practices they implement are sustainable ones. The difference between sustainable and unsustainable proactive support could be seen in an anecdote shared by April, who recalled struggling to obtain a laptop for her coursework.

> Until recently, I wasn't able to purchase my own laptop. . . . I was in a situation where I had no way to take my exams . . . and one of my professors actually helped me out. She loaned me her personal laptop, so that I could take the exams, which was staggering to me. It was really sweet.

April was incredibly grateful for this gesture from her professor, and it was certainly proactive for the faculty member to step in and provide help before one of her students missed an exam.[55] Yet this type of intervention represents a substantial burden that would probably be difficult or impossible for most university personnel.

As it turned out, there were multiple offices on campus where students like April could access computer labs or rent a laptop for class. Unfortunately, these resources were not well known. Procedures could have been employed to gather information from students regarding access to technology and connect individuals with the tools they needed. Such an approach represents a sustainable proactive practice that doesn't place emotional, material, or financial burdens on faculty and staff. These more sustainable arrangements also make it possible for students not to have to rely on the goodwill of others but instead to be able to count on resources that will be available on a consistent basis.

In addition to proactive practices, faculty and staff can work to create policies, procedures, and resource distributions that make students' college journeys more predictable. For instance, making course rotations visible multiple semesters in advance could support students' efforts to plan ahead. Georgia (a minimizer) drove this point home as she described being thrown off track in a course sequence when she was unable to register for a prerequisite class that wasn't offered in the spring semester. At the time of her interview in early December, she noted that although she was hoping the class would run the following fall, she wouldn't be sure until the course list was posted in March.

Those with oversight of financial aspects of college attendance should work in comparable ways to make paying for college more straightforward. Limiting the use of add-on charges for classes, labs, events, and other programs could help mitigate the financial precarity students confront in college. Lakshmi (a minimizer) recalled her frustration that CU seemed to be "sneaking so many fees" into the cost of her education through charges for required events, materials, and supplemental course fees. While it may not be possible to eliminate all add-on charges or fold them into standard tuition and fees, administrators should at the very least ensure they are easier for students to anticipate by identifying them multiple semesters in advance in plan-of-study documents.

Efforts to make students' journeys through college more predictable could show up in a variety of other ways as well. For instance, policies that distribute scholarships over multiple years would be helpful. Lance illustrated this point as he described the hardships that arose when a CU scholarship he'd thought would last for the duration of his studies turned out to be only for his first year.[56] Faculty and staff could bring similar approaches to supporting predictability into the ways they organize everything from classes and programs to campus housing and dining. Regardless of where these strategies show up, they can have a similar impact: by helping students anticipate their pathways through college with greater clarity, they can support the kinds of stability and continuity that foster student success.

Finally, faculty and staff should consider pedagogical strategies that can help students understand their lived experiences—especially experiences with insecurity during college—in dialogue with the broader social, historical, and political contexts that shape those experiences. When discussing academic achievement, campus involvement, or future careers, it will be helpful to do so in ways that acknowledge the impact of insecurity on students and the ways it infuses their lives. In other words, faculty and staff need to equip them with the tools for developing a sociological imagination, one that can make going to college less isolating, empower students to make change, and support them in building more equitable communities. This can happen in the classroom, when faculty engage topics through the lenses of social, historical, and political contexts. And this can happen beyond the classroom when practitioners create programs and resources that help students situate their lived experiences in those contexts.

The strategies outlined here are far from exhaustive. They are meant to illustrate how changes to the normative institutional arrangements of the university—both broad changes to university structure and more focused changes to everyday practice—can boost security. These new arrangements can eliminate the need for individuals to arrive in college with dominant resources; they can avoid tendencies to privilege students who are most comfortable with risk; and they can make college more predictable, helping students envision and follow more secure paths through higher education. Collectively, these strategies make it possible to promote success for diverse groups of students regardless of the types of resources, identities, and experiences they bring to college.

As students, scholars, and higher education leaders explore the lessons of precarity, I hope this book can play a part in bringing about positive change. I hope student readers might find in its pages concepts that will inform a sociological imagination, equipping them with tools for building and being part of strong communities. I hope scholars will come to account for inequality and insecurity in ways that support more critical understandings of our social world. And I hope university leaders will find useful insights about how to create more equitable and effective institutions.

Acknowledgments

There are many individuals and organizations deserving of thanks for their role in bringing this book to publication. First, this project benefitted from the early and ongoing support of the wonderful folks at the University of Chicago Press. Elizabeth Branch Dyson continues to foster the expansion of the sociology of higher education, bringing new and exciting ideas into the conversation. This book couldn't exist without her dedication and encouragement. Once again, Mollie McFee made each of the steps toward publication seamless, and I owe many thanks to Olivia Aguilar, Steve LaRue, Lindsy Rice, and the other members of the production and promotions teams.

I have been fortunate to have numerous mentors, colleagues, and friends at George Mason University who have championed my work and provided opportunities for me to expand and refine it. Dan Temple has been a supportive chair whose critical perspectives on higher education make the Department of Sociology and Anthropology a generative place to ask interesting questions and pursue answers. I am thankful for Jamie Clark, John Dale, Shannon Davis, Rutledge Dennis, Katherine Foarde, Nancy Hanrahan, Katy Hoepf, Cortney Hughes Rinker, Farhana Islam, Dae Young Kim, Haagen Klaus, Lester Kurtz, Brian Levy, Huwy-min Liu, Ben Manski, Patricia Masters, Christopher Morris, Manjusha Nair, Amaka Okechukwu, Rashmi Sadana, Anne Schiller, Joseph Scimecca, Rick Smith, Elizangela Storelli, Susan Trencher, and James Witte, who are always kind and generous with their time.

I am likewise grateful for the support of the Center for Social Science Research (CSSR) and the members of the Education and Health Research Hub. Amy Best, the center director and fellow sociologist, has been a dedicated mentor. In addition to supporting my work at every turn, Amy convened

CSSR's Friday Writing Group, where I had the opportunity to work alongside a supportive community of scholars including Marisa Allison, Michelle Dromgold-Sermen, LeNaya Hezel, Emily McDonald, Sara Montiel, Sarah Ochs, Carol Petty, Matthew Sedlar, Emma Vetter, Kellie Wilkerson, and others. Katharine Rupp, CSSR's office manager, coordinated logistical elements of grant administration for this project and facilitated access to technologies that made this research possible.

In Mason's Honors College, I am fortunate to have encouraging and steadfast colleagues. Their work to build more secure and effective educational pathways is always inspiring. Andy Hoefer and John Woolsey read and provided valuable feedback on chapters. Jan Allbeck, Eva Bramesco, Zofia Burr, Vanessa Correa, Melanie Fedri, Gaby Guzman, Tabatha Hargrove, Michael Hock, Nadeen Makhlouf, Holly Marvin, Una Murphy, Tahmina Rahman, Jasmyne Rogers, Richard Todd Stafford, Telecia Taylor, and Caroline West took time to discuss many of the complexities of student experiences explored in this book.

Matthew Ahlfs, Matthew Boero, and Fanni Farago provided incredible research assistance, conducting interviews, producing transcripts, and helping to gather some of the materials for the ethnographic archive. Kristopher Cleland and Tharuna Kalaivanan contributed their attention to detail to the process of finalizing transcripts.

I also want to thank colleagues and mentors beyond George Mason University who took the time to pass along their wisdom in support of this book. Josipa Roksa offered timely perspectives on the project design and preliminary findings. Allison Pugh and Lisa Nunn read portions of the book and provided insightful comments and suggestions. Rashawn Ray and Jenny Stuber shared their reflections on normative institutional arrangements. And, at an Eastern Sociological Society conference session, Geoff Harkness gave valuable feedback on the project's connections to literature and theory.

I want to express my gratitude to the American Sociological Association (ASA) for generously supporting data collection for this project through a Fund for the Advancement of the Discipline Grant. It was also at an ASA meeting that I first had the opportunity to present some of the findings of this project, and I am grateful to the attendees at that session for their helpful feedback.

Study participants play a unique role in making qualitative research, especially projects centered around interviews, possible and worthwhile. The students at Commonwealth University were generous with their time and perspectives. During the height of the COVID-19 pandemic, when so many

ACKNOWLEDGMENTS

other priorities were competing for their attention, these students sat down to talk about their journeys through college.

Finally, I am always thankful—and occasionally remember to say so—for my family and friends. This book was completed with their support and encouragement, especially Laurie, who proofread the manuscript; Nader and Oliver; Luisa, Novie, and Charlie; Wayne, Brett, Blair, Meghan, Andy, Judy, and Rollins; Nadia, Nick, Alex, Maci, Manal, Paul, Juliana, and Jack. Thank you all.

APPENDIX

Methods

Studying Precarity

Understanding how students experience and navigate insecurity in higher education required research methods that centered participants' voices while also illuminating relevant dimensions of the institutional context in which they found themselves. In other words, it was important to examine students' firsthand accounts of their college journeys as well as the university where those journeys took place. For this reason, I relied on ethnographic interviews that paired formal, in-depth interviewing with an archive of supporting materials and field notes.

The decision to use ethnographic interviews for this project was informed by the work of sociologists Rachel Rinaldo and Jeffrey Guhin, who situate qualitative methods on a spectrum ranging from survey-like interviews that are decoupled from a broader context to observations that do not involve talking to or interacting with participants.[1] In the middle of this spectrum sits the ethnographic interview, which pairs semistructured interviews with ethnographic detail. Specifically, my project relies on an approach where "formal interviews are the driving method, but they are supported by ethnographic context."[2] This makes it possible to understand both the social psychological dimensions of participants' lived experiences alongside specific mesolevel influences on those experiences—in this case, the ways the university and its normative institutional arrangements affect students.[3]

Research Site

This study began in the fall of 2020, during the first year of the COVID-19 pandemic. Knowing that conducting the research in a safe way would require virtual data collection opened up the possibility of studying almost any institution. A great deal of research on higher education takes place at a small swath of elite, highly resourced colleges and universities.[4] Yet my desire to understand student experiences with insecurity meant that it was important to select a research site that could illuminate the types of resource constraints that are common across a far wider segment of higher education. As the first chapter of this book describes, I decided to seek out what Hamilton and Nielsen call a "new university."[5] I also wanted to conduct this study at an institution with a diverse student body to ensure it would be feasible to examine variation in experiences at the intersections of socioeconomic status, race, gender, and other sociodemographic dimensions.

182   APPENDIX

With these priorities in mind, I chose an institution I refer to as Commonwealth University (CU), a pseudonym meant to evoke various meanings embedded in the word *commonwealth*. First, I wanted to emphasize for readers that CU represents a "common" type of institution as part of the largest segment of contemporary higher education: public four-year schools.[6] I also hoped this name could signal the ways this study complicates notions of the types of resources (wealth) universities believe to be widely accessible (common) for students. Finally, the word *commonwealth* has multiple meanings; one of these is "common well-being; esp. the general good, welfare, or prosperity of a community, country, etc., as a whole."[7] This pseudonym then also references the (often unfulfilled) ideal that this university and so many other public institutions claim to uphold of higher education as a public good.

The decision to use a pseudonym comes with trade-offs. While not naming the university risks losing certain kinds of insights about the particulars of the research site, it also makes it feasible to be more precise and detailed in discussing participants' experiences without using methods such as the creation of composite characters that would require sacrificing analytical leverage.[8] Additionally, students feel invested in the external reputation of their institution, and I have found that participants often seem more comfortable being honest and critical of their experiences when they are reassured that the name of the institution will not be featured in publications. I also agree with Anthony Jack's assertion that in many cases, revealing the identity of the research site can be a distraction that allows higher education leaders at other institutions to quickly claim that "we are different," ignoring transferable insights that extend well beyond the specific institution studied.[9]

I began describing CU in chapter 1, and subsequent chapters expanded on many of its features. However, there were other characteristics of the university that deserve mention here. The organization of student services at CU aligned with what scholars of higher education refer to as a "personnel model" or an "administration-centered model."[10] In other words, it featured a type of bureaucracy that prioritized the ways administrators think about their work rather than responding to students' needs. The result was that offices operated as distinct entities with few efforts to coordinate or create a more seamless experience. When students are imagined in this type of environment, they are understood as customers who desire abundant opportunities and few requirements. In addition to being one of the oldest ways of organizing student services, the administration-centered model remains one of the most common. Advocates for students continue to call for more effective integration of student services with academic affairs to foster student success, but change in this direction has been slow or nonexistent at many institutions.[11]

Though data collection for the study occurred virtually, I also took time to explore the physical campus in order to understand the place where so many students lived and studied—even in the midst of the pandemic. It was a lively environment. People filled the sidewalks and other open spaces. Modern buildings and beautiful gardens contributed to the aesthetic appeal of the campus. But they also obscured some of the hardship encountered by students. As I admired the stunning glass-walled atrium of a brand-new building, I could appreciate the frustration some students expressed that academic support services seemed to be stretched so thin while campus construction boomed. Of course, those familiar with funding for higher education know that money for a building is not the same as money to hire more academic advisors.[12] Yet seeing this place made it easy to understand the dissonance students might feel.

Commonwealth University's campus was also expansive. On just one walk, I spotted multiple student unions, gymnasiums, and dining halls. I noticed that the names of academic buildings did not correspond with departments or programs. Some brandished the surnames of university

METHODS   183

leaders or donors, while others sounded like motivational slogans with words that suggested curiosity, creativity, and success. There was no "Chemistry Building" or "Sciences Hall." And the dormitories sprinkled across campus were virtually indistinguishable from academic and administrative buildings. It wasn't hard to imagine feeling lost or overwhelmed in such a place.

Study Participants

When it was time to start collecting data for the project, I began reaching out to faculty, staff, and students who sent calls for participants to various email lists. These individuals shared my message with the programs they coordinated, the classes they taught, and the student organizations they led. Commonwealth University students who had been enrolled in college for at least one year were eligible to participate. Volunteers emailed me to schedule a time for a virtual interview. In all, 104 students took part in the study.

As I illustrated in chapter 1, these students reflected the diversity of CU, which facilitated analysis of the intersections of socioeconomic status, race, gender, and other sociodemographic dimensions. Table 1.1 portrayed the sample in terms of first-generation status, Pell Grant eligibility, race/ethnicity, and gender. It was also diverse in other respects. There were thirty-six working-class, twelve lower-middle-class, twenty-two middle-class, and thirty-four upper-middle-class students. In terms of major, 47 percent were in science, technology, engineering, math, and health fields; 32 percent were in the humanities, the arts, and the social sciences; 16 percent were in business or applied social and behavioral sciences; and 5 percent had double majors that spanned two of these categories. The sample was divided evenly between students who described themselves as "sophomores," "juniors," and "seniors" in terms of their accumulated course credits. Approximately half of the students were from immigrant families, and a third had transferred from another institution to attend CU.

While I relied on participants' self-identification of race, gender, immigrant generation, major, and other characteristics, the components of socioeconomic status deserve additional explanation here. Table A.1 offers a visual representation of the indicators of socioeconomic status and how they typically hung together. Gathering information on parental education was relatively straightforward, and I classified students whose parents or guardians had not completed a four-year college degree as first-generation college students. Those whose parents or guardians possessed bachelor's degrees (and sometimes graduate or professional degrees) were categorized as continuing-generation college students.

Defining family income and class background was more complex. Because of well-documented challenges with asking students about how much money their parents or guardians make, I used two indicators of income.[13] The first was students' eligibility for financial aid reserved for low-income families, especially Pell Grants. There were thirty-five students who mentioned such aid in their interviews. I classified an additional six students as low-income because although they did not claim eligibility for these forms of financial aid, they described having limited family finances. Income was therefore treated as binary. Students who met one of these criteria were classified as "low income," while those who did not were categorized as "middle or high income." As I note in chapter 1, not all participants were able to identify the specific grants they received, so it is possible that some recipients of financial aid for low-income students did not report these sources.

Finally, I defined social class background based on parental occupation. The four class backgrounds outlined in table A.1 include examples of typical occupations for each. Working-class

184   APPENDIX

TABLE A.1. Defining socioeconomic status

Socioeconomic status and social class	Typical parental education	Example occupations	Typical family income
LIFGWC			
Working	First generation: high school or less	Manual labor, seamstress, driver, mail carrier, food services, factory worker, childcare, custodial work	Low income: usually Pell eligible
Lower middle	First generation: some college or two-year degree	Sales/clerical position, desk manager, clinical assistant, pastor, sports coach	Low income: usually Pell eligible
Socioeconomically advantaged			
Middle	Continuing generation: four-year or graduate degree	Teacher, librarian, human resources, information technology, counselor, midlevel management	Middle or high income
Upper middle	Continuing generation: graduate, doctoral/ professional degree	Lawyer, engineer, therapist, professor, consultant, senior management, finance, military general	Middle or high income

Note: In instances where students' parents or guardians differed on education level and/or occupation type, their socioeconomic status was determined by the parent or guardian with the higher level of education. The only exception to this pattern was in cases where the parent with more education was deceased or did not live with the students' primary caregiver.

and lower-middle-class students had parents or guardians with blue-collar, care-work, or lower-level management jobs. Middle- and upper-middle-class students' parents or guardians typically worked in professionalized white-collar jobs.

Because of the ways income, parental education, and parental occupation often aligned, it was possible to observe broad differences between students based on socioeconomic status. Throughout much of the book, I therefore contrast low-income, first-generation, and working-/lower-middle-class (LIFGWC) students with students whom I refer to as "socioeconomically advantaged" (those who were middle or high income, continuing generation, and middle/upper-middle class).[14]

Sometimes the components of socioeconomic status did not align in assumed ways. As Elizabeth Armstrong and Laura Hamilton note in their book *Paying for the Party*, such indicators are "messy" and don't always coalesce neatly.[15] For instance, there were low-income students who were continuing generation as well as first-generation students who came from middle- or high-income families. For this reason, I use the collapsed socioeconomic categories ("LIFGWC" and "socioeconomically advantaged") to talk about broad patterns, but when I introduce students in the book, I do so with the specific characteristics they described as most central in informing their own experiences of socioeconomic advantage or marginalization.

Interviews and Interpretive Analysis

All interviews were conducted using a videoconferencing platform. As I noted in chapter 1, virtual interviews can be challenging in some respects. For instance, there were a few interviews where disrupted internet connections required participants and interviewers to slow down, clarifying dialogue. But for the vast majority of interviews, the technology worked well, providing a seamless connection. Moreover, it turned out that this approach had a major benefit: allowing participants to take part in the study from the spaces where they lived, worked, and studied. In this way, virtual interviews offered a glimpse of how students experienced the settings that were central to their everyday lives. This added to the ethnographic context that helped situate these interviews.

Data collection was supported by three research assistants. Their contributions to the project were invaluable. First, they made it possible to gather a larger dataset (I conducted sixty of the interviews myself, and the research assistants conducted the other forty-four). Additionally, their engagement provided greater scheduling flexibility for study participants. Between the four of us, we were able to accommodate almost any scheduling request. Finally, as students themselves— two graduate students and a college senior—the research assistants shared valuable perspectives that made it possible to collect a rich dataset. They suggested additional questions to add to the interview guide, and their firsthand experiences as students allowed them to empathize with participants in ways that built rapport.

The interviews covered a broad range of topics related to students' journeys through higher education. We asked questions about their transition to college, how they chose and sometimes changed majors, how they funded college, and what their everyday lives were like. We discussed uncertainties they'd faced and how they dealt with them. We inquired about paid work, other forms of cocurricular and extracurricular involvement, and how they navigated the transitions that came along with the COVID-19 pandemic. Finally, we talked about their intentions for the future, how they'd grown or developed during their time in college, and the influence of family, friends, mentors, and various institutional resources on the experiences they'd had so far.

These topics of conversation offered windows into various facets of insecurity in higher education. Some of the questions focused on manifestations of uncertainty or instability that could be traced to specific institutional policies, for instance, hearing about the ways students' encounters with insecurity were shaped by the organization of university resources. Other questions illuminated elements of insecurity culture that were linked to broad and sometimes abstract factors like family churn or labor market precarity that seeped into students' everyday experiences in college. Examples could be seen in the ways students selected majors in response to their perceptions of career prospects, for example.

Each interview lasted approximately sixty to ninety minutes, and participants received a $10 gift card for taking part. Audio recordings were transcribed for analysis. But these transcripts were not the only data I obtained from the interviews. After conducting or listening to an interview, I took notes that explored facets of the conversation that would not appear in a transcript. For instance, I wrote about nonverbal cues like students' gestures, tone, and affect. For the sixty interviews I conducted myself, I took notes about students' surroundings—what their environments were like and how they seemed to be interacting with those settings. These pages of descriptive text could be revisited alongside the transcript, preserving some of the texture of the interviews.

I used the transcripts and interview notes to begin answering my research questions through a process of interpretive analysis. Allison Pugh notes that such a process "involves several steps,

186 APPENDIX

in which the researcher turns to the interviewee's words again and again, coding them for persistent ideas, gleaning relevant themes from this data, repeatedly returning to the texts to check and recheck themes, and linking codes and themes into analytic memos."[16] After using open coding methods to identify concepts, emotions, strategies, and other experiences that appeared across interviews, I developed analytic memos to explore patterns in how these phenomena showed up.[17] For instance, I wrote memos about the interviewees who struggled to stay afloat in the face of rampant insecurity, those who worked to leverage opportunities, those who tried to avoid uncertainty, and those who basked in it. These memos eventually came together to illuminate the four ways students were positioned in relation to insecurity. Though these patterns turned out to be broad—forming the scaffolding for chapters 2, 3, 4, and 5—other analytic memos focused on finer points that were eventually explored within a single chapter section or subsection. For instance, I wrote multiple memos about the different strategies maximizers used to build an enterprising self, and I produced several that focused on how pioneers described resilience.

Ethnographic Archive

The interview transcripts, notes, and analytic memos were supplemented with an ethnographic archive collected over the course of the study. This archive included a range of content that emerged as relevant to the research. I used the analytic memos to identify materials based on details the students provided. For instance, when they mentioned academic advising and counseling services, I explored the university web pages for such resources to gather information about them. When students discussed welcome events at CU, I examined orientation schedules, videos, and materials. When students alluded to stories in newsletters and on the university homepage, I found and saved many of these. And when students mentioned messages they'd seen distributed through university social media accounts, I enlisted my research assistants to help me compile a year's worth of relevant social media posts.

Gathering this content often led to other insights. For instance, while exploring news stories on the CU homepage, I also found materials and videos for prospective applicants that offered new information on how the university presented itself to potential students and their families. In this way, I began with leads from students and traced my way through an array of content, some of which was immediately relevant, while some was tangential but provided broader perspectives on the university.

This content was compiled in digital format—text documents, video files, web page screenshots, and so forth—and organized by topic. In addition to assembling these materials, I also wrote field notes that made observations about the information and insights they offered. It was then possible to use the resulting archive to bring ethnographic detail to complement the interviews, with the materials and field notes informing my analytic memos as they expanded over the course of the project. In this way, the archive gave a clearer view of students' worlds, including the messages, resources, policies, and events they encountered in everyday life at CU. It was because of this ethnographic context that many of the findings presented in this book, especially those in chapters 6 and 7, were possible.

Notes

Prologue

1. To protect the confidentiality of participants, all names in this book are pseudonyms.

2. The tendencies of schools to emphasize grit, resilience, and other qualities of self-reliance are well documented in existing research (Blume Oeur 2018; Golann 2015, 2021). Importantly though, schools are not the only places where youths encounter these ideas. They confront related kinds of expectations and pressures in a broad range of settings, including families, neighborhoods, and peer groups where neoliberal sensibilities are taken for granted (McGuigan 2014; Pugh 2015; Silva 2013).

3. Some readers may recoil at the notion that colleges could or should adopt the highly structured pathways of contemporary US high schools. However, what Daniel was observing here was the sharp disconnect between the structure of high school, which offered few opportunities for students to practice navigating choices, and the daunting lack of structure at his university. Implications for responding to such critiques at both the high school and college levels are explored in the concluding chapter of this book.

4. Fullerton and Wallace 2007; Halpern-Meekin and Turney 2016; Kalleberg 2009; Sennett 1998; Shildrick et al. 2012; Smith 2010; Vallas and Christin 2018.

Chapter One

1. Shapin 2012; Tierney and Perkins 2014.

2. For accounts of these types of resources and how they operate in postsecondary education, see Schuh, Jones, and Harper (2011), Turner and Hurley (2014), and White (2015).

3. Research documents significant increases over time in the share of postsecondary spending dedicated to administrative functions (Desrochers and Hurlburt 2014).

4. These studies show how numerous social problems—racism, sexism, classism, exclusion, violence, hunger, and political polarization, for instance—show up within colleges and universities, where they complicate students' lives in myriad ways (Binder and Wood 2013; Binder and Kidder 2022; Byrd 2017; Reyes 2018; Sloan and Fisher 2010; Warikoo 2016). As graduates exit college, on average they are better positioned for economic opportunity in the form of high-paying white-collar jobs than their peers who did not attend college (Goldin and Katz 2018; Kim, Tamborini, and Sakamoto 2015). These graduates are also less likely to be fired from a job, get

188   NOTES TO PAGES 1–4

divorced, or have serious health problems (Pascarella and Terenzini 2005; Mayhew et al. 2016). Yet conversations about college outcomes often neglect the fact that many students who enroll in college never make it to graduation.

5. National Student Clearinghouse 2020.

6. Causey et al. 2020. Notably, scholars have critiqued a narrow focus on retention and graduation rates as metrics of student success, arguing that this narrow focus stems from neoliberal pressures to move students through college cheaply and efficiently (Isserles 2021). The result, they claim, is that students from less socioeconomically advantaged backgrounds may have limited access to enriching experiences within college. In this book I respond to these critiques by taking a more expansive view of the types of experiences and outcomes that matter for students.

7. Ma, Pender, and Libassi 2020.

8. This type of stress can be especially acute for less socioeconomically advantaged students, including low-income, first-generation, and working-class students (Deckard, Goosby, and Cheadle 2022; Dwyer, McCloud, and Hodson 2011; McCabe and Jackson 2016).

9. Goldrick-Rab 2016; Quadlin and Powell 2022.

10. Evans et al. 2010.

11. Oreopoulos and Petronijevic 2013.

12. Arum and Roksa 2011.

13. Brewer et al. 2020; McCabe 2009; Winkle-Wagner 2009.

14. Silver 2020a.

15. Kirp 2019; Silva 2013.

16. Bowen, Chingos, and McPherson 2009; Rosenbaum 2001, 2011.

17. Though research on the extensive impact of the pandemic on student experiences is only just emerging, several recent studies highlight the way COVID-19 elevated uncertainty for college students (Fruehwirth, Biswas, and Perreira 2021; Marek, Chew, and Wu 2021; Son et al. 2020).

18. This was apparent in reviewing materials from the ethnographic archive for this project. In various university-wide announcements, the university attributed disruptions and uncertainties of various sorts to the pandemic without acknowledging the impact of their own structures or policies.

19. Hamilton and Nielsen 2021.

20. Arum et al. 2018.

21. Beck 1986; Giddens 2003. Sociologist Zygmunt Bauman (2012) described the advent of liquid modernity characterized by a state of constant change and widespread uncertainty. He observed that liquid modernity replaced a period of solid modernity exemplified by a more predictable organization of society.

22. Though it can be tempting to romanticize the stability of the past, sociologists observe that a decline in rigid social formations has also brought about new kinds of freedoms for groups that were marginalized or oppressed in solid modernity (Gerson 2010; Pugh 2015).

23. See for instance, Giroux (2014), Halpern-Meekin and Turney (2016), and Shildrick et al. (2012).

24. Pugh 2015.

25. Bauman 2012; Cooper and Pugh 2020; Fullerton and Wallace 2007; Kalleberg 2009; Sennett 1998; Smith 2010; Urry 2007; Vallas and Christin 2018.

26. Eaton 2022; Hamilton and Nielsen 2021; Harvey 2005.

27. Childress 2019; Labaree 2017; State Higher Education Executive Officers 2015.

NOTES TO PAGES 4–7   189

28. Houle and Addo 2022.

29. See for instance, Houle and Addo (2022), McMillan Cottom (2017), Mettler (2014), and Price (2004). Along the way, institutions have invested in marketable research and worked to appeal to affluent students and donors (Armstrong and Hamilton 2013; Geiger 2004; Kirp 2003; Slaughter and Rhoades 2004) while allowing the academic mission of teaching and learning to fade into the background (Arum and Roksa 2011).

30. Anctil 2008; Harrison and Risler 2015.

31. Holland 2019; McMillan Cottom 2017; Saichaie and Morphew 2014.

32. McMillan Cottom 2017.

33. Labaree 1997; Roksa and Robinson 2016.

34. Saunders 2014.

35. Roksa and Silver 2019.

36. Of the sixty-two students, just fifteen described using a university resource to support their transition to postbaccalaureate life; notably, eight of the fifteen only used the university's career fair (Roksa and Silver 2019).

37. Some scholars also refer to a "cafeteria-style model" of higher education administration (Bailey, Jaggars, and Jenkins, 2015), which aligns with conceptions of students as consumers while also cutting costs (Isserles 2021; Mettler 2014). When resources are not integrated into the curriculum, few students will make use of them, thereby saving an institution money (Kuh 2009). In a setting where students are treated as consumers and resources are scarce, the cafeteria-style, self-service model becomes the default.

38. Bailey, Jaggars, and Jenkins, 2015.

39. A growing body of literature in sociology and psychology documents the changing nature of this transition, which became significantly more precarious in the latter part of the twentieth century (see, e.g., Arnett 2014; Cebulko 2014; Chesters and Cuervo 2019; Hardie 2022; Nelson 2019a; Settersten, Furstenberg, and Rumbaut 2008; Silva 2013; Waters et al. 2011).

40. Furstenberg, Rumbaut, and Settersten 2005; Latz 2012; Newman 2012.

41. Arnett 2014.

42. Rosenbaum 2001; Schneider and Stevenson 1999.

43. Frank Furstenberg and his colleagues (2005, 6) observe, "It is no great mystery why these changes [in the timing of adult role markers] have come about. Education and training are more valuable than ever before because jobs are less permanent and work careers have become more fluid." See also Aronson (2017), Bauman (2012), and Vallas and Christin (2018).

44. Bills 2004; Saunders and Machell 2000. Notably, Moss-Pech (in progress) documents important exceptions found in some business and engineering programs where staff and employers have developed relationships to support students' transitions from school to work.

45. Goerisch 2019.

46. Aronson 2017, 397.

47. Silva 2013.

48. Cabrera 2011; Goerisch 2019.

49. These interviews align with an approach that Rinaldo and Guhin (2022) describe as "primary ethnographic interviews," which are formal interviews supported by ethnographic context gathered from the research site. My research methods are described in greater detail in the Methods appendix, where I also elaborate on the choice of the pseudonym "Commonwealth University." This pseudonym signals that (1) CU represents a "common" institution type, part of the largest segment of higher education; (2) this research complicates understandings of the

resources (wealth) higher education leaders perceive as accessible (common) for students; and (3) the book engages with notions of education as a public good.

50. "The new university" is a phrase Hamilton and Nielsen (2021) borrow from Michael Crow and William Dabars (2015), who use the term in their book, *Designing the New American University*. Hamilton and Nielsen (2021) theorize and provide social and historical context for this institutional form in their book *Broke: The Racial Consequences of Underfunding Public Universities*.

51. Hamilton and Nielsen (2021, 4) describe new universities, as "schools that pair high research ambitions with predominately disadvantaged student populations." These institutions are broad access and enroll high proportions of students of color, low-income students, and first-generation college students.

52. Not only have elite institutions been a focal point of the majority of this research but also scholars often present studies on elite schools as representative of broader patterns in education rather than acknowledging the fact that they are nonrepresentative in many ways (Khan 2018). Of course, there is much we can learn from studying the schooling of elites, but Khan (2018, 196) argues that such research could be more productive if studies of elite education were willing to "treat exceptional cases as exceptional . . . rather than couch them in a veneer of representativeness." The challenge with existing research is that it frequently neglects the institutions attended by most college students today.

53. Byrd 2021, 152.

54. National Center for Education Statistics 2021.

55. Because only 5 percent of CU students were international students, the 40 percent who grew up in a home where a language other than English was spoken are probably primarily students from immigrant families.

56. Rinaldo and Guhin (2022) describe the value of supporting in-depth interviews with ethnographic context in order to account for mesolevel public culture. In the case of this study, such an approach allowed me to situate my interviews in the broader organizational context in which they were grounded.

57. See, for instance, Lareau (2021) and Pugh (2013).

58. Pugh 2015. Similarly, Bauman (2012) distinguishes between "tourists," who are advantaged by liquid modernity and have their standard of living improved, and "vagabonds," who are immobile or forced to be mobile because of changes in the structure of employment (see also, Auyero and Swistun 2008; Kalleberg 2009; Urry 2007).

59. Settersten 2015, 122.

60. Armstrong and Hamilton 2013.

61. Roksa and Silver 2019.

62. Hamilton, Roksa, and Nielsen 2018.

63. Beattie 2018; Benson and Lee 2020; Nunn 2021.

64. In a study of college students in Wisconsin, sociologist Sara Goldrick-Rab (2016) found that over half of the low-income students in her sample took out loans.

65. Silver and Roksa 2017.

66. Lee and Zhou 2015; Louie 2004; Xie and Goyette 2003.

67. Silver and Roksa 2017.

68. Beasley 2011; Brooms 2017, 2020; Deckman 2022; Druery and Brooms 2019; Johnson 2019.

69. Bourdieu 1986.

70. Coleman 1988.

NOTES TO PAGES 11–17   191

71. Dumais and Ward 2010; Lareau and Weininger 2003.

72. Yosso 2005.

73. Yosso 2005, 77–81.

74. Yosso 2005, 80–81.

75. In recent years, scholars working in the cultural capital tradition have begun to extend greater recognition to the cultural resources of marginalized groups, even when those resources are not recognized by dominant institutions (see, e.g., Lo 2015; Wallace 2018).

76. Rodriguez et al. 2022; Squire and McCann 2018.

77. Richards 2020. Black feminist scholars have referred to the mutual constitution of socio-demographic characteristics as intersectionality (Collins [2000] 2009). There is a well-established tradition of using intersectional framework to study student experiences in K–12 schools (Bettie 2003; Ispa-Landa 2013; Ispa-Landa and Conwell 2015; Morris 2005; 2007), and in recent years, scholars increasingly have begun to employ intersectional frameworks to understand college student experiences (Byrd, Brunn-Bevel, and Ovink 2019; Duran and Jones 2019; Lee and LaDousa 2015; Ray and Rosow 2010).

78. Carter 2005; Lopez 2003.

79. Benson and Lee 2020; Dumais and Ward 2010; Jack 2019; Roksa et al. 2020; Stuber 2009, 2011a.

80. See, for instance, Gonzales (2012) and Musoba and Baez (2009).

81. Roksa, Silver, and Wang 2022.

82. O'Shea 2016.

83. Hinton 2015.

84. Vallas and Christin (2018) observe that many studies and theories of how social actors navigate insecurity leave agency and resistance undertheorized. Their study of the ways professionals engage with personal branding literature indicates that while some individuals adopt elements of neoliberal ideology, some merely perform compliance, and others actively resist this ideology. Additionally, recent sociological research has begun working to deal with the previously "unbalanced theoretical toolkit" (Streib 2017) by examining social and cultural resources that inform both social reproduction and social mobility (see also, Jack 2019; Streib 2018).

85. In this work, Bourdieu (1986) makes clear that schools are not neutral institutions. Rather, they value, prioritize, and reward the cultural dispositions and social resources of some students over others.

86. Ray and Rosow 2010; Reyes 2018; Stuber 2016.

87. For a discussion of how institutional isomorphism shapes contemporary higher education, see Croucher and Woelert (2016) and Fay and Zavattaro (2016).

88. Ray and Rosow 2010, 3.

89. See, for instance, George (2007), Labaree (1997); Titus (2008). Instead of dedicating resources to the provision of services needed by students—especially those from less socioeconomically advantaged families—to learn and succeed in college (Hamilton and Nielsen 2021), universities divert funding to support the trappings of an enjoyable college experience (Armstrong and Hamilton 2013). When institutions conceive of students as customers, university personnel are pressured to shift from an emphasis on intellectual rigor to focus on ensuring student satisfaction (Hayes and Wynyard 2002).

90. Armstrong and Hamilton (2013) offer a detailed account of the ways upper-middle-class, out-of-state students became an important source of revenue for public universities.

91. Blumenstyk 2003; Toma 2007.

92. In *Paying for the Party*, Armstrong and Hamilton (2013, 15) provide examples of three types of pathways and explore their accessibility at a flagship university. Specifically, they describe a "party pathway" focused on providing diversion for socioeconomically advantaged students who desire a primarily social college experience, a "mobility pathway" meant to provide opportunities for less socioeconomically advantaged students to achieve upward mobility, and a "professional pathway" designed to support motivated students from socioeconomically advantaged families in preparing for high-status occupations. Calls from scholars to replace the widespread "pipeline" metaphor with a focus on educational "pathways" are increasingly drawing attention to the ways available opportunities and resources come together with student decision-making to shape the routes individuals take through higher education (Kizilcec et al. 2023).

93. Armstrong and Hamilton 2013, 15.

94. Mullen 2010.

95. Roksa and Robinson 2016; Stuber 2011a.

96. For instance, Armstrong and Hamilton (2013) show how a focus on affluent out-of-state students is responsible for the blocked mobility pathway they document in their research. Other studies of low-income, first-generation, and working-class students at elite universities find evidence of similar resource omissions (Gable 2021; Jack 2019; Lee 2016).

97. Mills (1959) 2000.

Chapter Two

1. While I refer to "low-income, first-generation, and working-class students" and use the acronym LIFGWC throughout this chapter, not every student shared all three of these characteristics. For instance, Drew's mother completed a master's degree, so he did not fit the typical definition of a first-generation college student. Yet his experience aligned with those described in this chapter as his mother lost her job and his parents divorced during his high school years, after which time his mother was not very involved in his life. In the case of students who do not share all three of these identities, I introduce them with whichever sociodemographic characteristics were most salient for informing their experiences.

2. Scholars have observed that first-generation college students' sense of being atypical is actually cultivated in part by university discourse that frames these students as "academically deficient" or "in need of cultural transformation" (Wildhagen 2015, 285).

3. Reynolds 2014; Saichaie and Morphew 2014.

4. Holland 2019, 2020; Nichols 2020; Soria and Stebleton 2012.

5. Armstrong and Hamilton 2013, 152.

6. Beattie 2018; Benson and Lee 2020; McCabe 2016; Nunn 2021; Silver 2020b; Stuber 2011b.

7. Hurst 2010; Lee and Kramer 2013; Rondini 2016.

8. Studies show that for many students, economic prospects are cited as the primary reason for college attendance (Aronson 2017; Binder, Davis, and Bloom 2016; Lehmann 2009), a finding that aligns with broader trends in how education is understood in the United States (Labaree 1997).

9. Houle and Addo 2022.

10. For a thorough account of the complexities of paying for college that can complicate LIFGWC students' ability to remain enrolled, see Goldrick-Rab (2016).

11. Roksa and Silver 2019.

NOTES TO PAGES 29–42

12. Armstrong and Hamilton 2013; Jack 2019; Lee 2017; Lehmann 2007.

13. These types of challenges are well documented in studies of the transition into college (Ardoin 2017; Duncheon 2018; Johnson 2019).

14. Collier and Morgan 2008; Nunn 2021; Soria 2012.

15. See, for instance, Childress (2019) and Murray (2019).

16. Curtis 2013.

17. While Amal was not clear on how other students had learned about these resources, previous research suggests that information about academic success strategies may be more readily accessible for socioeconomically advantaged students whose social capital can help convey such information (Collier and Morgan 2008; McCabe 2016).

18. Notably, adjunct faculty at CU were required to hold office hours even if they did not have a formal office space on campus. For a discussion of the obstacles LIFGWC college students encounter related to participating in faculty office hours, see Jack's (2019) book, *The Privileged Poor*.

19. Notably, even those faculty employed in full-time positions often find themselves overextended with research and service commitments that leave less time for teaching and mentoring (Arum and Roksa 2011).

20. The precarity induced by the coming out process has been documented in a range of studies on LGBTQ+ youth (see, e.g., Patrón 2021; Robinson 2020; Silver, Krietzberg, and Kalaivanan. 2021).

21. Gallagher 2015.

22. While Alyssa did not disclose whether she shared the specific details of this missing grant with her father, their experience aligns with existing research finding that the parents of LIFGWC students are often reluctant to intervene with college and university administrations (Hamilton 2016).

23. See for instance, Mehta, Newbold, and O'Rourke (2011); Nora (2004); Salas (2016).

24. See for instance, Capannola and Johnson (2020); Hope and Quinlan (2021); O'Shea (2015).

25. Roksa, Silver, and Wang 2022.

26. See also Beattie (2018) and Yee (2016).

27. McCabe 2016; Stuber 2011a.

28. Jayakumar, Vue, and Allen 2013; Pérez 2017; Sáenz et al. 2017; Samuelson and Litzler 2016.

29. Yosso 2005, 77.

30. Azmitia et al. 2018.

31. Hamilton 2016.

32. For a rich account of this diversity, see Benson and Lee's (2020) *Geographies of Campus Inequality: Mapping the Diverse Experiences of First-Generation Students*, which illustrates the diverse range of ways first-generation students engage academically and socially in college.

33. This is not to suggest that pioneers never received support from their families. Alyssa, for instance, asked her father to take out a parent PLUS loan to cover an unpaid balance on her account. In moments like these, even pioneers received tangible benefits from family members. Nonetheless, they did not have the consistent support theorized by scholars of community cultural wealth.

34. McGuigan 2014; Pugh 2015; Silva 2013.

35. Pugh 2015, 9.

36. Yosso 2005, 77.

37. Blume Oeur 2018, 6.

38. Aronson 2017; Webster and Rivers 2019.

39. Nunn 2021; Yee 2016.

40. Nunn 2021.

41. As the previous chapter described, approximately a quarter of the students who begin higher education leave college before their second year of study (National Student Clearinghouse 2020).

42. While CU did not publish data on further educational enrollment, research demonstrates that LIFGWC students are less likely to enroll in graduate and professional school than their more socioeconomically advantaged peers (Mullen, Goyette, and Soares, 2003; Pyne and Grodsky 2020).

Chapter Three

1. By some definitions, Noah may also be considered a first-generation college student. Although his father completed a college degree before immigrating to the US from Peru, Noah described him as being relatively unfamiliar with the US system of higher education. His father was currently employed as a truck driver, and his mother occasionally worked in childcare.

2. Best 2006.

3. Psychologists have similarly conceptualized encounters with insecurity as a means of self-discovery and exploration. This is often used to explain engagement with what clinicians often refer to as high-risk behaviors (see, e.g., Lightfoot 1997).

4. Best 2006, 89.

5. Here I conceive of these resources to include elements of several forms of community cultural wealth described by Yosso (2005), including "navigational capital," "resistant capital," and "familial capital." While these are distinct resources in some ways, they coalesce to inform a broader capacity to draw from community support and familial resources to successfully navigate exclusive social institutions (see also Lo 2015).

6. Hamilton and Nielsen 2021; Ray 2019.

7. Capannola and Johnson 2020; Hope and Quinlan 2021; O'Shea 2015.

8. Silver et al. 2020.

9. Chapter 7 explores the University Honors Program and its impact in greater detail.

10. This study and others examining the use of university services find that when resources are integrated into the curriculum, they tend to be more widely accessed and have the potential to mitigate inequality (see also Roksa and Silver 2019).

11. The general tendency to avoid more rigorous instructors is not limited to minimizers. Other scholars have documented this tendency among a broader group of students (Grigsby 2009; Johnson 2003). Yet minimizers used this as a primary strategy not just for choosing between instructors but for choosing courses and majors as well.

12. For further insight into the ways families affect major selection, see Hamilton, Roksa, and Nielsen (2018) and Ma (2009, 2020).

13. For discussion of high-impact learning experiences, see Kilgo, Ezell Sheets, and Pascarella (2015) and Kuh (2008).

14. Beck (1986) argued that changes to science and industry brought both prosperity and new risks. As awareness of the limits of control grows, individuals and groups often become concerned about uncertainty. His work raises questions about how people understand and try to manage these risks. Minimizers offer new perspectives on how risks are experienced, interpreted, and resisted as well as the consequences of prioritizing risk avoidance.

NOTES TO PAGES 68-76

15. Cheatham 2019; West et al. 2021.

16. Arum and Roksa 2011.

17. Arum and Roksa 2014.

18. In her book, *The Costs of Completion*, Isserles (2021) explains how this emphasis on completion is driven by performance metrics that attempt to quantify success in narrow ways that fail to account for students' broader needs or life circumstances.

19. Research indicates that it may in fact be beneficial for students to engage in a degree of content repetition when it increases confidence and GPA (Harrison, Hernandez, and Stevens 2022). Yet Patrice and other minimizers were not typically engaging in content repetition. Rather, they avoided even entry-level courses in subjects where they felt less confident in their abilities.

20. Moss-Pech, in progress.

21. For instance, Armstrong and Hamilton (2013) show the challenges faced by less socioeconomically advantaged students who major in "business-lite" fields (management-focused programs like arts or sports management outside of business schools) but do not have the family connections to land jobs in these fields. For further discussion of some of the negative outcomes of such majors, see Arum and Roksa (2011, 2014), Brint (2002), and Carnevale, Cheah, and Hanson (2015).

22. Bozick and DeLuca 2005; Elman and O'Rand 2004; Roksa and Velez 2012; Zarifa et al. 2018.

23. Rivera 2011, 2012; Takacs 2020. Although the social and cultural capital gained from these types of experiences can be beneficial, minimizers felt compelled to prioritize the acquisition of economic capital through paid employment. This tendency aligns with Bourdieu's (1986) observation that while different forms of capital (cultural, social, and economic) convert to one another, those forms that are not economic introduce a certain degree of risk if they are misrecognized or refused recognition. In other words, investing in dominant cultural capital can be riskier than investing in paid labor, especially for individuals whose displays of capital may not be recognized because of various kinds of discrimination.

24. McCabe 2016.

25. In our research on college seniors, my coauthors and I documented working-class students' use of a vigilant self-narrative to alleviate concerns about the future. However, we show that this self-narrative made it challenging for students to make progress toward specific career plans (Silver et al. 2022).

26. Aciman 2021, 201.

27. In doing so, this book builds on the work of Benson and Lee (2020), who documented the diverse range of experiences first-generation students have, in contrast to widespread notions of less socioeconomically advantaged students as a monolithic group.

28. Gast 2021; Jack 2019; George Mwangi 2018; Nunn 2021.

29. This tendency is part of what McMillan Cottom (2017, 11) has described as a broader "risk shift" that corresponded with the reallocation of risks for workforce training "from states and companies to individuals and families."

30. Jacob, McCall, and Stange 2018; Levin 2005; Titus 2008.

31. These struggles may be surprising in some respects, given the fact that CU was a broad-access public university. When Armstrong and Hamilton (2013, 152) described the "blocked mobility pathway," they attributed its barriers to LIFGWC student success to the fact that the institution they studied was a flagship university that drew much of its enrollment from regional

elites. Meanwhile, they found that some of the most positive LIFGWC student outcomes documented in their research were among four students who transferred to regional public universities (Armstrong and Hamilton 2013, 177). It is noteworthy then that students at CU, a very different type of university, faced comparable obstacles to upward mobility.

Chapter Four

1. Khan 2011, 15.

2. Khan 16.

3. Their words illustrate what Grodsky and Riegle-Crumb (2010) have called a "college-going habitus," the durable conviction—inculcated during childhood—that one will pursue higher education.

4. George 2007; Roksa and Robinson 2016; Saunders and Kolek 2017.

5. Heller and Marin 2002; Perna and Steele 2011.

6. Notably, not all continuing-generation and middle- and upper-middle-class college students had a foundation of financial security. Some minimizers had socioeconomically advantaged parents who were not able or willing to transfer economic resources to their children (see also Streib 2020). For instance, Layne, a nonbinary continuing-generation Asian student, had two parents who worked in white-collar occupations, and their mother had completed a JD. Yet when they arrived in college, their parents stopped providing financial support. Without the economic stability and other forms of parental support that benefitted maximizers, Layne engaged in the risk-minimizing strategies described in the previous chapter.

7. Bourdieu and Passeron 1977; Lareau and Weininger 2003.

8. Coleman 1988.

9. Bourdieu 1973, 1986.

10. Jack 2019; Lee 2016; Stuber 2011a.

11. In other words, maximizers had the types of parents that Hamilton, Roksa, and Nielsen (2018, 116) call "college concierges," a phrase they use to refer to "parents who were in regular contact with their children, monitored their children's well-being, contributed substantial funds, and offered academic, social, and career advice in times of need." Hamilton (2016) distinguishes between two types of engaged parents: helicopters and paramedics. While not all maximizers had helicopter parents, most of their parents at least served as paramedics, stepping in when students perceived they were needed.

12. Khan (2011, 2012). According to Khan, "ease" is an "embodied" disposition, meaning that it involves both internal feelings (like a sense of comfort) as well as external self-presentation (like a casual or easygoing appearance). Maximizers lacked both elements of ease, as they struggled to feel comfortable or to demonstrate ease externally because of experiences with marginalization. Making their effort visible appeared to be part of a strategy to alleviate some of this marginalization.

13. Khan 2012, 112–13.

14. In his study of St. Paul's School, Khan (2012) also documents the ways the embodiment of ease is gendered, with girls at the school encountering unique contradictions and constraints that did not affect boys. The findings presented in this chapter show how ease could be similarly inaccessible for others, including students of color, LGBTQ+ students, and students who identified with a marginalized religious group.

15. McCabe 2016; Silver 2020b; Silver and Krietzberg 2023.

16. Streib 2020.

17. These students' experiences with a mixture of privilege and vulnerability parallel broader changes in elite identity over recent decades where the "new elite" has come to represent a more diverse group of socioeconomically advantaged individuals (e.g., in terms of race and ethnicity) than was historically the case (Khan 2012; Khan and Jerolmack 2013).

18. This pattern resonates with the findings of studies showing how socioeconomically advantaged youth and their parents work to demonstrate merit in K–12 schools. Stevens (2007, 247–48), for instance, describes "the production of demonstrated accomplishment" as a common strategy whereby advantaged families engage in a process of "laundering privilege."

19. See for instance, Vallas and Christin (2018), who build on Foucault's (2008) lectures at the Collège de France from 1978–1979 on human capital theory as evidence of a cultural shift that positioned the individual as an economic enterprise through practices that cultivate specific forms of subjectivity or "technologies of the self."

20. Although the interview guide included a follow-up question about minors, most maximizers had already described their academic minor(s) before we arrived at this question.

21. While Neville's suggestion that he might even add a second major may sound unusual, several maximizers had done just that, including Valerie, who double majored in math and computer science, and Zoey, who combined psychology and education (see also Mcdossi 2022).

22. See for instance, Mcdossi (2022) and Moss-Pech (in progress).

23. Kilgo, Ezell Sheets, and Pascarella 2015; Kuh 2008.

24. Armstrong and Hamilton 2013; Arum and Roksa 2011.

25. This is not to say that all maximizers avoided the party scene. There were maximizers who acknowledged that some of their engagement was informed by a desire to enjoy themselves after working hard. Yet these students were usually clear that partying came second to academic and professional "résumé-building" experiences.

26. This pattern aligns with Wolfgram and Ahrens's (2022, 139) finding that there is a "particular culture [among college students] of the multiple internship economy, representing multiple internships as a linear, progressive, goal-oriented cultural project to accumulate a marketable self" (see also Wright and Mulvey 2021).

27. Literature often describes these behaviors as "opportunity hoarding" (Hamilton, Roksa, and Nielsen 2018; Stich 2018). Research on higher education extends work on opportunity hoarding facilitated by parents in K–12 schooling (Calarco 2018; Hagerman 2018; Lewis and Diamond 2015; Warikoo 2020; 2022).

28. Moss-Pech 2021; Silva et al. 2016.

29. Roksa (2011) shows that these types of disparities in employment during college represent an important element of inequality in higher education. Less socioeconomically advantaged students tend to spend more time on paid employment, a gap that has increased in recent decades for students at four-year institutions (Weiss and Roksa 2016) but have fewer internship experiences (Armstrong and Hamilton 2013; Stuber 2009). While internships are often professionally advantageous (Moss-Pech 2021; Wolfgram and Ahrens 2022), spending greater time working for pay off campus is associated with lower likelihood of degree completion (Bozick 2007; Roksa 2011).

30. Roksa and Silver 2019.

31. Warikoo 2016.

32. Warikoo 2016, 90. Such beliefs align with contemporary pressures to justify socioeconomic advantage through narratives of hard work (Khan 2012; Khan and Jerolmack 2013).

33. See also, Roksa and Silver (2019).

34. Hamilton, Roksa, and Nielsen 2018; Roksa and Silver 2019.

35. Takacs 2020, 255.

36. Urry 2007.

37. Pugh 2015, xi.

38. Ma 2020.

39. Byrd 2017; Warikoo 2016.

Chapter Five

1. Notably, explorers and maximizers both claimed to appreciate flexibility, but they understood and leveraged it in different ways. Maximizers saw flexibility as a way to engage with a range of quantifiable opportunities and frame their accomplishments as the result of initiative. Explorers, meanwhile, appreciated having the flexibility to navigate college in a leisurely and open way with few requirements for specific kinds of engagement. In other words, different dispositions and strategies led these two groups to a shared appreciation for limited structure in higher education.

2. Khan 2011.

3. Evans et al. 2010.

4. Abes, Jones, and Stewart 2019; Miller, Nachman, and Wynn 2020; Wijeyesinghe and Jackson 2012.

5. Hamilton (2016, 35) observes that of the five ways of understanding college that she documents, the hybridized experience was "the only vision of college that touched on college as offering broader life enrichment—not just instrumental career or social network development." Such perspectives on what college can or should offer similarly reflect tendencies toward broad cultural participation, sometimes referred to as "cultural omnivorousness," among contemporary elites (Peterson and Kern 1996; Warde and Gayo-Cal 2009).

6. Grodsky and Riegle-Crumb 2010.

7. Bourdieu and Passeron 1977; Lareau and Weininger 2003.

8. Though scholars critique students for pursuing fun rather than learning in higher education (see, e.g., Arum and Roksa 2011), explorers show us that in broad-access institutions the students who are able to make claims to valuing deep engagement with academic material and emphasize learning are those who are advantaged in many respects.

9. Rivera 2015.

10. Elsewhere, I have documented the ways socioeconomically advantaged White men's focused involvement in just one or two extracurricular settings is made possible by these students' encounters with welcoming social outlets on campus (Silver 2020b). The findings presented here show how these patterns can also be attributed to a logic of approaching outlets to pursue depth of engagement in a couple settings rather than sufficient engagement in many outlets, as maximizers did.

11. Warikoo 2016, 96–97.

12. Nunn 2021, 147.

13. Jay 2012; Settersten, Furstenberg, and Rumbaut 2008.

14. See, for instance, Armstrong and Hamilton (2013), Byrd (2021), and Cabrera (2018).

15. Silva and Corse 2018; Silver et al. 2022.

16. Rivera 2011, 2012.

NOTES TO PAGES 123–131   199

17. Rivera 2011, 83.

18. Bonilla-Silva 2018, 2.

19. This finding aligns with Khan's (2012) claim that elites have come to embrace the notion that ascriptive characteristics should not determine opportunities; they have used rhetoric about equal rights to emphasize individual capacities, thereby reproducing inequality even as they rhetorically position themselves as champions of equal opportunity.

Chapter Six

1. Hartley and Morphew 2008; Saichaie and Morphew 2014.

2. Armstrong and Hamilton 2013; Kahlenberg 2010.

3. Ray and Best 2015; Ray and Rosow 2010; Stuber 2016.

4. Stuber 2016.

5. Geiger 2011.

6. Byrd 2021; Hamilton and Nielsen 2021.

7. Goldin, Katz, and Kuziemko 2006.

8. Attewell and Lavin 2007; Bowen, Kurzweil, and Tobin 2005.

9. Hamilton and Nielsen 2021, 20.

10. Harvey 2005; Saunders 2010.

11. Levin 2005; Slaughter and Rhoades 2004.

12. Servage 2009. As described in the first chapter, these trends shape how universities organize requirements (or a lack thereof) with a result that Robinson (2011, 601) describes as the "decline of prescription and the rise of choice."

13. For instance, Hamilton and Nielsen (2021) show how administrators endorse practices like "tolerable suboptimization" in order to sustain operations with limited resources.

14. Roksa and Silver 2019.

15. Desrochers and Hurlburt 2014.

16. Hamilton and Nielsen 2021.

17. National Center for Education Statistics 2022.

18. Armstrong and Hamilton 2013.

19. Brulé 2004; Roksa and Robinson 2016.

20. For instance, Kamenetz (2015) argues that neoliberal universities foster innovation, while scholars like Giroux (2014), Hamilton and Nielsen (2021), and Slaughter and Rhoades (2004) illustrate their more problematic outcomes.

21. Arum and Roksa 2014; Brand and Xie 2010; Goldin and Katz 2018.

22. Houle and Addo 2022; Silva 2013.

23. Taylor and Cantwell 2019, 110. Their dataset documents growing tuition reliance at public institutions, where they argue that increasing rates of access have failed to produce greater opportunity.

24. Harrison and Risler 2015; Melear 2003.

25. Bailey, Jaggars, and Jenkins 2015.

26. Deil-Amen and Rosenbaum (2003, 123) note that while having "more options sometimes leads to better decisions, they can also increase the need for information and may create confusion and mistaken choices" (see also, Person, Rosenbaum, and Deil-Amen 2006; Roksa, Silver, and Wang 2022).

27. Arum and Cook 2018.

28. Roksa and Silver 2019.

29. Settersten 2015, 122.

30. Lareau and Weininger 2003; Roksa and Silver 2021.

31. As one illustration, CU created a pie chart that indicated how each full-time student's $3,500 "mandatory student fee" was allocated across various expenses. Based on this data, more than $600 of each student's annual fee was allocated toward athletics, and an additional $400 went to student activities. By contrast, student health services was allocated less than $100 of this fee.

32. Of course, directors in the residence halls and staff at the campus gymnasium may sometimes provide students with support in challenging times. Yet the primary purpose of their roles was not presented as such by the university, and few students saw these personnel as outlets for academic or social support.

33. Berrey 2015; Thomas 2020.

34. Ahmed 2012; Thomas 2020.

35. Byrd 2021.

36. Lerma, Hamilton, and Nielsen (2020) refer to these efforts as "racialized equity labor."

37. Goerisch 2019; Lee and Maynard 2017.

38. Research on the impact of "intrusive" or "proactive" advising and student support practices has expanded rapidly over the past decade (see, e.g., Braxton et al. 2013; Donaldson et al. 2016; Museus 2021; Van Jura and Prieto 2021).

39. For statistics on academic advisor caseloads, see Carlstrom (2013) and Robbins (2013). Notably, the majors where caseloads appeared to be especially high were those where LIFGWC students were concentrated, such as information technology, where three advisors divided a caseload of nearly 1,800 students. My method of calculating these ratios did not factor in students who were minoring in a particular field. For this reason, these calculations probably underestimated the true extent of advisors' caseloads.

40. Jack 2019; Nunn 2021.

41. See chapter 4 for a discussion of maximizers' opportunity hoarding.

42. These findings align with patterns observed by Hamilton (2016) and Hamilton, Roksa, and Nielsen (2018).

43. Blimling 2001; Manning, Kinzie, and Schuh 2006.

44. Thomas 2020.

45. While a growing body of research demonstrates the value of connecting support services to the curriculum (Roksa and Silver 2019), surprisingly few other resources at CU took this approach.

46. While there is currently no nationwide data on representation in honors colleges and programs, various sources document issues of limited access and underrepresentation for students of color and LIFGWC students in honors education (see, e.g., Harper 2019; MacDonald 2019; Pulido Villanueva, Priede, and Thien 2021).

47. Lee and Harris (2020, 1136) refer to these services as "counterstructures."

48. Eaton 2022; Hamilton and Nielsen 2021.

Chapter Seven

1. Byrd 2021. For a few recent exceptions to this trend, see Hamilton and Nielsen (2021), McCabe (2016), and McMillan Cottom (2017).

NOTES TO PAGES 153–159

2. Arum and Roksa 2011; Arum and Roksa 2014. These findings may be unsurprising, given well-documented trends indicating that twenty-first-century students spend significantly less time studying than their counterparts from earlier decades (see, e.g., Babcock and Marks 2011).

3. Mills (1959) 2000, 3–4.

4. Mills, 8.

5. Mills, 8.

6. Hackstaff 2010; Hirshfield 2022; Olsen 2016.

7. Ghidina 2019; Hironimus-Wendt and Wallace 2009; Massengill 2011; Nell Trautner and Borland 2013; Scimecca 2021.

8. Arum, Roksa, and Cook 2016, 40.

9. Aldegether 2017.

10. Pascarella and Terenzini 2005. Student development theories argue that participants in the cocurriculum and extracurriculum will learn to socially, politically, and historically situate aspects of individual identity by recognizing how patterns of advantage and oppression inform individual experiences (Evans et al. 2010).

11. Sociological research on LIFGWC students and students from immigrant families illuminates the structural inequality that shapes the college-going experiences of these youth and their broader transitions to adulthood (Cebulko 2014; Gonzales 2015; Gunther and Benson 2021; Hurst 2019; Kalaivanan et al. 2022; Kasinitz et al. 2009; Kim 2013; Rumbaut 2005; Sánchez-Connally 2018; Warnock and Hurst 2016).

12. Though the vast majority of minimizers did not acknowledge the impact of broad social structures on their lived experiences, there were a couple students who represented exceptions to this trend. For instance, Ellie noted that "some Black people tend to get the end of the stick as far as like job placements or being in hierarchical positions and things like that." Such a remark signaled at least a tentative recognition of systemic racism. Notably, though, most of her discussion focused on prejudiced individuals and the strategies she adopted for avoiding them.

13. This "no excuses" discourse has become widespread in a range of settings, and some students may encounter it well before college, including in K–12 charter schools (see, e.g., Golann 2015, 2021; Golann and Torres 2020). The analysis presented here does not assume that students fully adopt and internalize individualistic explanations of lived experiences. It may be the case that the lesson students are learning is how to rely on an individualized discourse about personal accountability even if their internal beliefs may be more complex. Mills (1940) made clear that discussion of motive is often driven by talk or "vocabularies" that are more acceptable in certain settings than in others. Perhaps these students have learned that they are expected to employ individualistic explanations of their experiences or the experiences of others. Regardless, the fact that students are adopting such perspectives—in belief or in rhetoric—has important consequences for their college journeys and for the reproduction of inequality.

14. As chapter 2 notes, this could be seen clearly in the way students adopted the "one-way honor system" that Pugh (2015) describes, imposing "strict rules" on themselves, while expecting little accountability from institutions.

15. After all, this is a moment that many scholars and practitioners describe as a time to gain experience doing new kinds of things—everything from making important decisions to doing laundry—for oneself (Chambliss and Takacs 2014; Cuba et al. 2016; Nathan 2005).

16. Blume Oeur 2018; Nunn 2021.

17. Bombaci and Pejchar 2022; Schmaling et al. 2015. Many such efforts align with superficial attempts by organizations to "quantify diversity" and signal support for racial and/or gender

equity that do not always align with the actual practices of those organizations (Byrd 2021; Laursen and Austin 2020).

18. Other research similarly shows that understanding concepts of racial privilege or advantage does not necessarily lead to an ability to understand one's own role in the reproduction of such advantages (Crowley 2019).

19. This finding contributes to understandings of the consequences of socioeconomic inequality in student involvement within higher education (Benson and Lee 2020; Silver 2020b; Stuber 2009; 2011a).

20. See also Goyette and Mullen (2006), Ma (2009), and Mullen (2010).

21. The pattern of universities missing opportunities to help students learn to engage as members of a community aligns with existing research. I documented comparable trends in my first book, *The Cost of Inclusion* (Silver 2020a). Similarly, other scholars have critiqued universities' failures to contribute to civic education, preparing students to be part of a diverse democratic society (Aries and Berman 2013; Byrd 2017; Warikoo 2016).

22. Notably, there are a few exceptions to this trend. For instance, Roksa, Silver, Deutschlander, and Whitley (2020) explore the notion of cultural capital as a family resource rather than simply a personal resource (see also Roksa and Deutschlander 2018). Nonetheless, like other studies, this project bracketed questions of variation in individual and institutional resources in order to understand the distinct properties of family resources.

23. Hamilton 2016, 6.

24. Exceptions include Ray and Best (2015), Ray and Rosow (2010), Reyes (2018), Richards (2022), and Stuber (2016).

25. Richards (2020, 2) critiques such tendencies, noting that research in the cultural capital tradition often "elevates a one-dimensional view of inequality as rooted primarily in class-based stratification" that fails "to interrogate explicitly and problematize the racist hierarchies and power dynamics which amplify the value of (White) cultural capital, while devaluing the cultural competencies and currencies of historically marginalized groups, positing that they lack such cultural capital" (see also Bettie 2003; Carter 2005; Wallace 2017, 2018).

26. Yosso 2005.

27. Though there is a dearth of research on this topic, recent studies are attempting to rectify this neglect (see for instance, Patrón 2021).

28. Aronson 2017.

29. Roksa et al. 2020.

30. Lee and Kramer 2013; Nelson 2019b; Rondini 2016, 2018.

31. Benson and Lee 2020, 165–66.

32. Davies and Rizk 2018; Lamont and Lareau 1988.

33. Deutschlander 2017. For scholarly discussions of the concept of "college knowledge," see Bell, Rowan-Kenyon, and Perna (2009), Gast (2021); George Mwangi (2018); and Kiyama (2010).

34. Khan 2011.

35. Ardoin 2017; Roderick, Coca, and Nagaoka 2011. An important critique of these tendencies can be found in Rios-Aguilar and Kiyama's (2012) article on funds of knowledge and Latina/o college students (see also, Kiyama and Rios-Aguilar 2018).

36. These dispositions can be thought of as representative of habitus, a set of deeply internalized preferences, styles, and ways of being first cultivated in early childhood (Bourdieu 1973). When one's habitus aligns with the contours of a given institution, it can be thought of as a form

of cultural capital. Notably though, for many LIFGWC students the habitus acquired through childhood socialization may feel unwelcome in school settings (Latz 2012; Lehmann 2014).

37. These insights show that many of the recurring debates between those following in the traditions of Bourdieu and Yosso stem from failure to consider structure and agency simultaneously (see also Roksa, Silver, and Wang 2022).

38. DiMaggio and Powell 1983.

39. Notably, many of the policies and practices that become widespread because of institutional isomorphism fail to adequately serve even those students enrolled at highly resourced institutions (see, e.g., Armstrong and Hamilton 2013).

40. Taylor and Cantwell 2019.

41. See, for instance, Eaton (2022), Hamilton and Nielsen (2021), and Goldrick-Rab (2016).

42. See also Mullen (2010).

43. To say that an emphasis on extracurricular and cocurricular engagement was problematic is not to say that these forms of engagement aren't valuable. There is a great deal of evidence to demonstrate the positive impact of such engagement (Mayhew et al. 2016; Pascarella and Terenzini 2005). The issue is that universities currently tout extracurricular and cocurricular involvement without making them accessible to all students.

44. Even in those rare moments when universities think beyond the desires of affluent students to consider the experiences of LIFGWC students, they often rely on problematic perspectives. For instance, CU's website sometimes included praise for these students' "grit" or "resilience" without acknowledging that the need for these traits was sometimes prompted by the institution's inadequate support.

45. See, for instance, Buchmann and DiPrete (2006); DiPrete and Buchmann (2013); Nielsen and Hamilton (2022). With regard to assuming a White student body, for example, Nielsen and Hamilton (2022, 24) explain how "institutional whiteness," which can be observed when "demography, policies, and practices that assume a white 'typical' student, blocks the potential for democratic higher education."

46. Roksa and Robinson 2016; Titus 2008.

47. Armstrong and Hamilton 2013; Labaree 1997.

48. Hayes and Wynyard 2002.

49. See also Roksa and Silver (2019).

50. Arum and Cook 2018.

51. In his book *Where Colleges Fail*, Sanford (1967) articulated the value of strategically pairing challenge and support. Unfortunately, while this model continues to be recommended by much of the student affairs literature (Evans et al. 2010; Longerbeam 2016), studies like this one show that it rarely translates into practice.

52. Research demonstrates that mandatory support services built into one's program of study often work better for LIFGWC students than opt-in services (Bassett 2021).

53. Roksa and Silver 2019; Roksa, Silver, and Wang 2022.

54. Studies of the experiences of adjunct faculty or advisors with high caseloads underscore this point (Bryan, Kim, and Liu 2022; Holland 2015; Murray 2019; Woods and Domina 2014).

55. Other students similarly expressed gratitude for faculty and staff members who had accommodated their schedules with late night or early morning meetings, offered extra tutoring sessions, loaned them various materials, and in one case provided a place to live when a student was unhoused.

56. The practice at many institutions of giving one-time, first-year scholarships has various negative outcomes (Goldrick-Rab 2016; Nunn 2021). In addition to creating financial precarity, such practices can undermine belonging in college. See, for instance, Nunn's (2021, 40) discussion of the experiences of students like Violet, whose loss of a university scholarship had the effect of disrupting her sense of belonging.

Appendix

1. Rinaldo and Guhin 2022.

2. Rinaldo and Guhin (2022, 41) describe this type of ethnographic interviewing as "primary ethnographic interviews" in contrast to "contextual ethnographic interviews," where interviews support ethnographic data.

3. This project not only seeks to understand "meso-level public culture," as described by Rinaldo and Guhin (2022), but it also aims to understand the specific impact of policies and practices employed by the university in ways that reflect elements of case study methods commonly used in educational research (Merriam and Grenier 2019).

4. Byrd 2021.

5. Hamilton and Nielsen 2021.

6. Silver 2020a.

7. *Oxford English Dictionary* online, s.v. "commonwealth, n.2."

8. For a discussion of this trade-off, see Hamilton (2016, 215) and Khan (2011, 202–3). While I often changed unique department and program names to more generic ones, using these pseudonyms meant that I was able to maintain the rich details of students' stories, my top priority for this study.

9. Jack 2019, 199.

10. Blimling 2001; Manning, Kinzie, and Schuh 2006.

11. Bowman, Mohebali, and Jarratt 2022; Kuk and Banning 2009.

12. For further reading on this subject, see Eaton (2022).

13. Bowman and Hill 2011; Smith and McCann 1998.

14. While I opted not to add "LMC" to the already lengthy LIFGWC initialism, it is important to note that lower-middle-class students—who were typically first generation and low income—were also among this group.

15. Armstrong and Hamilton 2013, 264–65.

16. Pugh 2015, 214.

17. Corbin and Strauss 2008; Emerson, Fretz, and Shaw 1995.

References

Abes, Elisa S., Susan R. Jones, and D-L Stewart, eds. 2019. *Rethinking College Student Development Theory Using Critical Frameworks*. Sterling, VA: Stylus.

Aciman, André. 2021. *Homo Irrealis: Essays*. New York: Farrar, Straus and Giroux.

Ahmed, Sara. 2012. *On Being Included: Racism and Diversity in Institutional Life*. Durham, NC: Duke University Press.

Aldegether, Reem A. 2017. "'What Every Student Should Know': General Education Requirements in Undergraduate Education." *World Journal of Education* 5 (3): 14.

Anctil, Eric J. 2008. *Selling Higher Education: Marketing and Advertising America's Colleges and Universities*. San Francisco: Jossey-Bass.

Ardoin, Sonja. 2017. *College Aspirations and Access in Working-Class Rural Communities: The Mixed Signals, Challenges, and New Language First-Generation Students Encounter*. Lanham, MD: Lexington Books.

Aries, Elizabeth, and Richard Berman. 2013. *Speaking of Race and Class: The Student Experience at an Elite College*. Philadelphia: Temple University Press.

Armstrong, Elizabeth A., and Laura T. Hamilton. 2013. *Paying for the Party: How College Maintains Inequality*. Cambridge, MA: Harvard University Press.

Arnett, Jeffrey Jensen. 2014. *Emerging Adulthood: The Winding Road from the Late Teens through the Twenties*. 2nd ed. New York: Oxford University Press.

Aronson, Pamela. 2017. "'I've Learned to Love What's Going to Pay Me': A Culture of Despair in Higher Education during a Time of Insecurity." *Critical Sociology* 43 (3): 389–403.

Arum, Richard, and Amanda Cook. 2018. "What's Up with Assessment?" In *Education in a New Society: Renewing the Sociology of Education*, edited by Jal Mehta and Scott Davies, 200–219. Chicago: University of Chicago Press.

Arum, Richard, and Josipa Roksa. 2011. *Academically Adrift: Limited Learning on College Campuses*. Chicago: University of Chicago Press.

Arum, Richard, and Josipa Roksa. 2014. *Aspiring Adults Adrift: Tentative Transitions of College Graduates*. Chicago: University of Chicago Press.

Arum, Richard, Josipa Roksa, and Amanda Cook. 2016. *Improving Quality in American Higher Education: Learning Outcomes and Assessments for the 21st Century*. San Francisco: Jossey Bass.

Arum, Richard, Josipa Roksa, Jacqueline Cruz, and Blake Silver. 2018. "Student Experiences in College." In *Handbook of the Sociology of Education in the 21st Century*, edited by Barbara Schneider, 385–403. Cham, Switzerland: Springer International.

Attewell, Paul, and David Lavin. 2007. *Passing the Torch: Does Higher Education for the Disadvantaged Pay Off across the Generations?* New York: Russell Sage Foundation.

Auyero, Javier, and Debora Swistun. 2008. "The Social Production of Toxic Uncertainty." *American Sociological Review* 73 (3): 357–79.

Azmitia, Margarita, Grace Sumabat-Estrada, Yeram Cheong, and Rebecca Covarrubias. 2018. "'Dropping Out Is Not an Option': How Educationally Resilient First-Generation Students See the Future." *New Directions for Child and Adolescent Development* 160: 89–100.

Babcock, Phillip, and Mindy Marks. 2011. "The Falling Time Cost of College: Evidence from Half a Century of Time Use Data." *Review of Economics and Statistics* 93 (2): 468–78.

Bailey, Thomas R., Shanna S. Jaggars, and Davis Jenkins. 2015. *Redesigning America's Community Colleges*. Cambridge, MA: Harvard University Press.

Bassett, Becca S. 2021. "Big Enough to Bother Them? When Low-Income, First-Generation Students Seek Help from Support Programs." *Journal of College Student Development* 62 (1): 19–36.

Bauman, Zygmunt. 2012. *Liquid Modernity*. Malden, MA: Polity Press.

Beasley, Maya A. 2011. *Opting Out: Losing the Potential of America's Young Black Elite*. Chicago: University of Chicago Press.

Beattie, Irenee R. 2018. "Sociological Perspectives on First-Generation College Students." In *Handbook of the Sociology of Education in the 21st Century*, edited by Barbara Schneider, 171–91. New York: Springer.

Beck, Ulrich. 1986. *Risk Society: Towards a New Modernity*. London: Sage.

Bell, Angela D., Heather T. Rowan-Kenyon, and Laura W. Perna. 2009. "College Knowledge of 9th and 11th Grade Students: Variation by School and State Context." *Journal of Higher Education* 80 (6): 663–85.

Benson, Janel E., and Elizabeth M. Lee. 2020. *Geographies of Campus Inequality: Mapping the Diverse Experiences of First-Generation Students*. New York: Oxford University Press.

Berrey, Ellen. 2015. *The Enigma of Diversity: The Language of Race and the Limits of Racial Justice*. Chicago: University of Chicago Press.

Best, Amy L. 2006. *Fast Cars, Cool Rides: The Accelerating World of Youth and Their Cars*. New York: New York University Press.

Bettie, Julie. 2003. *Women without Class: Girls, Race, and Identity*. Berkeley: University of California Press.

Bills, David B. 2004. *The Sociology of Education and Work*. New York: Blackwell.

Binder, Amy J., Daniel B. Davis, and Nick Bloom. 2016. "Career Funneling: How Elite Students Learn to Define and Desire 'Prestigious' Jobs." *Sociology of Education* 89 (1): 20–39.

Binder, Amy J., and Jeffrey L. Kidder. 2022. *The Channels of Student Activism: How the Left and Right Are Winning (and Losing) in Campus Politics Today*. Chicago: University of Chicago Press.

Binder, Amy J., and Kate Wood. 2013. *Becoming Right: How Campuses Shape Young Conservatives*. Princeton, NJ: Princeton University Press.

Blimling, Gregory S. 2001. "Uniting Scholarship and Communities of Practice in Student Affairs." *Journal of College Student Development* 42 (4): 381–96.

Blumenstyk, Goldie. 2003. "Auxiliary Services: Colleges Look for More Revenue." *Chronicle of*

REFERENCES

Higher Education, December 19. https://www.chronicle.com/article/auxiliary-services-colleges-look-for-more-revenue/.

Blume Oeur, Freeden. 2018. *Black Boys Apart: Racial Uplift and Respectability in All-Male Public Schools*. Minneapolis: University of Minnesota Press.

Bombaci, Sara P., and Liba Pejchar. 2022. "Advancing Equity in Faculty Hiring with Diversity Statements." *BioScience* 72 (4): 365–71.

Bonilla-Silva, Eduardo. 2018. *Racism without Racists: Color-Blind Racism and the Persistence of Racial Inequality in America*. Lanham, MD: Rowman and Littlefield.

Bourdieu, Pierre. 1973. "Cultural Reproduction and Social Reproduction." In *Knowledge, Education and Cultural Change*, edited by R. Brown, 71–112. London: Tavistock.

Bourdieu, Pierre. 1986. "The Forms of Capital." In *Handbook of Theory and Research for the Sociology of Education*, edited by John G. Richardson, 241–58. New York: Greenwood Press.

Bourdieu, Pierre, and Jean-Claude Passeron. 1977. *Reproduction in Education, Society, and Culture*. Thousand Oaks, CA: Sage.

Bowen, William G., Matthew M. Chingos, and Michael S. McPherson. 2009. *Crossing the Finish Line: Completing College at America's Public Universities*. Princeton, NJ: Princeton University Press.

Bowen, William G., Martin A. Kurzweil, and Eugene M. Tobin. 2005. *Equity and Excellence in American Higher Education*. Charlottesville: University of Virginia Press.

Bowman, Nicholas A., and Patrick L. Hill. 2011. "Measuring How College Affects Students: Social Desirability and Other Potential Biases in College Student Self-Reported Gains." *New Directions for Institutional Research* 150: 73–85.

Bowman, Nicholas A., Milad Mohebali, and Lindsay Jarratt. 2022. "An Interdisciplinary Theory of College Student Success." In *How College Students Succeed: Making Meaning across Disciplinary Perspectives*, edited by Nicholas Bowman, 238–72. Sterling, VA: Stylus.

Bozick, Robert. 2007. "Making It Through the First Year of College: The Role of Students' Economic Resources, Employment, and Living Arrangements." *Sociology of Education* 80 (3): 261–85.

Bozick, Robert, and Stefanie DeLuca. 2005. "Better Late than Never? Delayed Enrollment in the High School to College Transition." *Social Forces* 84 (1): 531–54.

Brand, Jennie E., and Yu Xie. 2010. "Who Benefits Most from College? Evidence for Negative Selection in Heterogeneous Economic Returns to Higher Education." *American Sociological Review* 75 (2): 273–302.

Braxton, John M., William R. Doyle, Harold V. Hartley III, Amy S. Hirschy, Willis A. Jones, and Michael K. McLendon. 2013. *Rethinking College Student Retention*. San Francisco: John Wiley and Sons.

Brewer, Alexandra, Melissa Osborne, Anna S. Mueller, Daniel M. O'Connor, Arjun Dayal, and Vineet M. Arora. 2020. "Who Gets the Benefit of the Doubt? Performance Evaluations, Medical Errors, and the Production of Gender Inequality in Emergency Medical Education." *American Sociological Review* 85 (2): 247–70.

Brint, Steven. 2002. *The Future of the City of Intellect: The Changing American University*. Stanford, CA: Stanford University Press.

Brooms, Derrick R. 2017. *Being Black, Being Male on Campus: Understanding and Confronting Black Male Collegiate Experiences*. Albany: State University of New York Press.

Brooms, Derrick R. 2020. "'It's the Person, but Then the Environment, Too': Black and Latino Males' Narratives about Their College Successes." *Sociology of Race and Ethnicity* 6 (2): 195–208.

Brulé, Elizabeth. 2004. "Going to Market: Neoliberalism and the Social Construction of the University Student as an Autonomous Consumer." In *Inside Corporate U: Women in the Academy Speak Out*, edited by Marilee Reimer, 247–64. Toronto, Ontario: Canadian Scholars' Press.

Bryan, Julia, Jungnam Kim, and Chang Liu. 2022. "School Counseling College-Going Culture: Counselors' Influence on Students' College-Going Decisions." *Journal of Counseling and Development* 100 (1): 39–55.

Buchmann, Claudia, and Thomas A. DiPrete. 2006. "The Growing Female Advantage in College Completion: The Role of Family Background and Academic Achievement." *American Sociological Review* 71 (3): 515–41.

Byrd, W. Carson. 2017. *Poison in the Ivy: Race Relations and the Reproduction of Inequality on Elite College Campuses*. New Brunswick, NJ: Rutgers University Press.

Byrd, W. Carson. 2021. *Behind the Diversity Numbers: Achieving Racial Equity on Campus*. Cambridge, MA: Harvard Education Press.

Byrd, W. Carson, Rachelle J. Brunn-Bevel, and Sarah M. Ovink. 2019. *Intersectionality and Higher Education: Identity and Inequality on College Campuses*. New Brunswick, NJ: Rutgers University Press.

Cabrera, Nolan L. 2011. "Using a Sequential Exploratory Mixed-Method Design to Examine Racial Hyperprivilege in Higher Education." *New Directions for Institutional Research* 151: 77–91.

Cabrera, Nolan L. 2018. *White Guys on Campus: Racism, White Immunity, and the Myth of "Post-Racial" Higher Education*. New Brunswick, NJ: Rutgers University Press.

Calarco, Jessica M. 2018. *Negotiating Opportunities: How the Middle Class Secures Advantages in School*. New York: Oxford University Press.

Capannola, Amanda L., and Elizabeth I. Johnson. 2020. "On Being the First: The Role of Family in the Experiences of First-Generation College Students." *Journal of Adolescent Research* 37 (1). https://doi.org/10.1177/0743558420979144.

Carlstrom, Aaron. 2013. *NACADA National Survey of Academic Advising*. Manhattan, KS: National Academic Advising Association.

Carnevale, Anthony P., Ban Cheah, and Andrew R. Hanson. 2015. "The Economic Value of College Majors." Washington, DC: Georgetown University Center on Education and the Workforce.

Carter, Prudence L. 2005. *Keepin' It Real: School Success beyond Black and White*. New York: Oxford University Press.

Causey, J., F. Huie, R. Lang, M. Ryu, and D. Shapiro. 2020. *Completing College 2020: A National View of Student Completion Rates for 2014 Entering Cohort: Signature Report 19*. Herndon, VA: National Student Clearinghouse Research Center.

Cebulko, Kara. 2014. "Documented, Undocumented, and Liminally Legal: Legal Status during the Transition to Adulthood for 1.5-Generation Brazilian Immigrants." *Sociological Quarterly* 55 (1): 143–67.

Chambliss, Daniel F., and Christopher G. Takacs. 2014. *How College Works*. Cambridge, MA: Harvard University Press.

Cheatham, Dennis. 2019. "Rewarding Risk: Exploring How to Encourage Learning that Comes from Taking Risks." *Teaching and Learning Design: Re:Research* 1 (1): 105–16.

Chesters, Jenny, and Hernan Cuervo. 2019. "Adjusting to New Employment Landscapes: Consequences of Precarious Employment for Young Australians." *Economic and Labour Relations Review* 30 (2): 222–40.

Childress, Herb. 2019. *The Adjunct Underclass: How America's Colleges Betrayed Their Faculty, Their Students, and Their Mission*. Chicago: University of Chicago Press.

REFERENCES

Coleman, James S. 1988. "Social Capital in the Creation of Human Capital." In "Organizations and Institutions: Sociological and Economic Approaches to the Analysis of Social Structure." Supplement, *American Journal of Sociology* 94: S95–S120.

Collier, Peter J., and David L. Morgan. 2008. "'Is That Paper Really Due Today?': Differences in First-Generation and Traditional College Students' Understandings of Faculty Expectations." *Higher Education* 55 (4): 425–46.

Collins, Patricia Hill. (2000) 2009. *Black Feminist Thought: Knowledge, Consciousness, and the Politics of Empowerment*. New York: Routledge.

Cooper, Marianne, and Allison J. Pugh. 2020. "Families across the Income Spectrum: A Decade in Review." *Journal of Marriage and Family* 82 (1): 272–99.

Corbin, Juliet, and Anselm Strauss. 2008. *The Basics of Qualitative Research: Techniques and Procedures for Developing Grounded Theory*. Thousand Oaks, CA: Sage.

Croucher, Gwilym, and Peter Woelert. 2016. "Institutional Isomorphism and the Creation of the Unified National System of Higher Education in Australia: An Empirical Analysis." *Higher Education* 71 (4): 439–53.

Crow, Michael M., and William B. Dabars. 2015. *Designing the New American University*. Baltimore: Johns Hopkins University Press.

Crowley, Ryan. 2019. "White Teachers, Racial Privilege, and the Sociological Imagination." *Urban Education* 54 (10): 1462–88.

Cuba, Lee, Nancy Jennings, Suzanne Lovett, and Joseph Swingle. 2016. *Practice for Life: Making Decisions in College*. Cambridge, MA: Harvard University Press.

Curtis, John W. 2013. "Trends in Instructional Staff Employment Status, 1975–2011." Washington, DC: American Association of University Professors Research Office.

Davies, Scott, and Jessica Rizk. 2018. "The Three Generations of Cultural Capital Research: A Narrative Review." *Review of Educational Research* 88 (3): 331–65.

Deckard, Faith M., Bridget J. Goosby, and Jacob E. Cheadle. 2022. "Debt Stress, College Stress: Implications for Black and Latinx Students' Mental Health." *Race and Social Problems* 14 (3): 238–53.

Deckman, Sherry L. 2022. *Black Space: Negotiating Race, Diversity, and Belonging in the Ivory Tower*. New Brunswick, NJ: Rutgers University Press.

Deil-Amen, Regina, and James E. Rosenbaum. 2003. "The Social Prerequisites of Success: Can College Structure Reduce the Need for Social Know-How?" *The Annals of the American Academy of Political and Social Science* 586 (1): 120–43.

Desrochers, Donna M., and Steven Hurlburt. 2014. "Trends in College Spending: 2001–2011; A Delta Data Update." Washington, DC: Delta Cost Project at American Institutes for Research.

Deutschlander, Denise. 2017. "Academic Undermatch: How General and Specific Cultural Capital Structure Inequality." *Sociological Forum* 32 (1): 162–85.

DiMaggio, Paul J., and Walter W. Powell. 1983. "The Iron Cage Revisited: Institutional Isomorphism and Collective Rationality in Organizational Fields." *American Sociological Review* 48 (2): 147–60.

DiPrete, Thomas A., and Claudia Buchmann. 2013. *The Rise of Women: The Growing Gender Gap in Education and What It Means for American Schools*. New York: Russell Sage.

Donaldson, Paul, Lyle McKinney, Mimi Lee, and Diana Pino. 2016. "First-Year Community College Students' Perceptions of and Attitudes toward Intrusive Academic Advising." *NACADA Journal* 36 (1): 30–42.

Druery, Jarrod E., and Derrick R. Brooms. 2019. "'It Lit Up the Campus': Engaging Black Males in Culturally Enriching Environments." *Journal of Diversity in Higher Education* 12 (4): 330–40.

Dumais, Susan A., and Aaryn Ward. 2010. "Cultural Capital and First-Generation College Success." *Poetics* 38 (3): 245–65.

Duncheon, Julia C. 2018. "'You Have to Be Able to Adjust Your Own Self': Latinx Students' Transitions into College from a Low-Performing Urban High School." *Journal of Latinos and Education* 17 (4): 358–72.

Duran, Antonio, and Susan R. Jones. 2019. "Using Intersectionality in Qualitative Research on College Student Identity Development: Considerations, Tensions, and Possibilities." *Journal of College Student Development* 60 (4): 455–71.

Dwyer, Rachel E., Laura McCloud, and Randy Hodson. 2011. "Youth Debt, Mastery, and Self-Esteem: Class-Stratified Effects of Indebtedness on Self-Concept." *Social Science Research* 40 (3): 727–41.

Eaton, Charlie. 2022. *Bankers in the Ivory Tower: The Troubling Rise of Financiers in US Higher Education*. Chicago: University of Chicago Press.

Elman, Cheryl, and Angela O'Rand. 2004. "The Race Is to the Swift: Socioeconomic Origins, Adult Education, and Wage Attainment." *American Journal of Sociology* 110 (1): 123–60.

Emerson, Robert M., Rachel I. Fretz, and Linda L. Shaw. 1995. *Writing Ethnographic Fieldnotes*. 2nd ed. Chicago: University of Chicago Press.

Evans, Nancy J., Deanna S. Forney, Florence M. Guido, Lori D. Patton, and Kristen A. Renn. 2010. *Student Development in College: Theory, Research, and Practice*. 2nd ed. San Francisco: John Wiley and Sons.

Fay, Daniel L., and Staci M. Zavattaro. 2016. "Branding and Isomorphism: The Case of Higher Education." *Public Administration Review* 76 (5): 805–15.

Foucault, Michel. 2008. *The Birth of Biopolitics: Lectures at the Collège de France, 1978–1979*. New York: Palgrave Macmillan.

Fruehwirth, Jane C., Siddhartha Biswas, and Krista Perreira. 2021. "The Covid-19 Pandemic and Mental Health of First-Year College Students: Examining the Effect of Covid-19 Stressors Using Longitudinal Data." *PLoS One* 16 (3): e0247999. https://doi.org/10.1371/journal.pone.0247999.

Fullerton, Andrew S., and Michael Wallace. 2007. "Traversing the Flexible Turn: US Workers' Perceptions of Job Security, 1977–2002." *Social Science Research* 36 (1): 201–21.

Furstenberg, Frank F., Rubén G. Rumbaut, and Richard A. Settersten. 2005. "On the Frontier of Adulthood: Emerging Themes and New Directions." In *On the Frontier of Adulthood: Theory, Research, and Public Policy*, edited by Richard A. Settersten, Frank F. Furstenberg, and Rubén G. Rumbaut, 3–25. Chicago: University of Chicago Press.

Gable, Rachel. 2021. *The Hidden Curriculum: First Generation Students at Legacy Universities*. Princeton, NJ: Princeton University Press.

Gallagher, Robert P. 2015. *National Survey of College Counseling Centers 2014*. Monograph Series no. 9V. Pittsburgh, PA: The International Association of Counseling Services.

Gast, Melanie Jones. 2021. "Reconceptualizing College Knowledge: Class, Race, and Black Students in a College-Counseling Field." *Sociology of Education* 95 (1): 43–60.

Geiger, Robert L. 2004. *Knowledge and Money: Research Universities and the Paradox of the Marketplace*. Stanford, CA: Stanford University Press.

Geiger, Robert L. 2011. "The Ten Generations of American Higher Education." In *American

Higher Education in the Twenty-First Century: Social, Political, and Economic Challenges, edited by Phillip G. Altbach, Patricia J. Gumport, and Robert O. Berdahl, 37–68. Baltimore: Johns Hopkins University Press.

George, David. 2007. "Market Overreach: The Student as Customer." *Journal of Socio-Economics* 36 (6): 965–77.

George Mwangi, Chrystal A. 2018. "'It's Different Here': Complicating Concepts of College Knowledge and First Generation through an Immigrant Lens." *Teachers College Record* 120 (11): 1–36.

Gerson, Kathleen. 2010. *The Unfinished Revolution: Coming of Age in a New Era of Gender, Work, and Family.* Oxford: Oxford University Press.

Ghidina, Marcia. 2019. "Deconstructing Victim-Blaming, Dehumanization, and Othering: Using Empathy to Develop a Sociological Imagination." *Teaching Sociology* 47 (3): 231–42.

Giddens, Anthony. 2003. *Runaway World: How Globalization Is Reshaping Our Lives.* New York: Taylor and Francis.

Giroux, Henry A. 2014. *Neoliberalism's War on Higher Education.* New York: Haymarket Books.

Goerisch, Denise. 2019. "Doing Less with Less: Faculty Care Work in Times of Precarity." In *Intersectionality and Higher Education: Identity and Inequality on College Campuses,* edited by W. Carson Byrd, Rachelle J. Brunn-Bevel, and Sarah M. Ovink, 122–35. New Brunswick, NJ: Rutgers University Press.

Golann, Joanne W. 2015. "The Paradox of Success at a No-Excuses School." *Sociology of Education* 88 (2): 103–19.

Golann, Joanne W. 2021. *Scripting the Moves: Culture and Control in a "No-Excuses" Charter School.* Princeton, NJ: Princeton University Press.

Golann, Joanne W., and A. Chris Torres. 2020. "Do No-Excuses Disciplinary Practices Promote Success?" *Journal of Urban Affairs* 42 (4): 617–33.

Goldin, Claudia, and Lawrence F. Katz. 2018. "The Race between Education and Technology." In *Inequality in the 21st Century,* edited by David B. Grusky and Jasmine Hill, 49–54. New York: Routledge.

Goldin, Claudia, Lawrence F. Katz, and Ilyana Kuziemko. 2006. "The Homecoming of American College Women: The Reversal of the College Gender Gap." *Journal of Economic Perspectives* 20 (4): 133–56.

Goldrick-Rab, Sara. 2006. "Following Their Every Move: An Investigation of Social-Class Differences in College Pathways." *Sociology of Education* 79 (1): 67–79.

Goldrick-Rab, Sara. 2016. *Paying the Price: College Costs, Financial Aid, and the Betrayal of the American Dream.* Chicago: University of Chicago Press.

Gonzales, Leslie D. 2012. "Stories of Success: Latinas Redefining Cultural Capital." *Journal of Latinos and Education* 11 (2): 124–38.

Gonzales, Roberto G. 2015. Lives in Limbo: Undocumented and Coming of Age in America. Berkeley: University of California Press.

Goyette, Kimberly A., and Ann L. Mullen. 2006. "Who Studies the Arts and Sciences? Social Background and the Choice and Consequences of Undergraduate Field of Study." *Journal of Higher Education* 77 (3): 497–538.

Grigsby, Mary. 2009. *College Life through the Eyes of Students.* Albany: State University of New York Press.

Grodsky, Eric, and Catherine Riegle-Crumb. 2010. "Those Who Choose and Those Who Don't: Social Background and College Orientation." *Annals of the American Academy of Political and Social Science* 627 (1): 14–35.

Gunther, Hannah, and Janel Benson. 2021. "Divergent Approaches to Access: How Selective College Admissions Offices Recruit Lower-Income, First-Generation, and Working-Class Students." *Journal of Working-Class Studies* 6 (2): 36–49.

Hackstaff, Karla B. 2010. "Family Genealogy: A Sociological Imagination Reveals Intersectional Relations." *Sociology Compass* 4 (8): 658–72.

Hagerman, Margaret A. 2018. *White Kids: Growing Up with Privilege in a Racially Divided America*. New York: New York University Press.

Halpern-Meekin, Sarah, and Kristin Turney. 2016. "Relationship Churning and Parenting Stress among Mothers and Fathers." *Journal of Marriage and Family* 78 (3): 715–29.

Hamilton, Laura T. 2016. *Parenting to a Degree: How Family Matters for College Women's Success*. Chicago: University of Chicago Press.

Hamilton, Laura T., and Kelly Nielsen. 2021. *Broke: The Racial Consequences of Underfunding Public Universities*. Chicago: University of Chicago Press.

Hamilton, Laura T., Josipa Roksa, and Kelly Nielsen. 2018. "Providing a 'Leg Up': Parental Involvement and Opportunity Hoarding in College." *Sociology of Education* 91 (2): 111–31.

Hardie, Jessica Halliday. 2022. *Best Laid Plans: Women Coming of Age in Uncertain Times*. Oakland: University of California Press.

Harper, Graeme. 2019. *Diversity, Equity and Inclusion in Honors Education*. New York: Cambridge Scholars.

Harrison, Laura M., and Laura Risler. 2015. "The Role Consumerism Plays in Student Learning." *Active Learning in Higher Education* 16 (1): 67–76.

Harrison, Monique H., Philip A. Hernandez, and Mitchell L. Stevens. 2022. "'Should I Start at MATH 101?' Content Repetition as an Academic Strategy in Elective Curriculums." *Sociology of Education* 95 (2): 133–52.

Hartley, Matthew, and Christopher C. Morphew. 2008. "What's Being Sold and to What End? A Content Analysis of College Viewbooks." *Journal of Higher Education* 79 (6): 671–91.

Harvey, David. 2005. *A Brief History of Neoliberalism*. New York: Oxford University Press.

Hayes, Dennis, and Robin Wynyard. 2002. *The McDonaldization of Higher Education*. Westport, CT: Bergin and Garvey.

Heller, Donald E., and Patricia Marin. 2002. *Who Should We Help? The Negative Social Consequences of Merit Scholarships*. Cambridge, MA: Civil Rights Project, Harvard University.

Hinton, Kip A. 2015. "Should We Use a Capital Framework to Understand Culture? Applying Cultural Capital to Communities of Color." *Equity and Excellence in Education* 48 (2): 299–319.

Hironimus-Wendt, Robert J., and Lora Ebert Wallace. 2009. "The Sociological Imagination and Social Responsibility." *Teaching Sociology* 37 (1): 76–88.

Hirshfield, Laura E. 2022. "The Promise of a Health Professions Education Imagination." *Medical Education* 56 (1): 64–70.

Holland, Megan M. 2015. "Trusting Each Other: Student-Counselor Relationships in Diverse High Schools." *Sociology of Education* 88 (3): 244–62.

Holland, Megan M. 2019. *Divergent Paths to College: Race, Class, and Inequality in High Schools*. New Brunswick, NJ: Rutgers University Press.

Holland, Megan M. 2020. "Framing the Search: How First-Generation Students Evaluate Colleges." *Journal of Higher Education* 91 (3): 378–401.

Hope, Julia, and Kathleen M. Quinlan. 2021. "Staying Local: How Mature, Working-Class Students on a Satellite Campus Leverage Community Cultural Wealth." *Studies in Higher Education* 46 (12): 2542–55.

Houle, Jason N., and Fenaba R. Addo. 2022. *A Dream Defaulted: The Student Loan Crisis among Black Borrowers*. Cambridge, MA: Harvard Education Press.

Hurst, Allison. 2010. *The Burden of Academic Success: Loyalists, Renegades, and Double Agents*. Latham, MD: Lexington Books.

Hurst, Allison L. 2019. *Amplified Advantage: Going to a "Good" College in an Era of Inequality*. Lanham, MD: Lexington Books.

Ispa-Landa, Simone. 2013. "Gender, Race, and Justifications for Group Exclusion: Urban Black Students Bussed to Affluent Suburban Schools." *Sociology of Education* 86 (3): 218–33.

Ispa-Landa, Simone, and Jordan Conwell. 2015. "'Once You Go to a White School, You Kind of Adapt': Black Adolescents and the Racial Classification of Schools." *Sociology of Education* 88 (1): 1–19.

Isserles, Robin G. 2021. *The Costs of Completion: Student Success in Community College*. Baltimore: Johns Hopkins University Press.

Jack, Anthony Abraham. 2019. *The Privileged Poor: How Elite Colleges Are Failing Disadvantaged Students*. Cambridge, MA: Harvard University Press.

Jacob, Brian, Brian McCall, and Kevin Stange. 2018. "College as Country Club: Do Colleges Cater to Students' Preferences for Consumption?" *Journal of Labor Economics* 36 (2): 309–48.

Jay, Meg. 2012. *The Defining Decade: Why Your Twenties Matter—And How to Make the Most of Them Now*. New York: Hachette Book Group.

Jayakumar, Uma, Rican Vue, and Walter Allen. 2013. "Pathways to College for Young Black Scholars: A Community Cultural Wealth Perspective." *Harvard Educational Review* 83 (4): 551–79.

Johnson, Anthony M. 2019. "'I Can Turn It on When I Need To': Pre-College Integration, Culture, and Peer Academic Engagement among Black and Latino/a Engineering Students." *Sociology of Education* 92 (1): 1–20.

Johnson, Valen E. 2003. *Grade Inflation: A Crisis in College Education*. New York: Springer Science and Business Media.

Kahlenberg, Richard D. 2010. *Rewarding Strivers: Helping Low-Income Students Succeed in College*. New York: Century Foundation Press.

Kalaivanan, Tharuna, Lily Krietzberg, Blake R. Silver, and Bianca Kwan. 2022. "The Senior-Year Transition: Gendered Experiences of Second-Generation Immigrant College Students." *Journal of Women and Gender in Higher Education* 15 (1): 21–40.

Kalleberg, Arne L. 2009. "Precarious Work, Insecure Workers: Employment Relations in Transition." *American Sociological Review* 74 (1): 1–22.

Kamenetz, Anya. 2015. "DIY U: Higher Education Goes Hybrid." In *Remaking College: The Changing Ecology of Higher Education*, edited by Michael W. Kirst and Michell L. Stevens, 39–60. Stanford, CA: Stanford University Press.

Karabel, Jerome. 2006. *The Chosen: The Hidden History of Admission and Exclusion at Harvard, Yale, and Princeton*. Boston: Houghton Mifflin.

Kasinitz, Philip, Mary C. Waters, John H. Mollenkopf, and Jennifer Holdaway. 2009. *Inheriting the City: The Children of Immigrants Come of Age*. New York: Russell Sage Foundation.

Khan, Shamus R. 2011. *Privilege: The Making of an Adolescent Elite at St. Paul's School*. Princeton, NJ: Princeton University Press.

Khan, Shamus. 2012. "Elite Identities." *Identities* 19 (4): 477–84.

Khan, Shamus. 2018. "Talking Pigs? Lessons from Elite Schooling." In *Education in a New Society: Renewing the Sociology of Education*, edited by Jal Mehta and Scott Davies, 183–99. Chicago: University of Chicago Press.

Khan, Shamus, and Colin Jerolmack. 2013. "Saying Meritocracy and Doing Privilege." *Sociological Quarterly* 54 (1): 9–19.

Kilgo, Cindy A., Jessica K. Ezell Sheets, and Ernest T. Pascarella. 2015. "The Link between High-Impact Practices and Student Learning: Some Longitudinal Evidence." *Higher Education* 69 (4): 509–25.

Kim, Chang Hwan, Christopher R. Tamborini, and Arthur Sakamoto. 2015. "Field of Study in College and Lifetime Earnings in the United States." *Sociology of Education* 88 (4): 320–39.

Kim, Dae Young. 2013. *Second-Generation Korean Americans: The Struggle for Full Inclusion*. El Paso, TX: LFB Scholarly.

Kirp, David L. 2003. *Shakespeare, Einstein, and the Bottom Line: The Marketing of Higher Education*. Cambridge, MA: Harvard University Press.

Kirp, David L. 2019. *The College Dropout Scandal*. New York: Oxford University Press.

Kiyama, Judy Marquez. 2010. "College Aspirations and Limitations: The Role of Educational Ideologies and Funds of Knowledge in Mexican American Families." *American Educational Research Journal* 47 (2): 330–56.

Kiyama, Judy Marquez, and Cecilia Rios-Aguilar. 2018. *Funds of Knowledge in Higher Education*. New York: Routledge.

Kizilcec, René F., Rachel B. Baker, Elizabeth Bruch, Kalena E. Cortes, Laura T. Hamilton, David Nathan Lang, Zachary A. Pardos, Marissa E. Thompson, and Mitchell L. Stevens. 2023. "From Pipelines to Pathways in the Study of Academic Progress." *Science* 380 (6643): 344–47.

Kuh, George D. 2008. *High-Impact Educational Practices: What They Are, Who Has Access to Them, and Why They Matter*. Washington, DC: Association of American Colleges and Universities.

Kuh, George D. 2009. "What Student Affairs Professionals Need to Know about Student Engagement." *Journal of College Student Development* 50 (6): 683–706.

Kuk, Linda, and James H. Banning. 2009. "Designing Student Affairs Organizational Structures: Perceptions of Senior Student Affairs Officers." *NASPA Journal* 46 (1): 94–117.

Labaree, David F. 1997. "Public Goods, Private Goods: The American Struggle over Educational Goals." *American Educational Research Journal* 34 (1): 39–81.

Labaree, David F. 2017. *A Perfect Mess: The Unlikely Ascendancy of American Higher Education*. Chicago: University of Chicago Press.

Lamont, Michele, and Annette Lareau. 1988. "Cultural Capital: Allusions, Gaps and Glissandos in Recent Theoretical Developments." *Sociological Theory* 6 (2): 153–68.

Lareau, Annette. 2021. *Listening to People: A Practical Guide to Interviewing, Participant Observation, Data Analysis, and Writing It All Up*. Chicago: University of Chicago Press.

Lareau, Annette, and Elliott B. Weininger. 2003. "Cultural Capital in Educational Research: A Critical Assessment." *Theory and Society* 32 (5/6): 567–606.

Latz, Amanda O. 2012. "Understanding the Educational Lives of Community College Students: A Photovoice Project, a Bourdieusian Interpretation, and Habitus Dissonance Spark Theory." *Current Issues in Education* 15 (2). https://cie.asu.edu/ojs/index.php/cieatasu/article/view/836.

Laursen, Sandra, and Ann E. Austin. 2020. *Building Gender Equity in the Academy: Institutional Strategies for Change*. Baltimore: Johns Hopkins University Press.

REFERENCES

Lee, Elizabeth M. 2016. *Class and Campus Life: Managing and Experiencing Inequality at an Elite College*. Ithaca, NY: Cornell University Press.

Lee, Elizabeth M. 2017. "'Where People Like Me Don't Belong': Faculty Members from Low-Socioeconomic-Status Backgrounds." *Sociology of Education* 90 (3): 197–212.

Lee, Elizabeth M., and Jacob Harris. 2020. "Counterspaces, Counterstructures: Low-Income, First-Generation, and Working-Class Students' Peer Support at Selective Colleges." *Sociological Forum* 35 (4): 1135–56.

Lee, Elizabeth M., and Rory Kramer. 2013. "Out with the Old, in with the New? Habitus and Social Mobility at Selective Colleges." *Sociology of Education* 86 (1): 18–35.

Lee, Elizabeth M., and Chaise LaDousa. 2015. *College Students' Experiences of Power and Marginality: Sharing Spaces and Negotiating Differences*. New York: Routledge.

Lee, Elizabeth, and Tonya Maynard. 2017. "In Class, Sharing Class: Faculty Members from Low-Socioeconomic Status Backgrounds and Status Visibility." *Journal of Working-Class Studies* 2 (2): 36–53.

Lee, Jennifer, and Min Zhou. 2015. *The Asian American Achievement Paradox*. New York: Russell Sage Foundation.

Lehmann, Wolfgang. 2007. "'I Just Didn't Feel Like I Fit In': The Role of Habitus in University Drop-Out Decisions." *Canadian Journal of Higher Education* 37 (2): 89–110.

Lehmann, Wolfgang. 2009. "University as Vocational Education: Working-Class Students' Expectations for University." *British Journal of Sociology of Education* 30 (2): 137–49.

Lehmann, Wolfgang. 2014. "Habitus Transformation and Hidden Injuries: Successful Working-Class University Students." *Sociology of Education* 87(1): 1–15.

Lerma, Veronica, Laura T. Hamilton, and Kelly Nielsen. 2020. "Racialized Equity Labor, University Appropriation and Student Resistance." *Social Problems* 67 (2): 286–303.

Levin, John S. 2005. "The Business Culture of the Community College: Students as Consumers; Students as Commodities." *New Directions for Higher Education* 129: 11–26.

Lewis, Amanda E., and John B. Diamond. 2015. *Despite the Best Intentions: How Racial Inequality Thrives in Good Schools*. New York: Oxford University Press.

Lightfoot, Cynthia. 1997. *The Culture of Adolescent Risk-Taking*. New York: Guilford Press.

Lo, Ming-Cheng Miriam. 2015. "Conceptualizing 'Unrecognized Cultural Currency': Bourdieu and Everyday Resistance among the Dominated." *Theory and Society* 44 (2): 125–52.

Longerbeam, Susan. 2016. "Challenge and Support for the 21st Century: A Mixed-Methods Study of College Student Success." *Journal of the First-Year Experience and Students in Transition* 28 (2): 33–51.

Lopez, Nancy. 2003. *Hopeful Girls, Troubled Boys: Race and Gender Disparity in Urban Education*. New York: Routledge.

Louie, Vivian S. 2004. *Compelled to Excel: Immigration, Education, and Opportunity among Chinese Americans*. Stanford, CA: Stanford University Press.

Ma, Jennifer, Matea Pender, and CJ Libassi. 2020. *Trends in College Pricing and Student Aid 2020*. New York, NY: College Board.

Ma, Yingyi. 2009. "Family Socioeconomic Status, Parental Involvement, and College Major Choices: Gender, Race/Ethnic, and Nativity Patterns." *Sociological Perspectives* 52 (2): 211–34.

Ma, Yingyi. 2020. *Ambitious and Anxious: How Chinese College Students Succeed and Struggle in American Higher Education*. New York: Columbia University Press.

MacDonald, Kathryn M. 2019. "Taking on the Challenges of Diversity and Visibility: Thoughts from a Small Honors Program." *Journal of the National Collegiate Honors Council* 20 (1): 19–24.

Manning, Kathleen, Jillian Kinzie, and John H. Schuh. 2006. *One Size Does Not Fit All: Traditional and Innovative Models of Student Affairs Practice*. New York: Routledge.

Marek, Michael W., Chiou Sheng Chew, and Wen-chi Vivian Wu. 2021. "Teacher Experiences in Converting Classes to Distance Learning in the COVID-19 Pandemic." *International Journal of Distance Education Technologies* 19 (1): 40–60.

Massengill, Rebekah Peeples. 2011. "Sociological Writing as Higher-Level Thinking: Assignments That Cultivate the Sociological Imagination." *Teaching Sociology* 39 (4): 371–81.

Mayhew, Matthew J., Alyssa N. Rockenbach, Nicholas A. Bowman, Tricia A. Seifert, and Gregory C. Wolniak. 2016. *How College Affects Students: 21st Century Evidence That Higher Education Works*. Vol. 1. San Francisco: John Wiley and Sons.

McCabe, Janice M. 2009. "Racial and Gender Microaggressions on a Predominantly-White Campus: Experiences of Black, Latina/o and White Undergraduates." *Race, Gender and Class* 16 (1): 133–51.

McCabe, Janice M. 2016. *Connecting in College: How Friendship Networks Matter for Academic and Social Success*. Chicago: University of Chicago Press.

McCabe, Janice M., and Brandon A. Jackson. 2016. "Pathways to Financing College: Race and Class in Students' Narratives of Paying for School." *Social Currents* 3 (4): 367–85.

Mcdossi, Oded. 2022. "Inequality Reproduction, Higher Education, and the Double Major Choice in College." *Higher Education* 85: 1–30.

McGuigan, Jim. 2014. "The Neoliberal Self." *Culture Unbound* 6 (1): 223–40.

McMillan Cottom, Tressie. 2017. *Lower Ed: The Troubling Rise of For-Profit Colleges in the New Economy*. New York: New Press.

Mehta, Sanjay S., John J. Newbold, and Matthew A. O'Rourke. 2011. "Why Do First-Generation Students Fail?" *College Student Journal* 45 (1): 20–36.

Melear, Kerry B. 2003. "From *in loco parentis* to Consumerism: A Legal Analysis of the Contractual Relationship between Institution and Student." *NASPA Journal* 40 (4): 124–48.

Merriam, Sharan B., and Robin S. Grenier. 2019. *Qualitative Research in Practice: Examples for Discussion and Analysis*. San Francisco: John Wiley and Sons.

Mettler, Suzanne. 2014. *Degrees of Inequality: How the Politics of Higher Education Sabotaged the American Dream*. New York: Basic Books.

Miller, Ryan A., Brett Ranon Nachman, and Richmond D. Wynn. 2020. "'I Feel Like They Are All Interconnected': Understanding the Identity Management Narratives of Autistic LGBTQ College Students." *College Student Affairs Journal* 38 (1): 1–15.

Mills, C. Wright. 1940. "Situated Actions and Vocabularies of Motive." *American Sociological Review* 5 (6): 904–13.

Mills, C. Wright. (1959) 2000. *The Sociological Imagination*. New York: Oxford University Press.

Morris, Edward W. 2005. "'Tuck in That Shirt!' Race, Class, Gender, and Discipline in an Urban School." *Sociological Perspectives* 48 (1): 25–48.

Morris, Edward W. 2007. "'Ladies' or 'Loudies'? Perceptions and Experiences of Black Girls in Classrooms." *Youth and Society* 38 (4): 490–515.

Moss-Pech, Corey. 2021. "The Career Conveyor Belt: How Internships Lead to Unequal Labor Market Outcomes among College Graduates." *Qualitative Sociology* 44 (1): 77–102.

Moss-Pech, Corey. In progress. "Major Tradeoffs: Separating Fact from Myth about College Majors and Entry-level Jobs." Unpublished manuscript.

Mullen, Ann L. 2010. *Degrees of Inequality: Culture, Class, and Gender in American Higher Education*. Baltimore: Johns Hopkins University Press.

REFERENCES

Mullen, Ann L., Kimberly A. Goyette, and Joseph A. Soares. 2003. "Who Goes to Graduate School? Social and Academic Correlates of Educational Continuation after College." *Sociology of Education* 76 (2): 143–69.

Murray, Darrin S. 2019. "The Precarious New Faculty Majority: Communication and Instruction Research and Contingent Labor in Higher Education." *Communication Education* 68 (2): 235–45.

Museus, Samuel D. 2021. "Revisiting the Role of Academic Advising in Equitably Serving Diverse College Students." *Journal of the National Academic Advising Association* 41 (1): 26–32.

Musoba, Glenda, and Benjamin Baez. 2009. "The Cultural Capital of Cultural and Social Capital: An Economy of Translations." In *Higher Education: Handbook of Theory and Research*, edited by John C. Smart, 151–82. New York: Springer.

Nathan, Rebekah. 2005. *My Freshman Year: What a Professor Learned by Becoming a Student.* Ithaca, NY: Cornell University Press.

National Center for Education Statistics. 2021. "Digest of Education Statistics: Table 303.70. Total Undergraduate Fall Enrollment in Degree-Granting Postsecondary Institutions, by Attendance Status, Sex of Student, and Control and Level of Institution: Selected Years, 1970 through 2030." Institute of Education Sciences. https://nces.ed.gov/programs/digest/d21/tables/dt21_303.70.asp.

National Center for Education Statistics. 2022. "Postsecondary Institution Expenses." Institute of Education Sciences. https://nces.ed.gov/programs/coe/indicator/cue.

National Student Clearinghouse. 2020. *First-Year Persistence and Retention: 2018 Beginning Cohort.* Herndon, VA: National Student Clearinghouse Research Center.

Nell Trautner, Mary, and Elizabeth Borland. 2013. "Using the Sociological Imagination to Teach about Academic Integrity." *Teaching Sociology* 41 (4): 377–88.

Nelson, Ingrid A. 2019a. "Social Capital and Residential Decision Making among Rural and Nonrural College Graduates." *Sociological Forum* 34 (4): 926–49.

Nelson, Ingrid A. 2019b. "Starting Over on Campus or Sustaining Existing Ties? Social Capital during College among Rural and Non-Rural College Graduates." *Qualitative Sociology* 42 (1): 93–116.

Newman, Katherine S. 2012. *The Accordion Family: Boomerang Kids, Anxious Parents, and the Private Toll of Global Competition.* Boston: Beacon Press.

Nichols, Laura. 2020. *The Journey before Us: First-Generation Pathways from Middle School to College.* New Brunswick, NJ: Rutgers University Press.

Nielsen, Kelly, and Laura T. Hamilton. 2022. "Democracy's Experiment Station." *Change: The Magazine of Higher Learning* 54 (1): 24–32.

Nora, Amaury. 2004. "The Role of Habitus and Cultural Capital in Choosing a College, Transitioning from High School to Higher Education, and Persisting in College among Minority and Nonminority Students." *Journal of Hispanic Higher Education* 3 (2): 180–208.

Nunn, Lisa M. 2021. *College Belonging: How First-Year and First-Generation Students Navigate Campus Life.* New Brunswick, NJ: Rutgers University Press.

Olsen, Lauren D. 2016. " 'It's on the MCAT for a Reason': Premedical Students and the Perceived Utility of Sociology." *Teaching Sociology* 44 (2): 72–83.

Oreopoulos, Philip, and Uros Petronijevic. 2013. "Making College Worth It: A Review of Research on the Returns to Higher Education." National Bureau of Economic Research Working Paper Series 19053. Cambridge, MA: National Bureau of Economic Research.

O'Shea, Sarah. 2015. "Arriving, Surviving, and Succeeding: First-in-Family Women and Their

Experiences of Transitioning into the First Year of University." *Journal of College Student Development* 56 (5): 499–517.

O'Shea, Sarah. 2016. "Avoiding the Manufacture of 'Sameness': First-in-Family Students, Cultural Capital and the Higher Education Environment." *Higher Education* 72 (1): 59–78.

Pascarella, Ernest T., and Patrick T. Terenzini. 2005. *How College Affects Students*. Vol. 2, *A Third Decade of Research*. Indianapolis, IN: Jossey-Bass.

Patrón, Oscar E. 2021. "Precarious Familismo among Latinas/os/xs: Toward a Critical Theoretical Framework Centering Queer Communities." *Journal of Social and Personal Relationships* 38 (3): 1085–102.

Pérez, David. II. 2017. "In Pursuit of Success: Latino Male College Students Exercising Academic Determination and Community Cultural Wealth." *Journal of College Student Development* 58 (2): 123–40.

Perna, Laura W., and Patricia Steele. 2011. "The Role of Context in Understanding the Contributions of Financial Aid to College Opportunity." *Teachers College Record* 113 (5): 895–933.

Person, Ann E., James E. Rosenbaum, and Regina Deil-Amen. 2006. "Student Planning and Information Problems in Different College Structures." *Teachers College Record* 108 (3): 374–96.

Peterson, Richard A., and Roger M. Kern. 1996. "Changing Highbrow Taste: From Snob to Omnivore." *American Sociological Review* 61 (5): 900–907.

Price, Derek V. 2004. *Borrowing Inequality: Race, Class, and Student Loans*. Boulder, CO: Lynne Rienner.

Pugh, Allison J. 2013. "What Good Are Interviews for Thinking about Culture? Demystifying Interpretive Analysis." *American Journal of Cultural Sociology* 1 (1): 42–68.

Pugh, Allison J. 2015. *The Tumbleweed Society: Working and Caring in an Age of Insecurity*. New York: Oxford University Press.

Pulido Villanueva, Brenda, Alejandra Priede, and Deborah Thien. 2021. "Racial Equity and Healing in Honors." In *Honors Education and the Foundation of Fairness: A Question of Equity*, edited by Graeme Harper, 46–65. Newcastle: Cambridge Scholars.

Pyne, Jaymes, and Eric Grodsky. 2020. "Inequality and Opportunity in a Perfect Storm of Graduate Student Debt." *Sociology of Education* 93 (1): 20–39.

Quadlin, Natasha, and Brian Powell. 2022. Who Should Pay? Higher Education, Responsibility, and the Public. New York: Russell Sage Foundation.

Ray, Rashawn, and Bryant Best. 2015. "Diversity Does Not Mean Equality: De Facto Rules That Maintain Status Inequality among Black and White Fraternity Men." In *College Students' Experiences of Power and Marginality: Sharing Spaces and Negotiating Differences*, edited by Elizabeth M. Lee and Chaise LaDousa, 152–68. New York: Routledge.

Ray, Rashawn, and Jason A. Rosow. 2010. "Getting Off and Getting Intimate: How Normative Institutional Arrangements Structure Black and White Fraternity Men's Approaches toward Women." *Men and Masculinities* 12 (5): 523–46.

Ray, Victor. 2019. "A Theory of Racialized Organizations." *American Sociological Review* 84 (1): 26–53.

Reyes, Daisy V. 2018. *Learning to Be Latino: How Colleges Shape Identity Politics*. New Brunswick, NJ: Rutgers University Press.

Reynolds, Pauline J. 2014. *Representing "U": Popular Culture, Media, and Higher Education*. ASHE Higher Education Report 40: 4. San Francisco: John Wiley and Sons.

Richards, Bedelia Nicola. 2020. "When Class Is Colorblind: A Race-Conscious Model for Cultural Capital Research in Education." *Sociology Compass* 14 (7): 1–14.

REFERENCES

Richards, Bedelia Nicola. 2022. "Help-Seeking Behaviors as Cultural Capital: Cultural Guides and the Transition from High School to College among Low-Income First Generation Students." *Social Problems* 69 (1): 241–60.

Rinaldo, Rachel, and Jeffrey Guhin. 2022. "How and Why Interviews Work: Ethnographic Interviews and Meso-Level Public Culture." *Sociological Methods and Research* 51 (1): 3–67.

Rios-Aguilar, Cecilia, and Judy Marquez Kiyama. 2012. "Funds of Knowledge: An Approach to Studying Latina(o) Students' Transition to College." *Journal of Latinos and Education* 11 (1): 2–16.

Rivera, Lauren A. 2011. "Ivies, Extracurriculars, and Exclusion: Elite Employers' Use of Educational Credentials." *Research in Social Stratification and Mobility* 29 (1): 71–90.

Rivera, Lauren A. 2012. "Hiring as Cultural Matching: The Case of Elite Professional Service Firms." *American Sociological Review* 77 (6): 999–1022.

Rivera, Lauren A. 2015. *Pedigree: How Elite Students Get Elite Jobs*. Princeton, NJ: Princeton University Press.

Robbins, Rich. 2013. "Advisor Load." NACADA Clearinghouse. https://nacada.ksu.edu/Resources/Clearinghouse/View-Articles/Advisor-Load.aspx.

Robinson, Brandon A. 2020. *Coming Out to the Streets: LGBTQ Youth Experiencing Homelessness*. Berkeley: University of California Press.

Robinson, Karen J. 2011. "The Rise of Choice in the US University and College: 1910–2005." *Sociological Forum* 26 (3): 601–22.

Roderick, Melissa, Vanessa Coca, and Jenny Nagaoka. 2011. "Potholes on the Road to College: High School Effects in Shaping Urban Students' Participation in College Application, Four-Year College Enrollment, and College Match." *Sociology of Education* 84 (3): 178–211.

Rodriguez, Sarah L., Erin E. Doran, Mackenzie Sissel, and Nia Estes. 2022. "Becoming *La Ingeniera*: Examining the Engineering Identity Development of Undergraduate Latina Students." *Journal of Latinos and Education* 21 (2): 181–200.

Roksa, Josipa. 2011. "Differentiation and Work: Inequality in Degree Attainment in US Higher Education." *Higher Education* 61 (3): 293–308.

Roksa, Josipa, and Denise Deutschlander. 2018. "Applying to College: The Role of Family Resources in Academic Undermatch." *Teachers College Record* 120 (6): 1–30.

Roksa, Josipa, and Karen Robinson. 2016. "From *in loco parentis* to Consumer Choice: Patterns and Consequences of the Changing Relationship between Students and Institutions." In *Handbook of the Sociology of Higher Education*, edited by James Cote and Andy Furlong, 106–15. New York: Routledge.

Roksa, Josipa, and Blake R. Silver. 2019. "'Do-It-Yourself' University: Institutional and Family Support in the Transition out of College." *Review of Higher Education* 42 (3): 1051–71.

Roksa, Josipa, and Blake R. Silver. 2021. "Higher Education." In *Inequality in America: Causes and Consequences*, edited by Kimberley Kinsley and Robert Rycroft, 95–106. Santa Barbara, CA: Greenwood, ABC-CLIO.

Roksa, Josipa, Blake R. Silver, Denise Deutschlander, and Sarah E. Whitley. 2020. "Navigating the First Year of College: Siblings, Parents, and First-Generation Students' Experiences." *Sociological Forum* 35 (3): 565–86.

Roksa, Josipa, Blake R. Silver, and Yapeng Wang. 2022. "Inequality in Higher Education: Sociological Understandings of Student Success." In *How College Students Succeed: Making Meaning across Disciplinary Perspectives*, edited by Nicholas Bowman, 179–207. Sterling, VA: Stylus.

Roksa, Josipa, and Melissa Velez. 2012. "A Late Start: Delayed Entry, Life Course Transitions and Bachelor's Degree Completion." *Social Forces* 90 (3): 769–94.

Rondini, Ashley C. 2016. "Healing the Hidden Injuries of Class? Redemption Narratives, Aspirational Proxies, and Parents of Low-Income, First-Generation College Students." *Sociological Forum* 31 (1): 96–116.

Rondini, Ashley C. 2018. Cautionary Tales: Low-Income First-Generation College Students, Educational Mobility, and Familial Meaning-Making Processes. In *Clearing the Path for First-Generation College Students: Qualitative and Intersectional Studies of Educational Mobility*, edited by Ashley C. Rondini, Bedelia Nicola Richards, and Nicholas P. Simon, 19–50. Lanham, MD: Lexington Books.

Rosenbaum, James E. 2001. *Beyond College for All: Career Paths for the Forgotten Half.* New York: Russell Sage Foundation.

Rosenbaum, James E. 2011. "The Complexities of College for All: Beyond Fairy-Tale Dreams." *Sociology of Education* 84 (2): 113–17.

Rumbaut, Rubén G. 2005. "Turning Points in the Transition to Adulthood: Determinants of Educational Attainment, Incarceration, and Early Childbearing among Children of Immigrants." *Ethnic and Racial Studies* 28 (6): 1041–86.

Sáenz, Victor B., Carmen de las Mercédez, Sarah G. Rodriguez, and Claudia García-Louis. 2017. "Latino Men and Their Fathers: Exploring How Community Cultural Wealth Influences Their Community College Success." *Association of Mexican American Educators Journal* 11 (2): 89–110.

Saichaie, Kem, and Christopher C. Morphew. 2014. "What College and University Websites Reveal about the Purposes of Higher Education." *Journal of Higher Education* 85 (4): 499–530.

Salas, Braulio. 2016. "College Knowledge as Cultural Capital: Reshaping Parental Involvement to Increase College Attainment." *Harvard Journal of Hispanic Policy* 28: 93–104.

Samuelson, Cate C., and Elizabeth Litzler. 2016. "Community Cultural Wealth: An Assets-Based Approach to Persistence of Engineering Students of Color." *Journal of Engineering Education* 105 (1): 93–117.

Sánchez-Connally, Patricia. 2018. "Latinx First Generation College Students: Negotiating Race, Gender, Class, and Belonging." *Race, Gender and Class* 25 (3/4): 234–51.

Sanford, Nevitt. 1967. *Where Colleges Fail: The Study of the Student as a Person.* San Francisco: Jossey-Bass.

Saunders, Daniel B. 2010. "Neoliberal Ideology and Public Higher Education in the United States." *Journal for Critical Education Policy Studies* 8 (1): 41–77.

Saunders, Daniel B. 2014. "Exploring a Customer Orientation: Free- Market Logic and College Students." *Review of Higher Education* 37 (2): 197–219.

Saunders, Daniel, and Ethan Kolek. 2017. "Neoliberal Ideology and College Students: Developing a Customer Orientation While in College." *Critical Education* 8 (8). https://doi.org//10.14288/ce.v8i8.186175.

Saunders, Murray, and Joan Machell. 2000. "Understanding Emerging Trends in Higher Education Curricula and Work Connections." *Higher Education Policy* 13 (3): 287–302.

Schmaling, Karen B., Amira Y. Trevino, Justin R. Lind, Arthur W. Blume, and Dana L. Baker. 2015. "Diversity Statements: How Faculty Applicants Address Diversity." *Journal of Diversity in Higher Education* 8 (4): 213–24.

Schneider, Barbara L., and David Stevenson. 1999. *The Ambitious Generation: America's Teenagers, Motivated but Directionless.* New Haven, CT: Yale University Press.

REFERENCES

Schuh, John H., Susan R. Jones, Shaun R. Harper, and associates. 2011. *Student Services: A Handbook for the Profession*. 5th ed. San Francisco: John Wiley and Sons.

Scimecca, Joseph A. 2021. "Public Sociology and the Lost Legacy of C. Wright Mills." In *The Routledge International Handbook of C. Wright Mills Studies*, edited by Jon Frauley, 107–14. New York: Routledge.

Sennett, Richard. 1998. *The Corrosion of Character: The Personal Consequences of Work in the New Capitalism*. New York: W. W. Norton.

Servage, Laura. 2009. "The Scholarship of Teaching and Learning and the Neo-liberalization of Higher Education: Constructing the 'Entrepreneurial Learner.'" *Canadian Journal of Higher Education* 39, no. 2 (2009): 25–43.

Settersten, Richard A., Jr. 2015. "The New Landscape of Early Adulthood: Implications for Broad-Access Higher Education." In *Remaking College: The Changing Ecology of Higher Education*, edited by Michael W. Kirst and Mitchell L. Stevens, 113–33. Stanford, CA: Stanford University Press.

Settersten, Richard A., Jr., Frank F. Furstenberg, and Rubén G. Rumbaut. 2008. *On the Frontier of Adulthood: Theory, Research, and Public Policy*. Chicago: University of Chicago Press.

Shapin, Steven. 2012. "The Ivory Tower: The History of a Figure of Speech and Its Cultural Uses." *British Journal for the History of Science* 45 (1): 1–27.

Shildrick, Tracy, Robert MacDonald, Colin Webster, and Kayleigh Garthwaite. 2012. *Poverty and Insecurity: Life in Low-Pay, No-Pay Britain*. Bristol, UK: Policy Press.

Silva, Jennifer M. 2013. *Coming Up Short: Working-Class Adulthood in an Age of Uncertainty*. New York: Oxford University Press.

Silva, Jennifer M., and Sarah M. Corse. 2018. "Envisioning and Enacting Class Mobility: The Routine Constructions of the Agentic Self." *American Journal of Cultural Sociology* 6 (2): 231–65.

Silva, Patrícia, Betina Lopes, Marco Costa, Dina Seabra, Ana I. Melo, Elisabeth Brito, and Gonçalo Paiva Dias. 2016. "Stairway to Employment? Internships in Higher Education." *Higher Education* 72 (6): 703–21.

Silver, Blake R. 2020a. *The Cost of Inclusion: How Student Conformity Leads to Inequality on College Campuses*. Chicago: University of Chicago Press.

Silver, Blake R. 2020b. "Inequality in the Extracurriculum: How Class, Race, and Gender Shape College Involvement." *Sociological Forum* 35 (4): 1290–1314.

Silver, Blake R., Tharuna Kalaivanan, Lily Krietzberg, and Jordan Hawkins. 2020. "Distance, Alignment, and Boundaries: How Second-Generation Immigrant College Seniors Negotiate Parental Involvement." *Journal of College Student Development* 61 (5): 558–73.

Silver, Blake R., and Lily Krietzberg. 2023. "Compartmentalizing Communities or Creating Continuity: How Students Navigate LGBQ+ Identity within and beyond College." *Sociological Focus* 56 (1): 1–19.

Silver, Blake R., Lily Krietzberg, and Tharuna Kalaivanan. 2021. "Transitioning OUT: Lesbian, Gay, Bisexual, and Queer Students' Concerns in the Senior Year." *Journal of the First-Year Experience & Students in Transition* 33 (2): 9–27.

Silver, Blake R., Freddy Lopez, Fanni Farago, and Tharuna Kalaivanan. 2022. "Focused, Exploratory, or Vigilant: Reproduction, Mobility, and the Self-Narratives of Second-Generation Immigrant Youth." *Qualitative Sociology* 45 (1): 123–47.

Silver, Blake R., and Josipa Roksa. 2017. "Navigating Uncertainty and Responsibility: Understanding Inequality in the Senior-Year Transition." *Journal of Student Affairs Research and Practice* 54 (3): 248–60.

Slaughter, Sheila, and Gary Rhoades. 2004. *Academic Capitalism and the New Economy: Markets, State and Higher Education*. Baltimore: Johns Hopkins University Press.

Sloan, John J., III, and Bonnie S. Fisher. 2010. *The Dark Side of the Ivory Tower: Campus Crime as a Social Problem*. New York: Cambridge University Press.

Smith, Kris M., and Claudia W. McCann. 1998. "The Validity of Students' Self-Reported Family Incomes." American Institutes for Research Annual Forum Paper.

Smith, Vicki. 2010. "Enhancing Employability: Human, Cultural, and Social Capital in an Era of Turbulent Unpredictability." *Human Relations* 63 (2): 279–300.

Son, Changwon, Sudeep Hegde, Alec Smith, Xiaomei Wang, and Farzan Sasangohar. 2020. "Effects of COVID-19 on College Students' Mental Health in the United States: Interview Survey Study." *Journal of Medical Internet Research* 22 (9): e21279. https://doi.org/10.2196/21279.

Soria, Krista M. 2012. "Creating a Successful Transition for Working-Class First-Year Students." *Journal of College Orientation, Transition, and Retention* 20 (1) 44–55.

Soria, Krista M., and Michael J. Stebleton. 2012. "First-Generation Students' Academic Engagement and Retention." *Teaching in Higher Education* 17 (6): 673–85.

Squire, Dian D., and Kristin McCann. 2018. "Women of Color with Critical Worldviews Constructing Spaces of Resistance in Education Doctoral Programs." *Journal of College Student Development* 59 (4): 404–20.

State Higher Education Executive Officers. 2015. *State Higher Education Finance: FY 2014*. https://sheeo.org/wp-content/uploads/2019/02/SHEF-FY-2014-20150410.pdf.

Stevens, Mitchell L. 2007. *Creating a Class: College Admissions and the Education of Elites*. Cambridge, MA: Harvard University Press.

Stich, Amy E. 2018. "Stratification with Honors: A Case Study of the 'High' Track within United States Higher Education." *Social Sciences* 7 (10): 175.

Streib, Jessi. 2017. "The Unbalanced Theoretical Toolkit: Problems and Partial Solutions to Studying Culture and Reproduction but Not Culture and Mobility." *American Journal of Cultural Sociology* 5 (1): 127–53.

Streib, Jessi. 2018. "Class, Culture, and Downward Mobility." *Poetics* 70 (1): 18–27.

Streib, Jessi. 2020. *Privilege Lost: Who Leaves the Upper Middle Class and How They Fall*. New York: Oxford University Press.

Stuber, Jenny M. 2009. "Class, Culture, and Participation in the Collegiate Extra-Curriculum." *Sociological Forum* 24 (4): 877–900.

Stuber, Jenny M. 2011a. *Inside the College Gates: How Class and Culture Matter in Higher Education*. Latham, MD: Lexington Books.

Stuber, Jenny M. 2011b. "Integrated, Marginal, and Resilient: Race, Class, and the Diverse Experiences of White First-Generation College Students." *International Journal of Qualitative Studies in Education* 24 (1): 117–36.

Stuber, Jenny M. 2016. "Normative Institutional Arrangements and the Mobility Pathway: How Campus-Level Forces Impact First-Generation Students." In *The Working Classes and Higher Education: Inequality of Access, Opportunity, and Outcome*, edited by Amy E. Stich and Carrie Freie, 110–27. New York: Routledge.

Takacs, Christopher George. 2020. "Becoming Interesting: Narrative Capital Development at Elite Colleges." *Qualitative Sociology* 43 (2): 255–70.

Taylor, Barrett J., and Brendan Cantwell. 2019. *Unequal Higher Education: Wealth, Status, and Student Opportunity*. New Brunswick, NJ: Rutgers University Press.

REFERENCES

Thomas, James M. 2020. *Diversity Regimes: Why Talk Is Not Enough to Fix Racial Inequality at Universities*. New Brunswick, NJ: Rutgers University Press.

Tierney, William G., and Jason F. Perkins. 2014. "Beyond the Ivory Tower: Academic Work in the 21st Century." In *Faculty Work and the Public Good: Philanthropy, Engagement, and Academic Professionalism*, edited by Genevieve G. Shaker, 185–98. New York: Teachers College Press.

Titus, Jordan J. 2008. "Student Ratings in a Consumerist Academy: Leveraging Pedagogical Control and Authority." *Sociological Perspectives* 51 (2): 397–422.

Toma, J. Douglas. 2007. "Expanding Peripheral Activities, Increasing Accountability Demands and Reconsidering Governance in US Higher Education." *Higher Education Research and Development* 26 (1): 57–72.

Turner, H. Spencer, and Janet L. Hurley. 2014. *The History and Practice of College Health*. Lexington: University Press of Kentucky.

Urry, John. 2007. *Mobilities*. Cambridge: Polity Press.

Vallas, Steven P., and Angèle Christin. 2018. "Work and Identity in an Era of Precarious Employment: How Workers Respond to 'Personal Branding' Discourse." *Work and Occupations* 45 (1): 3–37.

Van Jura, Matt, and Kaity Prieto. 2021. "Navigating College with MAAPS: Students' Perceptions of a Proactive Advising Approach." *NACADA Journal* 41 (2): 27–39.

Wallace, Derron. 2017. "Reading 'Race' in Bourdieu? Examining Black Cultural Capital among Black Caribbean Youth in South London." *Sociology* 51 (5): 907–23.

Wallace, Derron. 2018. "Cultural Capital as Whiteness? Examining Logics of Ethno-Racial Representation and Resistance." *British Journal of Sociology of Education* 39 (4): 466–82.

Warde, Alan, and Modesto Gayo-Cal. 2009. "The Anatomy of Cultural Omnivorousness: The Case of the United Kingdom." *Poetics* 37 (2): 119–45.

Warikoo, Natasha K. 2016. *The Diversity Bargain: And Other Dilemmas of Race, Admissions, and Meritocracy at Elite Universities*. Chicago: University of Chicago Press.

Warikoo, Natasha K. 2020. "Addressing Emotional Health While Protecting Status: Asian American and White Parents in Suburban America." *American Journal of Sociology* 126 (3): 545–76.

Warikoo, Natasha K. 2022. *Race at the Top: Asian Americans and Whites in Pursuit of the American Dream in Suburban Schools*. Chicago: University of Chicago Press.

Warnock, Deborah M., and Allison L. Hurst. 2016. "'The Poor Kids' Table': Organizing Around an Invisible and Stigmatized Identity in Flux." *Journal of Diversity in Higher Education* 9 (3): 261–76.

Waters, Mary C., Patrick J. Carr, Maria J. Kefalas, and Jennifer Holdaway. 2011. *Coming of Age in America: The Transition to Adulthood in the Twenty-First Century*. Berkeley: University of California Press.

Webster, David, and Nicola Rivers. 2019. "Resisting Resilience: Disrupting Discourses of Self-Efficacy." *Pedagogy, Culture and Society* 27 (4): 523–35.

Weiss, Felix, and Josipa Roksa. 2016. "New Dimensions of Educational Inequality: Changing Patterns of Combining College and Work in the US Over Time." *Research in Social Stratification and Mobility* 44: 44–53.

West, Stacia, Amy Castro Baker, Sukhi Samra, and Erin Coltrera. 2021. "Preliminary Analysis: SEED's First Year." Stockton, CA: Stockton Economic Empowerment Demonstration.

White, Eric R. 2015. "Academic Advising in Higher Education: A Place at the Core." *Journal of General Education* 64 (4): 263–77.

Wijeyesinghe, Charmaine, and Bailey W. Jackson. 2012. *New Perspectives on Racial Identity Development: Integrating Emerging Frameworks*. New York: New York University Press.

Wildhagen, Tina. 2015. "'Not Your Typical Student': The Social Construction of the 'First-Generation' College Student." *Qualitative Sociology* 38 (3): 285–303.

Winkle-Wagner, Rachelle. 2009. *The Unchosen Me: Race, Gender, and Identity among Black Women in College*. Baltimore: Johns Hopkins University Press.

Wolfgram, Matthew, and Vivien Ahrens. 2022. "'One Internship, Two Internships, Three Internships . . . More!': Exploring the Culture of the Multiple Internship Economy." *Journal of Education and Work* 35 (2): 139–53.

Woods, Chenoa S., and Thurston Domina. 2014. "The School Counselor Caseload and the High School-to-College Pipeline." *Teachers College Record* 116 (10): 1–30.

Wright, Ewan, and Benjamin Mulvey. 2021. "Internships and the Graduate Labour Market: How Upper-Middle-Class Students 'Get Ahead.'" *British Journal of Sociology of Education* 42 (3): 339–56.

Xie, Yu, and Kimberly Goyette. 2003. "Social Mobility and the Educational Choices of Asian Americans." *Social Science Research* 32 (3): 467–98.

Yee, April. 2016. "The Unwritten Rules of Engagement: Social Class Differences in Undergraduates' Academic Strategies." *Journal of Higher Education* 87 (6): 831–58.

Yosso, Tara J. 2005. "Whose Culture Has Capital? A Critical Race Theory Discussion of Community Cultural Wealth." *Race Ethnicity and Education* 8 (1): 69–91.

Zarifa, David, Jeannie Kim, Brad Seward, and David Walters. 2018. "What's Taking You So Long? Examining the Effects of Social Class on Completing a Bachelor's Degree in Four Years." *Sociology of Education* 91 (4): 290–322.

Index

ability, 14, 79, 87, 101, 108, 156, 165, 169
ableism, 53, 124, 156–60
academic probation, 30–31
accelerated master's degree, 91
Aciman, André, 74–75
adjunct faculty, 32–33, 193n18, 203n54
adolescence: and high-risk behaviors, 194n3; and insecurity culture, 23; and schooling, 131; and socioeconomic inequality, 23, 124; and transition to adulthood, 1, 6; and uncertainty, 6
adulthood: and COVID-19, 119; and do-it-yourself environments, 5; and employment, 2; and independence, 46, 105–6; and insecurity culture, 6, 9–10, 121; markers of, 6, 101, 121, 189n43; and metaphors about college, 1; perceptions of, 46, 84, 101, 122; and reproduction of inequality, 84, 124, 201n11; and resources, 33, 86; and role of higher education, 2, 6, 23, 49, 80, 88, 105–6; transition to, 1–3, 5–6, 9–10, 33, 80, 121, 189n39; and uncertainty, 1, 6, 106
advising, academic: barriers to accessing, 56; caseloads, 138–39, 200n39; finding support with, 3, 132; and planning for graduation, 55–56; and reactive support practices, 138; as resource, 1, 75, 141–42, 186; and selecting a major, 62; and socioeconomic inequality, 99, 140; as student support services, 134, 168
agency, 13, 41, 48, 68, 157, 166, 191n84, 203n37
Ahrens, Vivien, 197n26
alternative institutional arrangements, 144–51
Ambitious and Anxious (Ma), 101
anatomy, 63–64
anthropology, 154, 161, 173
anti-immigrant sentiment, 53, 101, 124, 156
archive, ethnographic, 9–10, 181, 186, 188n18

Armstrong, Elizabeth, 10, 18, 22–23, 184, 191n90, 192n92, 192n96, 195n21, 195n31, 198n14
Aronson, Pamela, 6, 189n43
arts, 71–72, 116, 160, 183, 195n21
Arum, Richard, 2, 69, 195n21
aspirational capital, 11, 41
athletics, 116, 122–23, 200n31

Bauman, Zygmunt, 188n21, 189n43, 190n58
Beck, Ulrich, 68, 194n14
Behind the Diversity Numbers (Byrd), 136
Bell, Angela, 202n33
belonging, 23, 31, 82, 204n56
Benson, Janel, 163, 193n32, 195n27
Best, Amy, 48
biology, 63–64, 71, 77, 86–88, 90, 115
Black feminist scholars, 191n77
Blume Oeur, Freeden, 41
Bonilla-Silva, Eduardo, 124
Bourdieu, Pierre, 11–13, 15, 81, 164, 191n85, 195n23, 203n37
branding, personal, 191n84
Brint, Steven, 195n21
broad-access institutions, 128, 198n8
Broke (Hamilton and Nielsen), 127, 190n50
buffet-style services, 29, 78, 89, 97–102, 130–33, 170–71. *See also* do-it-yourself environments
bureaucracy: and do-it-yourself environments, 29, 35, 130–31; navigating, 21, 29, 58, 150; and normative institutional arrangements, 75–76, 172, 182; and socioeconomic inequality, 34–35, 58–59, 108, 130–31, 150, 167; students' frustrations with, x, 111, 128; support navigating, 58
business, 61, 70–71, 90, 172, 183
"business-lite" fields, 195n21

Byrd, W. Carson, 7, 136, 198n14
bystander parents, 37

"cafeteria" colleges, 189n37
calendars, 42, 51–52
calibrated merit, 97
campus gymnasium, 21, 133–34, 182–83, 200n32
Cantwell, Brendan, 129
capital. *See* forms of capital
career fair, 98, 189n36
career services, 33, 39–40, 59, 75, 77–78
Carnevale, Anthony, 195n21
caseloads, advising, 15, 138–39, 165–66, 200n39, 203n54
challenge and support model, 203n51
charter schools, 201n13
Cheah, Ban, 195n21
chemistry, 63–64, 70–71
childcare, 184, 194n1
childhood, 12, 23, 131, 196n3, 196n6, 202n36
choice. *See* flexibility
Christin, Angèle, 189n43, 191n84, 197n19
civic education, 154, 202n21
class. *See* social class
classism, 124, 187n4
clubs. *See* student organizations
cocurricular involvement, 18, 48, 60–67, 73–76, 80, 93–95, 115–16, 148, 168, 201n10, 203n43. *See also* involvement, student
college-going habitus, 196n3
college knowledge, 81–83, 87, 107–8, 139, 164–66
color-blind racism, 124
coming out as LGBTQ+, 33–34, 86–87, 101, 134, 193n20
communications, 44–45, 71
community health, 90
completion. *See* degree completion
computer science, 29–31, 91, 197n21
concentrations in a major, 14, 23, 63–64, 90–92, 129, 170
constraint, 13, 26, 37, 53, 68, 72, 79, 101–2, 128, 166, 196n14, 203n37
consumers, students as, 5, 90–94, 127, 128–30, 167–71, 189n37
content repetition, 195n19
contextual ethnographic interviews, 204n2
contingent faculty, 32–33, 193n18, 203n54
continuing-generation college students: and careers, 85; and college choice, 79–80; and college experiences, 105–6; and college-going habitus, 77–80; and customer-service models of higher education, 79–80; definition of, 14, 82, 183; demographic characteristics of, 196n6; and family, 81–82, 86–87; and insecurity, 106–7; and insulated explorers, 14–15, 103–5, 107–11; navigating the university, 139–40; and op-

portunity maximizers, 14, 77–79, 83–84, 88–96; and resources, 79–80; stressors of, 100–101; and student organizations, 93–95, 116–17
Cost of Inclusion, The (Silver), 202n21
Costs of Completion, The (Isserles), 195n18
counseling: centers, 33–34; personnel, 33; resources for students, 34, 58–59, 132, 134, 168, 186
counterstructures, 200n47
COVID-19: and campus closures, 8, 25, 118; and college resources, 34–35; disruptions of, xii, 15, 96; and employment, 67, 118–19; and finances, 34–35; and insulated explorers, 118–20; and online classes, 47, 119–20; and opportunity maximizers, 95–96; and planning, 52–53; and precarious pioneers, 29–30, 34–35; and precarities of higher education, 3; and research methods, 181–82, 185; and risk minimizers, 47, 52–53; and socioeconomic inequality, 95; and uncertainty, 3, 29–30, 188n17
credits, x, 23–24, 28–31, 72, 116, 145–46, 168–69, 183
credit scores, 27
criminology, 61, 91–92
Crow, Michael, 190n50
cultural capital: as college knowledge, 81–83, 91, 107, 164–65; and community cultural wealth, 11, 153; and COVID-19, 96; and deficit perspectives, 12; definition of, 11, 164–66; different forms of, 81–82, 162; and do-it-yourself environments, 131; and ease, 82, 164–65; as family resource, 161, 202n22; and friendships, 82; and habitus, 202n36; and institutional recognition, 37, 41, 81, 191n75; and interactional styles, 84; and navigating institutions, 11, 18, 69, 107, 131–33, 143, 159; and office hours, 82; as personal resource, 161; programs for building, 12; and race, 12, 136; race-conscious theories of, 12, 202n25; as risky investment, 195n23; theories of, 164–66; used for self-protection, 84
cultural omnivorousness, 198n5
culture, public, 190n56, 204n3
cultures of risk, 48

Dabars, William, 190n50
debt: attempts to minimize, 48, 72–74; and challenges with repayment, 2, 10; constraining opportunities, 2, 128–29; and future plans, 74; student concerns about, xi, 2, 10, 25, 74. *See also* loans, student
decentralization, 140–43
decline of prescription, 199n12
degree completion: and changing majors, 62; and employment, 197n29; institutional emphasis on, 69–70, 195n18; and normative institutional arrangements, 126, 147; rates of, 1, 102, 126, 188n6; transfer students and, 147
Degrees of Inequality (Mullen), 18

INDEX

Designing the New American University (Crow and Dabars), 190n50
Deutschlander, Denise, 164, 202n22
disability, 53, 135
dispositions, 11, 79, 88, 106, 113–14, 148, 164–72, 191n85, 196n12, 198n1. *See also* habitus
Diversity Bargain, The (Warikoo), 117
Diversity Regimes (Thomas), 143
do-it-yourself environments: bureaucracy of, 35; and flexibility, 130–31; and insulated explorers, 133; navigating, 29, 43, 96–97; and personal resources, 39–40, 131; and one-way honor system, 68–69, 157; and opportunity maximizers, 96–97; and precarious pioneers, 29–31, 35, 39–43; and program resources, 149–50; and risk minimizers, 58–59, 68–69; and self-blame, 40; and self-serve resources, 42, 130–31; and socioeconomic inequality, 5, 31, 133, 150, 157; and students as consumers, 5; and transfer students, 31; and transition out of college, 5, 29
dormitories. *See* residence halls
double majoring, 90–91, 183, 197n21
downward mobility. *See* mobility, social

earth science, 109, 114
ease, 79, 82–87, 104, 108–15, 121–26, 159, 164–71, 196nn12–14
Eaton, Charlie, 203n41, 204n12
economic capital: and affluent families, 80–81, 83, 120–21, 165; and affording college, 27–28, 165; and employment, 195n23; expected by the university, 54; and low-income families, 13, 25–29; and parental income, 183; as shelter from precarity, 108; and student concerns, ix; and student success, 87; supporting résumé building, 164
economics, 99, 142, 154
educational pathways. *See* pathways, educational
emerging adulthood, 122
engineering, 47, 60, 106, 114, 183, 189n44
English, 8, 88, 160, 190n55
enterprising self, 88–96, 99–100, 115, 186
entrepreneurial learners, 127
environmental sciences, 71, 88, 92
environmental studies, 71
ethnographic archive. *See* archive, ethnographic
ethnographic interviews, 7–9, 161–62, 181–86, 189n49, 204n2
exercise science, 60–61, 71
explorers. *See* insulated explorers
extracurricular involvement, 18, 48, 65–66, 73–76, 80, 93–95, 112–17, 129–34, 168, 198n10, 203n43. *See also* involvement, student

faculty, 6, 10–12, 29–33, 137–38, 166–75, 203n55. *See also* student-faculty interactions

faculty mentorship, 33, 136, 149
FAFSA. *See* Free Application for Federal Student Aid (FAFSA)
familial capital, 11, 37, 194n5
family involvement, 14, 36–38, 54–56, 98–99, 161–64, 194n5
fashion, 71
Fast Cars, Cool Rides (Best), 48
fast food jobs, 48, 53, 66–67, 74, 95
fees, course, 18, 28–29, 34–35, 174
finances. *See* economic capital
first-generation college students: deficit perspectives on, 192n2; definition of, 7–8, 29, 183, 192n1, 194n1; demographics of, 7–8; and family, 29, 34, 82; and insecurity, 21–22, 50–51; and new universities, 7–8, 190n51, 192n1; and planning, 51; and precarious pioneers, 13–14, 21–22; and responsibility, 51; and risk minimizers, 14; and student-faculty interactions, 33; and transfer students, 31
first-year experience, 22–23, 31, 49–51, 139, 148, 185, 193n13
flexibility, xii–xiii, 4–5, 14–19, 45, 68, 80–83, 100–101, 110–11, 119–22, 129–33, 144–45, 170–71
food insecurity, ix, 21, 25, 66, 73
foreign languages, 89–92, 170
forensic biology, 77
forms of capital, 11, 36, 47, 54, 78, 108, 162–63, 195n23
Foucault, Michel, 88, 197n19
fraternities, 90, 117, 120, 123, 134
Free Application for Federal Student Aid (FAFSA), 26
friends. *See* peers
funding college: and employment, 39; and financial aid, 27, 34; and government policy, 127; through grants, 4; and low-income, first-generation, and working-class students, 150; navigating, 9, 28–29, 72, 75, 141–42, 185; and parents, 81, 107, 161, 196n11; and related supplies, 25; through scholarships, 38, 81; through student loans, 4, 10, 25–29, 34–35, 39, 60, 190n64. *See also* loans, student
funding institutions and offices, 19, 76, 127–28, 134, 168–73, 182, 190n50, 191n89
funds of knowledge, 202n35
Furstenberg, Frank, 189n43

Gast, Melanie Jones, 202n33
gender, 14, 79, 83, 87, 101, 108, 123, 153–56, 159–65, 168–69
Geographies of Campus Inequality (Benson and Lee), 163–64, 193n32
geography, 114
George, David, 191n89
George Mwangi, Chrystal, 202n33

Goldrick-Rab, Sara, 190n64, 192n10, 203n41
government, 90, 94, 106, 114, 154
Goyette, Kimberly, 202n20
grade point average, 30, 38–39, 72, 89, 92–93, 113, 195n19
grades, 38–39, 70–72, 111–14, 120, 169
graduate school, 5, 45, 72, 77–78, 91, 96, 101, 121
graduation: and academic advising, 55–56; and credit overloads, 39; and electives, 116; as event or marker, 74; and minors, 24; outcomes after, 69, 73; persistence to, 22; plans for after, 44–46, 74, 101, 120–22, 132; postponing, 24, 116; and resources, 128, 132; students' perceptions of progress toward, ix–xi, 24, 43–44, 52, 70. *See also* degree completion
grandparents, 38, 82
grit, xii, 42, 187n2, 203n44
Guhin, Jeffrey, 181, 189n49, 190n56, 204nn2–3
guidance counselors, 125
guided pathways, 5, 23, 130–31, 170–72

habitus, 196n3, 202n36. *See also* dispositions
Hamilton, Laura, 7, 10, 18, 22–23, 37, 105, 127, 161, 181, 184, 190nn50–51, 191n90, 192n92, 192n96, 194n12, 195n21, 195n31, 196n11, 198n5, 198n14, 199n13, 199n20, 200n36 (chap. 6), 200n42 (chap. 6), 200n1 (chap. 7), 203n41, 203n45, 204n8
Hanson, Andrew, 195n21
Harris, Jacob, 150, 200n47
helicopter parents, 196n11
high-impact learning, 73, 92, 147–49, 194n13
history, 154, 160, 171
Homo Irrealis (Aciman), 74–75
homophobia, 124, 158, 160
honors education, 58, 81, 147–50, 172–73, 194n9, 200n46
housing insecurity, 21, 25, 27, 34, 44
human capital, 197n19
humanities, 81, 154, 160, 183

immigrants: and community cultural wealth, 55–56, 85, 162–63; and cultural capital, 164–65; and marginalization, 11, 53–56, 79, 169; parents, 55, 158, 194n1; and stereotypes, 159; students from immigrant families, ix, 18, 37, 85, 101, 158, 183, 190n55, 201n11. *See also* second-generation immigrants
immigration, ix, 14, 55, 79, 84, 87, 156, 169
inadequate student support services, 133–38
inclusion, 23, 31, 33, 54, 82, 136–37, 171, 204n56
income, 7, 10, 25, 37, 183, 190n51, 190n64
individualistic perspectives, 19, 155–61, 170
inflation, 4
information technology, ix, 47–48, 60–61, 91, 200n39
insecurity amplifiers, 150–53, 167. *See also* normative institutional arrangements

institutional whiteness, 203n45
insulated explorers: and academic engagement, 112–13, 116, 198n8; and capital, 143, 159, 164; and college experience, 105; and COVID-19, 118–19; descriptions of, 14, 103–4; and diversity, 117–18; and ease, 105, 111–15, 125–26; and employment, 113–14; and extracurricular activities, 116–17, 166; and flexibility, 128, 130, 133, 198n1; and the future, 120–22; and growth/development, 105–7, 117–22, 125, 130; and merit, 104; and online courses, 120; and passion, 114–15; and racism, 123–24; and selectively sociological imagination, 158–61; and self-discovery, 104–7, 119, 166; sociodemographic characteristics of, 107–11, 124; and socioeconomic inequality, 104, 115, 124–26, 140–43, 158, 164
international affairs, 81, 91, 116, 154
internships: and academic advising, 139; avoiding, 66–67, 73, 165; and COVID-19, 95–96; and do-it-yourself environments, 130; enhancing résumés with, 73, 80–86, 92–96, 115, 197n26, 197n29; as high-impact educational opportunities, 64; searching for, 1, 67, 92, 139; unpaid, 48, 165
intersectionality: definition of, 191n77; and family, 86; and insecurity, 152; in K–12 education, 191n77; as lens, 164–65; and marginalization, 104, 164; and privilege, 108, 164; and social locations, 15, 83–84, 104, 152
interviews, in-depth, 181, 190n56. *See also* ethnographic interviews
intrusive advising, 138, 200n38
invisible student support services, 133–38
involvement, student: accessibility of, 168, 175, 203n43; benefits of, 73, 203n43; high levels of, 14, 78–81, 86, 92–96, 126; low levels of, 64–68; and marginalization, 86; and normative institutional arrangements, 165; offices, 60, 134; vs. paid employment, 66; and resources, 56; and risk, 65–68, 75–76; and socioeconomic inequality, 198n10, 202n19; and sociological imagination, 160; staffing for, 134; strategic use of, 98, 148; stressors of, 126; and student development, 117
isomorphism, institutional, 167, 191n87, 203n39
Isserles, Robin, 195n18

Jack, Anthony, 182, 193n18
journalism, 71

Khan, Shamus, 78–79, 82–83, 104, 164, 190n52, 196n12, 196n14, 199n19, 204n8
Kiyama, Judy Marquez, 202n33, 202n35

Labaree, David, 191n89
Lareau, Annette, 190n57
laundering privilege, 197n18

INDEX

law, 77, 121, 173
law school, 121, 173
learning, 2, 19, 69–73, 111–13, 120–22, 130, 148–55, 198n8. *See also* high-impact learning
learning communities, 129–30
learning services, 33, 75, 135, 142
Lee, Elizabeth, 150, 163, 193n32, 195n27, 200n47
Lerma, Veronica, 137, 200n36
lessons of privilege, 78–79
LGBTQ+ resource centers, 33–34, 134
LGBTQ+ students, 38, 86–87, 101, 109–10, 135, 164, 193n20, 196n14
liberal arts, 70–71, 91–92
library, 25, 98–99
linguistic capital, 11
liquid modernity, 188n21, 190n58
loans, student: and affluent students, 81; average amount of, 2; avoiding, 74, 76; and employment, 39, 74; federal vs. private, 26–27, 60; and government policy, 4; and income, 10, 190n64; and maintaining enrollment, 25–29, 60; navigating, 28–29; and parent PLUS loans, 34–35, 193n33; risks of, 60, 68, 74, 76; and stress, 2, 101; and summer classes, 29

Ma, Yingyi, 101, 194n12, 202n20
majors, academic: and academic advisors, 138–39, 147–48, 200n39; changing, 9, 23, 47–48, 62, 71, 106, 194n11; choosing, ix–x, 9–13, 29–30, 60–62, 77–78, 132, 194n11; and concentrations, 14, 23, 63–64, 90–92, 129, 170; and coursework, 116; customizing, 130; and employment, 71–72, 81–82, 89–90, 185, 195n21; exploring, 75; and family, 58, 71–72, 194n12; flexibility of, 45, 130; participants', 183; and passions, 114–15; practical, 60–62, 67–72; requirements of, 63, 139, 146; resources for selecting, 59, 91–92; and socioeconomic inequality, 160; supplementing, 90–92, 115. *See also* double majoring
marketization, 5, 15–16
mascots, 36
mathematics, 26, 61–63, 70–71, 114, 142, 183, 197n21
maximizers. *See* opportunity maximizers
McCabe, Janice, 73, 200n1
McMillan Cottom, Tressie, 189n29, 195n29, 200n1
medical school, 86–93, 148
meditation, 119–20
mental health, 34, 58–59, 132–34, 168. *See also* counseling
merit, 14, 78–79, 88–89, 97–104, 153, 164, 197n18. *See also* calibrated merit
Mills, C. Wright, 19, 153–54, 158, 201n13
minimizers. *See* risk minimizers
minors, academic, 14, 77, 90–92, 115, 122, 129–30, 197n20

mobility, social: and adulthood, 23; and educational pathways, 18, 22–23, 126, 192n92, 192n96, 195n31; and families, ix; and institutional marketing, 18; and institutional missions, 17, 23; and low-income, first-generation, and working-class students, 125, 192n92, 195n31; and perceived role of colleges, 23–24, 49, 125; and resources, 166, 191n84; and social reproduction, 36, 166
mobility pathway, 23, 126, 192n92, 192n96
Moss-Pech, Corey, 70–71, 189n44, 197n22
Mullen, Ann, 18, 202n20, 203n42
multiple internship economy, 197n26
museums, 44–45
music, 71–72

navigational capital, 11, 194n5
neoliberalism: and consumer choice, 128; and families, 4, 187n2; and higher education, 127–28, 150, 199n20; and identity, 40, 191n84; and innovation, 128; and insecurity culture, 4–7; and K–12 education, 187n2; and policymaking, 4–7; and retention and graduation rates, 188n6; understandings of, 127–28
neoliberal self, 40
neuroscience, 89–90
new elite, 197n17
New York City, ix
nice diversity, 118
Nielsen, Kelly, 7, 127, 181, 190nn50–51, 194n12, 196n11, 199n13, 199n20, 200n36 (chap. 6), 200n42 (chap. 6), 200n1 (chap. 7), 203n41, 203n45
No Child Left Behind Act, 131
"no excuses" discourse, 156–57, 201n13
normative institutional arrangements, 15–20, 126–29, 143–44, 150–51, 161, 166–75, 181
norms, 12, 56, 81, 107, 158, 163
Nunn, Lisa, 43, 118, 204n56
nursing, 60–62

office hours, 11, 33, 82, 165–66, 193n18
omnivorousness, cultural, 198n5
one-way honor system, 40–41, 68–69, 201n14
opportunity hoarding, 197n27, 200n41
opportunity maximizers: and anxiety, 99–103; building an enterprising self, 88–96; and careers, 77–78, 84–85, 94–96; and college choice, 79–80; and college-going habitus, 79; and college knowledge, 164–66; and COVID-19, 95–96; descriptions of, 14, 42, 77–79, 103; and do-it-yourself environments, 96–99; families of, 78–79, 82, 84–85; and internships, 94–95; and lessons of privilege, 78–79; and major choice, 90–92; and marginalization, 82–85; and options, 86–88, 99–102; resources of, 78–82,

230 INDEX

opportunity maximizers (*cont.*)
164–66; and socioeconomic inequality, 80–82,
97–102; and transition to adulthood, 80
opt-in services, 172, 203n52
opt-out services, 172

pandemic. *See* COVID-19
paramedic parents, 196n11
parental education, 183, 196n6
Parenting to a Degree (Hamilton), 37
parent PLUS loan, 34–35, 193n33
parents, paying for college, 81, 107
parties, 94, 126, 169, 192n92, 197n25
party pathway, 126, 192n92
pathways, educational: and academic rigor, 69;
anticipating, 175; and careers, 44; and choices,
171; definition of, 18; guided, 5, 131; and high
school, 171, 187n3; and insulated explorers,
130; and low-income, first-generation, and
working-class students, 22–23, 195n31; and
normative institutional arrangements, 18,
170–72; and opportunity maximizers, 130; and
partying, 126; and precarious pioneers, 22–23,
44; and resources, 72, 171–72; and risk minimizers, 51, 69–70; risky, 18; and social mobility, 23,
126, 192n96, 195n31; and social reproduction,
130; and structure, 130, 187n3, 170; and transfer
students, 144–47, 171; types of, 18, 171, 192n92
Paying for the Party (Armstrong and Hamilton),
22–23, 184, 192n92
peers, 2, 31, 61, 73, 88, 115–18, 137, 142, 156
Pell Grants, 8–10, 125, 183
Perna, Laura, 202n33
Peru, 124, 194n1
physics, 70–71
physiology, 63–64
pioneers. *See* precarious pioneers
pipeline metaphor, 2, 192n92
practical arts, 70–71
practical majors, 60–62, 67–72
precarious pioneers: and affording college, 25–29;
and beliefs about typical college students,
22–23; and college choice, 22–23; and college
involvement, 33–35; and contingent faculty, 32–
33; descriptions of, ix–xiii, 13, 21–22, 47, 74–75;
and do-it-yourself environments, 29–32, 35–36;
and insecurity culture, 22–24, 40–42, 47; looking toward the future, 44–46; and low-income,
first-generation, and working-class students,
22–23, 74–76; and personal resources, 36–38;
and progress toward graduation, 43–44; and
resilience, 38–43; and socioeconomic inequality, 22–23; and university resources, 33–35
predental, 63–64
prelaw, 173

premed, 86–87, 92–93, 115, 148
primary ethnographic interviews, 204n2
private institutions, 7, 128
private loans, 26–27, 60
Privileged Poor, The (Jack), 193n18
Privilege Lost (Streib), 86
proactive advising, 200n38
proactive practices, 19, 58, 97, 138–40, 144, 147–51,
163, 172–74
production of demonstrated accomplishment,
197n18
professional pathway, 192n92
psychology, 71, 77, 92, 105, 154, 161, 189n39
public administration, 71
public culture. *See* culture, public
public institutions, 1–7, 13–15, 25, 104, 127–29, 150–
54, 182, 191n90, 195n31, 199n23
Pugh, Allison, 4, 40, 100, 185–86, 190n57, 193n34,
201n14

race, 10–14, 79, 83, 87, 101, 108, 123–27, 137, 153–56,
162–69
Race to the Top grants, 131
racialized equity labor, 200n36
racism, 12, 53–54, 85, 124, 136–38, 156–60, 187n4,
201n12
Ray, Rashawn, 15, 126, 202n24
reactive student support practices, 138–40
recreation, 71, 133–34
rehearsals, 74–75
relatives, 25, 101, 115, 162–63
religion, 14, 79, 85–87, 101, 159, 165, 169
reproduction, social, 19, 36–37, 102, 160–66,
191n84, 201n13
research, undergraduate, 147–49
residence halls, 77, 170, 182–83, 200n32
resilience: as dimension of community cultural
wealth, 13; and institutions, xii, 166, 187n2,
203n44; and lessons learned in college, xi;
and precarious pioneers, 13, 22, 38–43, 125–
26, 186; and socioeconomic inequality, xi, 13,
125–26, 162–63; staff advocating for, xii, 166,
203n44
resistance: as dimension of community cultural
wealth, 11–12, 13, 37, 194n5; and families, 12,
56–58, 163; and neoliberal ideology, 191n84; and
risk minimizers, 37, 56–74, 194n14; and socioeconomic inequality, 150; under-theorization
of, 191n84
resistant capital, 11, 37, 194n5
résumé building, 14, 40, 66, 73–79, 92–102, 123,
164, 197n25
Reyes, Daisy, 202n24
Richards, Bedelia Nicola, 202nn24–25
Rinaldo, Rachel, 181, 189n49, 190n56, 204nn2–3

INDEX

Rios-Aguilar, Cecilia, 202n35
rise of choice, 199n12
risk minimizers: and academic advisors, 59–60, 99, 147–49; and backup plans, 52, 74; and community cultural wealth, 54–58, 75, 161–65; and COVID-19, 52–53, 95–96; demographic characteristics of, 56–58, 75; descriptions of, 14, 47–49; and educational pathways, 63–67, 174, 195n19; emotions of, 68–69; and employment, 49, 60–61, 64–67, 72–74, 94–95, 195n23; families of, 54–58, 126, 148, 163–64, 196n6; and high-impact learning, 148; in high school, 50–51; and individualistic perspectives, 155–57, 201n12; and information, 75; and internships, 94–95; and majors, 72, 90–91, 194n11; managing insecurity, 50–53, 60, 63–64, 166, 194n11; and marginalization, 53–54, 73; and mentors, 58; and migration, 54–56; narratives of, 55; and perceptions of risk, 60, 63, 76, 104, 121, 165, 168–69, 194n11, 194n14; and practical majors, 60–62; and program resources, 58–59, 75, 139, 148; and rehearsal, 74–75; and responsibility, 51–52; and self-blame, 155–56; self-description as "planners," 49–50, 78, 89; social mobility, 105, 121; and student loans, 74
risk narratives, 48
risk shift, 76, 195n29
rituals, 74–75
Roksa, Josipa, 2, 5, 29, 69, 163, 195n21, 196n11, 197n29, 198n33, 200n42, 202n22, 203n49
Rosow, Jason, 15, 202n24
Rowan-Kenyon, Heather, 202n33

Sanford, Nevitt, 203n51
scholarships, 10, 38, 81, 99, 141–42, 174, 204n56
school spirit, 36
school supplies, 25–26, 42, 51–52, 77, 91, 173–74
sciences, 63–64, 70–72, 88, 132, 183, 194n14
second-generation immigrants, ix, 11, 18, 158. See also immigrants
security boosters, 150–53, 167. See also normative institutional arrangements
selectively sociological imagination, 19, 102, 124, 155, 158–61, 170
self-narratives, 122, 195n25
senior-year transition, 5, 46, 74, 100, 159–60, 189n36
service learning, 64
Settersten, Richard, 9, 133
sexism, 53, 84–85, 124, 156–61, 187n4
sexual orientation, 14, 79, 87, 101, 108–10, 165, 169
siblings, 8–9, 21, 31, 56, 162–63
social capital, 11–13, 37, 71, 81–87, 108, 112, 164, 193n17, 198n5
social class, ix, 11, 37, 111, 127, 169, 183–84, 188n8, 192n96 (chap. 1), 192n1 (chap. 2), 195n25, 204n14

social mobility. See mobility, social
social networks, 13, 37, 112, 198n5
social reproduction. See reproduction, social
social sciences, 61–62, 71–72, 152, 154, 160–61, 183
sociological imagination, 19, 154–70, 175
sociology, 69, 91–92, 154, 160–61, 189n39
solid modernity, 188nn21–22
sororities, 120, 134
state funding, 4, 15
statistics, 63–64
stereotypes, 85, 158–59
Stevens, Mitchell, 197n18
stigma, 85
Streib, Jessi, 86, 191n84
strivers, 125–26, 151
Stuber, Jenny, 126, 202n24
student-faculty interactions, 10–12, 29–33, 43–47, 69–70, 82, 99, 137–38, 148, 156, 173–74, 203n55
student health services, 200n31
student involvement. See involvement, student
student organizations, 23, 64–65, 77, 89, 93–96, 123–29, 134, 142, 160, 168
students from immigrant families, ix, 11, 18, 37, 158, 162, 190n55, 201n11
students of color, 7, 10–11, 37, 127, 134–37, 150, 162–69, 190n51, 196n14, 200n46
study abroad, 14, 23, 48, 64–66, 78–80, 88, 93–97, 115, 129–30
studying, 24, 70, 112
suboptimization, tolerable, 199n13

Takacs, Christopher, 100
Taylor, Barrett, 129
teaching, 62, 74, 96, 154, 173, 189n29, 193n19
teaching assistantship, 96
technologies of the self, 197n19
technology, 3, 18, 24–25, 61, 174, 185
tenured and tenure-track faculty, 32
textbooks, 21, 25
Thomas, James, 143
Titus, Jordan, 191n89
tolerable suboptimization, 199n13
tourism, 71
tourists, 190n58
tracks, 63–64, 69, 115, 129–30
transfer students, 25–26, 31–32, 35–39, 66, 130, 141, 144–47, 183
tuition: dependence, 128, 167–68, 199n23; and employment, 38, 67, 72; and fees, 174; increases, 4; in-state vs. out-of-state, 17, 80, 123; and loans, 34–35; vs. opportunity, 129; reimbursement programs, 67, 72; and socioeconomic inequality, 18–19, 28–29; and state funding, 4, 167–68; and stopping out, 26; struggles anticipating, 25, 28–29
tutoring, 1, 30, 75, 99, 142, 168–70, 172, 203n55

undergraduate research, 147–49

Unequal Higher Education (Taylor and Cantwell), 129

upward mobility. *See* mobility, social

vagabonds, 190n58

Vallas, Steven, 189n43, 191n84, 197n19

veteran services, 33

vulnerability, 14, 82–88, 169, 197n17

Warikoo, Natasha, 97, 117

Where Colleges Fail (Sanford), 203n51

Whitley, Sarah, 202n22

Wisconsin, 190n64

Wolfgram, Matthew, 197n26

writing center, 98–99, 173

xenophobia. *See* anti-immigrant sentiment

Yosso, Tara, 11–13, 37, 41, 56, 162, 194n5, 203n37